WHAT is the nature of the mental activity in which we attribute goodness or value to things? By putting the problem of the value judgement in these terms Dr Lamont avoids the extremes of the objective and subjective approaches; the former of which holds that the " goodness " of a thing refers to some property which it has in itself; the latter that it exists only in relation to some other thing, or to an appreciating subject. Since the advocates of these views have failed to reach agreement, his fresh and neutral approach may produce important results.

In Part One the author deals with the comparative value judgement—that is, with " good " and " better "; in Part Two, with the positive value judgement, or attribution of goodness. In a final section he relates the theory of the value judgement to that of moral judgement and to the conception of freedom.

The fine-spun argument is clarified by the use of numerous examples, which in turn lighten the burden of analysis with the bubbles of their wit.

THE
VALUE
JUDGEMENT

By

W. D. LAMONT

M.A., D.Phil.

PHILOSOPHICAL LIBRARY
NEW YORK

Published 1955 by Philosophical Library, Inc.
15 East 40th Street, New York, 16 N.Y.

Printed in Great Britain for Philosophical Library by
Robert Cunningham & Sons, Ltd., Alva, Scotland.

CONTENTS

v

CONTENTS

CHAPTER VIII

THE EXPRESSION OF APPROVAL

CHAPTER IX

THE ULTIMATE GROUND OF THE ATTRIBUTION OF GOODNESS

PREFACE

A SURVEY of the history of moral philosophy will show that all its detailed problems fall under, or are directly related to, one or other of the three main problems: the problem of goodness or value, the problem of duty or obligation, and the problem of responsibility or freedom.

The third of these is predominantly a metaphysical question concerned with difficulties which arise from an apparent conflict between the presuppositions of moral experience and the postulates of scientific knowledge. This metaphysical question cannot, however, be properly formulated until we know what the fundamental presuppositions of moral experience are; and to understand them aright involves a thorough investigation of our first and second main problems.

Perhaps one of the greatest sources of confusion in moral philosophy is the failure to distinguish adequately between the first and the second. The theory of value or goodness and the theory of duty or obligation are often regarded as though they were dealing with aspects of a single issue. There is a tendency to regard 'moral judgement' as a form of 'value judgement'; and the perplexities to which this leads have suggested to some philosophers that the relationship is precisely the reverse—that the value judgement is a form of, or consequent upon, the moral judgement. If we consider these two forms of judgement, however, we find that they are very different.

The value judgement—the assertion that something is good or bad, better or worse than something else—employs concepts which are extraordinarily like those employed in the economic order. The moral judgement, however, which is expressed through such terms as 'duty', 'obligation', 'right', 'justice', 'imperative', and so forth, is obviously employing the concepts of the juridical order. In this connexion, it is significant that both economics and jurisprudence are specialised studies which, historically, have developed out of moral philosophy in the old comprehensive sense. How intimately the problems of ethics were bound up with those of economic and legal theory will be appreciated if we reflect upon the scope of moral philosophy as conceived from the time of Plato and Aristotle right up to the end of the eighteenth century. Inevitably, progress in knowledge has required the development of such specialised studies; but progress has not demanded that their connexion with ethics should be forgotten; and one of the greatest weaknesses of contemporary moral theory is directly due to the fact that moral philosophers are not sufficiently in the habit of asking themselves how far the results attained in these special inquiries—the sciences of economics and jurisprudence, particularly—may contribute to the solution of traditional questions in ethical theory. Had we been more alive to the possibility of such contributions, we should not, I think, be still involved in the ancient confusions surrounding the nature of the moral and value judgements.

The general position here adopted is that the two forms of judgement are so different, and employ such different concepts, that they can and should be treated as the subject matter of different inquiries. I shall be concerned exclusively with the analysis of the value judgement. The reader will be reminded of this from time to time; and it is conceived that the reminders will be necessary, the confusion between 'value' and 'moral' being so deep-rooted in ethical theory, both ancient and modern, that the reader will constantly be tempted to slip into the error of supposing that the argument has something to do with what we 'ought' to try to realise and why we 'ought' to do so. To suppose this would be to assume that the book is intended, partly at least, to provide a theory of obligation. Anyone looking for enlightenment on the theory of obligation must look elsewhere. So far as the moral judgement is discussed, it is not for the purpose of providing a theory of obligation but merely for the purpose of distinguishing between such a theory and the theory of the value judgement. I have, however, attempted in a concluding chapter to place the theory of the value judgement in perspective by showing how it is related to the theory of moral judgement and the conception of freedom.

It will be noted that I speak of a 'theory of the value judgement' rather than of a 'theory of value'. The distinction is important. Most philosophers who treat of the subject are primarily concerned with the question, 'What is goodness or value?'. The fate of ethics during the past half century suggests that this is not a very fruitful approach. I have therefore adopted, as my primary problem, the question, 'What is the nature of the mental activity in which we attribute goodness or value to things?'. I am not primarily concerned with the controversy between 'objectivists' and 'subjectivists' as to the status of 'goodness' in relation to the objective order (although my conclusions do, I think, have a very important bearing on this controversy). I am primarily concerned with the activity of 'valuation' and 'attribution of goodness'.

Attention to our value judgements shows that some of them are 'simply positive' (attributing 'goodness' or 'badness' to things), while others are 'comparative' (attributing 'degrees of goodness'). The plan of the argument of the book gives prominence to this distinction. After the Introduction, in which the problem of the value judgement is set forth, I deal in Part I with 'Valuation' (i.e. with the nature of the comparative value judgement), and in Part II with 'The Attribution of Goodness' (i.e. with the nature of the simply positive value judgement). A Summary of the main conclusions, covering both Parts, will be found at the end of Chapter IX.

The reader will find that Part I—the larger part of the book dealing with the comparative value judgement—is devoted almost entirely to the exposition and clarification of certain principles and concepts used in economics; and any economist will recognise that the treatment is on a very elementary level. I want to make it quite clear that I do not regard myself as competent to make any contribution to economic theory. I have indeed deliberately confined myself, so far as possible, to summarising the doctrines which may be found in introductory text-books so as to ensure that the 'economic theory' on which I rely will approximate to what is accepted by all economists. My business is to draw out the implications of this theory for the philosophical theory of the value judgement.

It may be asked whether a great deal of this elementary exposition might not have been dispensed with, and replaced by references to the appropriate literature for those who require them. But such 'exposition by reference' would have the disadvantages commonly found in 'legislation by reference'. While the economist provides the vital clues, and much of the actual working out of a theory of the comparative value judgement, his central problems are different from those of the philosopher. The economist is primarily concerned with production and distribution within a social order, with the exchange of goods and services, and his theory of valuation is developed only so far as is required from this point of view. The philosopher, on the other hand, is not concerned with the phenomena of the market but with the process of valuation in the individual mind; and if he believes that economic theory provides clues to this process and to the principles operative, however elementary may be the economic doctrines to which he wishes to draw attention, his exposition of these doctrines must be selective, emphasising those aspects of valuational theory which are directly concerned with the operations of the individual mind rather than with the creation of the complex world of industry and commerce.

A task of this sort would, I know, be best performed by one who has the necessary qualifications in both economics and philosophy. That I am not an economist has been a severe handicap. Beginning with a 'hunch' that disputes amongst philosophers on the theory of 'value' or 'goodness' are due, to some extent, to lack of pondering the principles of economic theory, I have been making the double effort of trying to correlate the economic and the philosophical problems and at the same time trying to learn something of economics itself. Consequently I have leaned very heavily on the assistance of friends whose guidance has resulted in the 'evolution' of the following chapters from the crude attempt represented by the first draft of the book. Philosophers and economists, and economist-philosophers, have been generous with their time and patience; and I am particularly grateful to

Professor A. Macbeath of Belfast, Professors A. L. Macfie, W. G. Maclagan and A. K. Cairncross of Glasgow, Professors H. D. Lewis and D. Black of Bangor, and, for suggestions in the final stage of preparing the work, to Professor N. Kemp Smith of Edinburgh. Indeed their shares in the ultimate result are of such a positive character that I cannot truthfully give them the customary clearance certificate by saying that I alone am responsible for what appears. I can only say this: if anyone, observing the blemishes—probably serious enough in all conscience—which still remain, is tempted to accuse any of that gallant band, I would remind him of the ill-tempered complaints of the eighteenth-century traveller on the road from Perth to Inverness, and the all-sufficient reply,

> If you'd seen these roads before they were made
> You'd lift up your hands and bless General Wade.

W. D. LAMONT

The University of Glasgow
January 1955

INTRODUCTION

THE PROBLEM OF THE VALUE
JUDGEMENT

I. WHAT IS THE NATURE OF VALUATION?

WHEN contemporary philosophers discuss the theory of value or goodness (the two terms are used, for the moment, interchangeably), they often take the main issue to be the status of 'value' as a 'quality' or 'property'. The main question is put in something like the following form: When we call a thing good or valuable, are we referring to some quality, property or characteristic which the thing has in itself, irrespective of its relations to other things or to an appreciating subject; or are we referring to a characteristic which it may be said to possess only when it stands in relation to some other thing or to some appreciating subject, or to both; or, finally, are we really indicating a state of mind in an appreciating subject? The answers given to this question have ranged from extreme 'objectivism' to extreme 'subjectivism'; but despite the wealth of intellectual effort which has been expended on the problem, we seem to be no nearer an agreed answer than we were when Moore's *Principia Ethica* was published about half-a-century ago. The position is one of stalemate.

It is, therefore, natural that we should ask whether the root of the trouble may not lie in the way the issue has been presented. It may be that the whole approach to the problem has been misguided. There seem to be two different ways in which we can approach the problem of value. We may start with the assumption that 'value' is a 'something'—a property, a relation, or what you will—and then go on to inquire about its status in the objective order. Or we may start with the fact that, in apprehending or attributing value, this apprehension or attribution is an activity occurring within the mind of a subject; and then go on to analyse the nature of this activity. That is to say, on this second approach, we put the issue, not as one concerning the status of value in the objective order, but as

3

one concerning the nature of the process called 'valuation'.

If it be suggested that, in distinguishing between these two approaches, I am merely restating in other words the objective and the subjective theories, a little reflection should show that this is not the case. Naturally, an objectivist will be more attracted by the first approach; for he will feel that, if value is intrinsic to its object, the only way of learning what it is will be to study the object rather than our psychical processes in apprehending it. Equally naturally, a subjectivist might be expected to be more interested in the second approach. But while there may be this initial bias as to the worthwhileness of the two different approaches, the point I am making is that the distinction between the approaches is not the same as the distinction between the two opposed theories; for the second approach—that which takes as its main problem the analysis of the nature of 'valuation'—does not presuppose the truth or falsity of either theory. It would be perfectly consistent for an objectivist to undertake an inquiry into the nature of the mental activity involved in the apprehension of 'the intrinsic quality, goodness', just as it would be perfectly consistent for anyone holding an extreme realist view of primary and secondary qualities to undertake an investigation of the psychical activity we call perception.

This second approach, then, provides a basis common to all parties to the controversy. The analysis of the nature of valuation may not help to settle the issue on which they are divided. It certainly does not presuppose that one of them is right and the others wrong. What it does is to pick out one problem of importance concerning the significance of the term 'value', and it enables us to start on a common basis, namely the common acceptance of the fact that, whether value be an intrinsic property or not, there is always a subjective activity involved in the 'apprehension' or 'attribution' of value. Our question is: What is the nature of this activity which we call 'valuation'? However they may assess the importance of this question relatively to other problems in theory of value, all parties can agree that it is a legitimate question. Let us assume that the subjectivist theory is true; then the subjectivist, having his main point conceded, will agree that all further advance in theory of value must be sought through the elucidation of the subjective activity of valuation. Let us, on the other hand, assume that the objectivist theory is true; then the objectivist, having his main point conceded, will surely agree that, even if the question be of quite minor importance, it is perfectly rational to ask about the nature of the activity which constitutes the apprehension of intrinsic qualities. The objectivist may deny that this is a philosophical question; he may say that it is 'merely psychological'. But he will agree that it is a rational question. He will probably also agree that a study of this sort may have considerable merit; for, assuming that value is an intrinsic quality, the fact that a given person believes something to be intrinsically good is not conclusive evidence that the thing is really intrinsically good. People may make mistakes; and, if we understand the nature of the process of apprehension, we shall presumably be able to assist immature minds towards correct apprehension of intrinsic qualities.

It is proper, however, that we should recognise the potential effects of an analysis of the process of valuation on the subjectivist-objectivist controversy. While this approach does not presuppose the truth or falsity of either theory, it may well be that, in the course of our analysis, we find the controversy being placed in a new perspective. It is possible that a theory of valuation will lead us to conclusions which decidedly favour one or other of the contending parties. An analysis of the nature of valuation—an analysis resulting in a theory so self-consistent, intellectually satisfying and illuminating for the interpretation of value judgements that it compels our assent—might show conclusively that we cannot possibly make any value judgement without assuming that value is intrinsic to the object. This would mean that intrinsic value is an *a priori* concept or postulate involved in all valuation, one therefore which must be accepted as true if valuation itself is to be regarded as real. It would have a status analogous to that which Kant believed himself to have established for certain 'principles of the understanding' as *a priori* postulates in all theoretical or scientific judgement. It would then be impossible to maintain the subjective theory without denying that there is any such thing as valuation—a curious contention for anyone putting forward a 'subjective theory of value', and one which could, in any case, be easily answered by quotations from almost any newspaper on almost any day of the year. On the other hand, of course, the results of the analysis of valuation might point in the opposite direction. They might show the nature of the process to be such as to render an objectivist theory meaningless—a flat contradiction of all that is implied in valuation.

We have, therefore, to be careful not to confuse the two questions: Does this approach to the problem of value presuppose the truth or falsity of the objective or subjective theory? and, May this approach lead to conclusions which imply the truth or falsity of the objective or the subjective theory? The answer to the first is 'No', and to the second 'Yes'.

In all that follows, we shall be primarily concerned with what I have called the second line of approach to the problems of value. That is to say, we shall be concerned with the question: What is the nature of the process or activity which goes on in our minds when we are apprehending or attributing goodness or value? So far as we touch upon the familiar controversy between the objectivists and subjectivists, it will be merely to draw attention to incidental implications of our theory of valuation. It will not, I trust, be taken as prejudicing the issue if I say now quite frankly that, in my view, an analysis of the process of valuation has implications which are directly opposed to what I regard as essential to the objectivist theory. Perhaps it would have been politic to conceal this fact for the present; but it seems fair to place objectivists on their guard from the outset.

2. 'Goodness' and 'Degree of Goodness'

Up to the present we have used the terms 'goodness' and 'value' interchangeably. Later we shall attach different meanings to these terms. How exactly they are to be differentiated we shall explain at the appropriate time; but it is necessary here to deal with a distinction which will, in fact, be the main basis of the special senses to be attached later to 'goodness' and 'value', or rather to 'the attribution of goodness' as distinguished from 'valuation'.

This basis is the distinction between the simple or 'positive' attribution of 'goodness' to a thing and the 'comparative' attribution of a 'degree of goodness'. This distinction has great theoretical importance because we are confronted, in dealing with 'the value judgement' in the comprehensive sense, by two different questions. These two questions are put with sufficient clarity by Moore. He asks, firstly, about the things which have intrinsic value, and observes that 'in order to arrive at a correct decision on . . . this question, it is necessary to consider what things are such that, if they existed by themselves, in absolute isolation, we should yet judge their existence to be good'.[1] Secondly, he notes that things may have different degrees of goodness, and tells us that 'in order to decide upon the relative degrees of value of different things, we must similarly consider what comparative value seems to attach to the isolated existence of each'.[2] Attention is directed to these passages from Moore, not because of the criterion he employs, but simply to indicate that he thinks the distinction between 'goodness' and 'degree of goodness' worthy of notice.

Again Ross, in discussing whether the 'intrinsically good things' —virtue, knowledge and pleasure—can be compared with each other in value, says: 'I do not pretend that the views I shall express are certainly true, still less that I can prove them to be so. I will only say that they are the result of a good deal of reflection about the comparative value of these things, and that they agree, so far as I can judge, with the views of many others who have reflected on it'.[3]

Thus Moore and Ross both recognise that there are two questions which we can ask about the goodness of a thing. We can ask, 'Is it good?'; and we can ask, 'What is its degree of goodness as compared with some other good thing or things?' The first is a question whether a thing belongs to a certain class or order (the class or order of 'good things'). The second is a question about the place which it occupies in that order (its

[1] *Principia Ethica*, par. 112.   [2] *Ibid.*   [3] *The Right and the Good*, p. 149.

degree of goodness) relatively to the places occupied by other things. Obviously, while 'goodness' may or may not be relative, 'degree of goodness' is relative in some important sense.

Now anything which has a degree of goodness attributed to it has necessarily goodness attributed to it, though the converse does not hold. To attribute goodness is a 'simply positive' attribution. To attribute a degree of goodness is a 'comparative' statement, implying that other things are good, but good to a higher or lower degree. Logically at least, it would be intelligible to say that x, and x alone, is good. It would be quite unintelligible to say that x, and x alone, possesses a degree of goodness. Degree involves comparison with some other thing or things possessing the same characteristic to a lesser or greater extent (we should never conceive of a 'degree' if we thought everything had, or must have, the characteristic to exactly the same extent). To attribute a degree, then, is to give a specific place in a series. To attribute goodness is to attribute membership of an order. To attribute degree of goodness is to attribute a relative or comparative place in that order.

Obviously, 'goodness' is a more fundamental notion than 'degree of goodness'; but the distinction between the 'simply positive' and the 'comparative' forms of the value judgement has been emphasised at this early stage because it is often easier to distinguish between the value judgement in general and various other forms of judgement—moral, efficiency and aesthetic judgements—if we take the 'comparative' rather than the 'simply positive' forms.

3. VALUE JUDGEMENT AND MORAL JUDGEMENT

The argument of this book is concerned with the value judgement only; but, unfortunately, to say this will not convey to many philosophers the precise limitations of our problem; for the term 'value judgement' is used in a very loose sense even by many writers on moral theory. This looseness is specially noticeable in those writers who nowadays are fond of talking about 'ethical sentences' and including, under this term, statements which are valuational as well as those which are imperative. It is difficult to know whether they really appreciate the distinction between a value judgement and a moral judgement.

The two forms of judgement are quite distinct, employing quite distinct sets of concepts. Even though, in popular usage, they seem to be of the same character (as, e.g. when we talk of 'moral goodness'), careful study shows that in the one case we are employing valuational concepts (normally indicated by the terms, 'good', 'bad', 'better', 'worse', and so on), and in the other case juridical concepts ('duty', 'obligation', 'right', 'wrong', and so forth). In ordinary usage the ambiguous use of valuational terms may not lead to serious confusions because the practical context in which terms are used generally assists us to the true interpretation. But in philosophical theory precision is important.

That there is a fundamental distinction between the value judgement and the moral judgement may best be brought out by considering the Socratic paradox that 'virtue is knowledge'. Socrates appears to have reached this view by combining two propositions: (i) we all do, as a matter of fact, strive to realise the 'good' as we apprehend it, and (ii) virtuous action is action directed to the promotion of what is truly good. If both of these propositions be true, then virtue and vice must follow from knowledge and ignorance—the knowledge and ignorance of what is truly good and of the technical means appropriate to the realisation of any given end. What troubled Plato and Aristotle —as it has troubled modern thinkers—was the feeling that, despite their inability to accept the Socratic conclusion without qualification, there is something true and important in what he said.

What, then, is true in the Socratic doctrine? What we seem to accept as fundamentally sound is proposition (i) —that we all do, as a matter of fact, strive to realise the 'good' as we apprehend it. It appears that the whole of modern economic theory is founded upon an *a priori* postulate which can be formulated approximately in terms of Socrates' proposition. Presumably all branches of economic theory, however specialised, assume the general principles which find expression in the 'laws of supply and demand'; and if we reflect upon the economist's formulation of these laws—

and especially upon his account of the rise and fall of demand —it seems beyond dispute that economic science assumes the universal validity of Socrates' proposition. We evaluate and buy and sell so as to economise resources for the satisfaction of our demands as a whole. Our effective choices are determined by— or are—our relative valuations (our estimates of degrees of goodness), because our behaviour is in all cases an expression of our striving for the 'good' as we (truly or mistakenly) apprehend it. Challenge the truth of this proposition, and you challenge the basis of all economic theory.

It will be noted that Socrates' first proposition implies that a theory of valuation is a theory of choice. Choice is the external or overt expression of the internal state of valuation. To regard x as better than y is to have the internal disposition to act for the realisation of x rather than y. This is to put very crudely a point which will be a major subject of discussion in the following chapters; but perhaps the crude statement may be allowed in these introductory remarks, in order to bring out the intimate relation between value judgement and choice.

But the more we emphasise the connexion between value judgement and choice, the more are we compelled to recognise a distinction between the value judgement and the moral judgement which asserts an obligation or duty. If Socrates' first proposition is assumed to be valid, we may reasonably suspect that the paradoxical nature of his conclusion that 'virtue is knowledge' arises from the fact that he has combined proposition (i) with proposition (ii)—that virtuous action is action directed to the promotion of what is truly good. Quite apart from difficulties over the distinction between what we apprehend to be good and what is truly good, it seems to us patently false to say that we always choose to do what we know or believe to be our duty. If Socrates' first proposition is true, then we always do choose what we think good in preference to what we think bad, and what we think better in preference to what we think worse; but it appears that we do not suppose that choice has the same necessary relation to what we know or think to be our duty. We are inclined to accept as axiomatic the Kantian view that, if I ought to do a thing, then I can do it; what is a duty for me is necessarily a *possible* choice, but it is not a *necessary* choice; and transgression of duty may be quite conscious and deliberate. What I consider good (or better) is what I choose; but what I consider my duty is what I may, but do not necessarily choose. The 'problem of freedom' then arises, not only when we consider the respective postulates of moral and scientific judgements, but also when we consider the respective characters of moral and value judgement. These characters seem to be radically different.

In point of fact, this fundamental difference seems to be accepted by us when we inflict punishment for the transgression of duty. If a person acts contrary to his duty, we may, in the first instance, try to secure his future conformity by making clear what his duty is. If he repeats the offence in circumstances which suggest conscious transgression, and if we are determined that he shall conform, we do not merely repeat that his duty is so-and-so. We adjust the objective situation to which his choice or value judgement will be the response, by promise of reward or threat of punishment, the assumption being that voluntary action, though not necessarily an expression of awareness of obligation, is necessarily an expression of valuation.

While it is not my intention to deal with the nature of moral judgement in the present volume, it may be useful if I say very briefly and dogmatically what I regard as the essence of the distinction between the value and the moral judgements. Valuation or choice is concerned with the correlation of ends within a total *personal* conception of 'the good'. The moral judgement, on the other hand, being the assertion of a duty or obligation (or at least of something to which the notion of obligation is always relevant), always carries a reference to the conception of 'right' and therefore to an *inter-personal* order. The former is what may be called, for convenience, an 'economic' assessment of modes of action, while the latter is a 'juridical' assessment. The theory of the value judgement is concerned with matters common to ethics and economics. The theory of the moral judgement is concerned with matters common to ethics and jurisprudence.

4. Value Judgement and Efficiency Judgement

Just as 'morally good' and 'morally better' erroneously suggest that we are dealing with a value judgement, so the 'efficiency' judgement is apt to be expressed as though it were a value judgement. We talk as though there were 'two kinds of goodness'— good-as-end (or, as some would say, intrinsically-good) and good-as-means. But there is a confusion here which will be best brought to light if we take the comparative forms of the 'efficiency' and the genuine 'value' judgement.

We may say: 'For smoothing the surface of a board, a plane is a better instrument than a chisel.' One would not quarrel with this statement as a mode of popular usage. But whether it is a value judgement depends upon what the comparative judgement is about. What are we comparing, in this statement, when we say that a plane is 'better' than a chisel? We are comparing the relative efficiencies of two instruments or two possible means to a given end; and precisely the same point could be put—and put more accurately—in non-valuational terms: 'The plane will more easily and effectively produce a certain state, namely smoothness in the board.' This is not a valuational statement; it is a statement of fact, or at least a prediction of alternative results which will follow the adoption of alternative means.

Why, then, do we feel the term 'better' to be natural and appropriate in this context? It is because of an antecedent, implicit, genuine value judgement: 'Smoothness of the board is desirable, and is desirable without unnecessary care and energy.' The so-called comparative value judgement is, therefore, a non-valuational comparative efficiency judgement which assumes an antecedent 'positive' (not 'comparative') value judgement.

This is not to say that it would be impossible to make any genuine comparative value judgement with respect to a plane and a chisel. The point is simply that the one given above is not such a judgement. As will be shown at length in a later chapter,[1] that which is valued is always a future state of affairs or 'content of demand' (such, for instance, as the smoothness of the board, or

---

[1] Chapter II, Propositions II, III and IV.

the possession of a plane or the sharpness of a chisel). The argument on this point must not be anticipated here; but the point is mentioned to bring out what seems to be accepted by all schools of thought, namely that a value judgement, whether positive or comparative, is not an ordinary statement of fact, such as a statement about a causal relationship. Neither objectivists nor subjectivists contend that it is a factual statement about 'natural qualities'. The subjectivist says that it expresses an 'attitude' (emotional or other attitude) of a subject, and the objectivist says that it refers to a 'non-natural' quality. We commit ourselves to neither of these views, at the moment. They are mentioned to show that both subjectivists and objectivists would contend that any purely factual statement about the plane and chisel cannot be a value judgement. But to say that the plane is better than the chisel for smoothing a board is a purely factual statement (assuming a genuine value judgement on the smoothness of the board). It is a statement of comparative efficiency in the production of a certain result, not a comparative value judgement.

The instance of the efficiency judgement used above was one concerning means and end. But an ostensible value judgement which is really just an efficiency judgement may also occur when we are comparing two things which are not means to some end but prospective constituents in a thing to be produced. Thus, if we say that mahogany is better than pine for making a bookcase, the wood (mahogany or pine) is not—like the plane or chisel— an instrument or means to an end. It is material which will be a constituent part of the bookcase when the latter is completed. Nevertheless, the comparative judgement, 'Mahogany is better than pine for making a bookcase', may be a mere efficiency judgement. It depends on the context. It will be an efficiency judgement in all cases where we are thinking of the function to be performed by the finished product. If we are thinking of the bookcase as a means to an end—the storing of books in an orderly and accessible fashion—and make our comparative judgement on mahogany and pine in that context of thought, the judgement will be an efficiency one. We are thinking of strength, durability, and so forth. We are thinking in terms of the 'natural qualities' of the woods. We set a value, presumably, upon a certain end—having books stored in an orderly and accessible fashion; we want a bookcase suitable to this end; and the selection of its constituents (from this point of view) is a matter of comparative efficiency. Here, again, it is not contended that there can be no true comparative value judgement concerning mahogany and pine. The contention is simply that what may look like a value judgement is not so when we are thinking of the function of the bookcase (means to end) and, in this context, say that 'mahogany is better than pine'.

5. VALUE JUDGEMENT AND AESTHETIC JUDGEMENT

We have seen that, when alternative materials proposed to be embodied in something (say a bookcase) are compared with a view to the function to be served by the completed article, the comparative judgement on these materials will be an efficiency judgement. But there is another way in which we can compare constituents proposed for inclusion in a whole. For example, good quality pine might be so near the quality of the mahogany available that, functionally, there would be little difference between them. But we might still select the mahogany because it 'looks' better and would fit in with the total furnishing scheme. Here the bookcase is being judged in relation to its place in a whole, and the type of wood is being judged in relation to its contribution to a whole (the bookcase) which is a constituent in a more inclusive whole. This is not the same as a judgement which attends primarily to function. The judgement, so to speak, looks no further than the 'wholeness' of the whole, and not beyond this to the function which the whole is to perform as means to an end.

There may be different types of this kind of judgement, but the best-known (many would say the only one) is the aesthetic judgement. Poetry or music could be judged functionally. We could ask whether 'John Brown's Body' or 'Solemn Melody' is 'better' as a marching tune; and this would be to judge different items of music comparatively on a functional basis. Poetry or music may also be judged on a genuinely comparative valuational basis. We could ask whether it is 'better' to get to the concert hall in time to hear a certain item (and do without dinner) or have dinner (and arrive too late for this part of the programme); and this could be—and, on the face of it at least, appears to be—a genuinely comparative valuation, weighing two things, both of which are felt to be good, but between which circumstances enforce a choice. But we can also judge the comparative merits of two compositions *qua* poetry or *qua* music; and this is the aesthetic judgement, which is quite different from both the functional and the value judgements.

To attempt to define the aesthetic judgement would be out of place here. That is a task which probably requires as much discussion as the task of explaining the nature of the value judgement. It will be sufficient if we point to what are generally agreed to be features of the aesthetic judgement, and show that these features preclude us from identifying the aesthetic and the value judgement. They may be sub-forms of a common form of judgement (we are not concerned with this question); but they are not the same.

It is, I think, generally agreed that, to be 'beautiful', a thing must have at least two characteristics: It must have some form or structure which the expert in that branch of art can discern and theoretically separate out from the matter in which it is embodied; and the embodied or materialised form must be capable of evoking a certain mood in the experiencing subject—a mood with a rhythm or pattern which is initiated and sustained as the whole of the thing contemplated unfolds itself in detail to the observer. Some may say that the aesthetic judgement is passed on the pure form; others may say that the aesthetic judgement is passed on the ability of the embodied form to create the mood (even though the observer may not be explicitly aware of the form); but everyone would, I think, agree that it is the embodiment of form in matter which stimulates and sustains what we call aesthetic appreciation. Without the form the thing would be a mere 'jumble'; without the ability to stimulate and sustain a mood the embodied form would not be called 'beautiful'.

Now, whatever we take to be the precise criterion of beauty—whether it be concerned simply with form, or with the ability of embodied form to create a mood—it seems clear that the aesthetic judgement, the judgement on poetry or music *qua* poetry or music, is different from the value judgement.

Take the following lines:

> The curfew rings at the end of the day.
> The bawling cows straggle over the pasture towards the byre.

These two statements are both intelligible; and if we reflect for a moment on their significance we can see that a person could intend to deepen the significance of the second statement by placing it after the first. The significance, however, is a 'matter of fact' significance. We are being enlightened on a matter of general routine in life on the farm. The second statement will not be likely to provoke any conscious aesthetic reaction in us.

But suppose that we alter the first line to

> The curfew tolls the knell of parting day.

This makes substantially the same statement of fact. But it does more. It conveys a suggestion of sweet solemnity in the occasion; it initiates a mood. Having induced this mood, if we then add, 'The bawling cows straggle over the pasture towards the byre', the mood is abruptly shattered; and what was before accepted as a plain statement of fact is felt to be crude and ugly. We can remedy this, sustaining and enriching the mood, by altering the second line to 'The lowing herd winds slowly o'er the lea'; again, substantially the same statement of fact, but a statement of fact which further 'unfolds' the sense of the occasion.

There may possibly be some aesthetic quality in the two original lines; but all would agree that, even if they have an aesthetic quality, the revised form is aesthetically 'better'.

But to call the second pair of lines 'aesthetically better' is to use the term 'better' in a non-valuational sense. We mean—perhaps amongst other things—that they are 'more formed', or 'more conducive to the sustenance of a rhythmic, patterned mood'. To make a 'value judgement' on the alternative pairs of lines we should say, 'It is better to have the second rather than the first pair of lines'. The comparative value judgement is a judgement as to which of the alternatives should exist. The comparative aesthetic judgement asserts certain characteristics (intrinsic or relational) to be present in the things to a greater or less degree; and a favourable comparative aesthetic judgement may well be a *reason* we give in support of a favourable comparative value judgement; but it is not itself a comparative value judgement.

That the aesthetic and value judgements are different kinds of judgement is well illustrated in Moore's discussion of the question whether 'beauty' is 'good' apart from any question of its being appreciated by a subject. Consider the following quotation[1]:

'No one', says Professor Sidgwick, 'would consider it rational to aim at the production of beauty in external nature apart from any possible contemplation of it by human beings.' Well, I may say at once that I, for one, do consider this rational. . . . Let us imagine one world exceedingly beautiful. . . . And then imagine the ugliest world you can possibly conceive. . . . Such a pair of worlds we are entitled to compare. . . . Is it irrational to hold that it is better that the beautiful world should exist than the one which is ugly? Would it not be well . . . to do what we could to produce it rather than the other?

Moore's criticism of Sidgwick obviously presupposes a distinction between the aesthetic and the value judgements, between 'This is beautiful' and 'This is good'; for, prior to inviting a value judgement, Moore postulates that a comparative aesthetic judgement has already been made. It is assumed as accepted that world *A* is 'beautiful' and world *B* 'ugly'; and the question is then asked, 'Which of these is good (or better)?' Moore's answer is, 'World *A*, the beautiful one.' The fact that he can call *A* beautiful and still ask whether it is also good makes it clear that the aesthetic and value judgements are not the same. If they were the same, to ask whether a beautiful thing is good would be like asking whether a beautiful thing is beautiful, or a good thing good. Moore's argument also suggests that he is coming perilously close to a 'conative' theory of the value judgement. He may have been writing without his usual caution, but it is interesting to find him putting the question, 'Is it irrational to hold that it is better

---

[1] From *P.E.*, par. 50.

that the beautiful world should exist, and that we should do what we could to produce it?', as though anyone answering that such a world should be produced if possible were necessarily affirming, with Moore, that such a world is good.

6. THE COMPARATIVE VALUE JUDGEMENT

From all that has been said in distinguishing the value judgement, in the proper sense, from the moral, efficiency and aesthetic judgements, it will be obvious that the value judgement is not, strictly speaking, about things and their qualities. It seems, rather, to be about their being, maintenance and destruction. In other words, the reference in the content of the value judgement is to 'ends' or some 'end'. It indicates a state of affairs which the judger has a disposition to bring into existence, maintain in existence, allow to go out of existence or destroy. It appears to be primarily (though never entirely) the expression of a conative disposition, the expression of a 'demand'. To call something good is (as is often said) to express approval, to express the disposition to create or maintain it in existence.

But if the simply positive value judgement ('X is good') expresses a demand or conative disposition to maintain something in existence, what is a 'comparative' value judgement? It is obvious that, since the comparative value judgement expresses an estimate of degrees of goodness, all the things compared must be regarded as 'good' (in some degree). That is to say, there must be conative dispositions or demands to create or maintain them all. But under what circumstances should we place in an *order* of value two or more things, both or all of which we demand? Only in such circumstances as enforce a choice between them. The comparative value judgement is an expression of 'choice' when objective circumstances (which are for the moment beyond our control) enforce on us the disagreeable necessity of renouncing one thing if the other is to be attained. Moore's illustration of the beautiful and ugly worlds is not a true instance of a 'comparative' value judgement unless he supposes that we attribute some degree of goodness to the ugly world, and would like both the beautiful and the ugly worlds if it were possible to have both. If he does not suppose this—if he really supposes that we should say, 'I want the beautiful world to exist and do not want the ugly world to exist'—then he is really dealing with a simply positive value judgement: 'A beautiful world is or would be good; an ugly world is or would be not–good or bad.' It is not here a question whether the former is 'better' than the latter. The question as to whether one is better only arises if we say they are both good.

It will be useful to clarify the precise point at issue here by taking a few examples.

Suppose that I have a large quantity of wood of various kinds, and want to make a bookcase. There is an ample supply of every kind of wood. Here no choice is enforced upon me. It is true that I cannot make the bookcase wholly of mahogany, and wholly of pine, and wholly of oak, and wholly of birch. But then I cannot want to do so. To attempt to formulate such a series of 'demands' would be to formulate something which is utterly meaningless. I may, of course, want to make several bookcases of different woods; but the assumption is that I have ample woods of different kinds for all purposes. Here again, therefore, there is no choice enforced. I do not range my demands in an order, since all can be realised. However many bookcases I want to make, provided that there is enough wood of all kinds, the only comparative judgements I shall make will be comparative efficiency or comparative aesthetic judgements.

But suppose that I want to make both a bookcase and a table, and that wood is scarce, sufficient to make only one of them. Then I shall make a comparative value judgement as between the creation of the table and the creation of the bookcase. I shall range the contents of the two 'competing demands' in an order of goodness, or—what is the same thing—in an order of choice.

The comparative value judgement, therefore, is the expression of 'choice' (real or hypothetical) when circumstances (really or by hypothesis) enforce such a choice between two or more conceived ends, both or all of which the subject is disposed to adopt. For the sake of clarity, 'choice' will be used in this strict sense throughout the rest of this work. When the reference is to any decision which does not involve choice in this sense, I shall use such terms as 'decide', 'select' and so forth. For instance, a person who has many kinds of wood will, on a comparative efficiency or aesthetic judgement, 'decide' on, or 'select', this kind of wood rather than that. He will never, in my use of the term, be said to 'choose' on the basis of a judgement other than a comparative value judgement.

7. 'Attribution of Goodness' and 'Valuation'

There is one further terminological point which may conveniently be dealt with here. I have used, in the title of this book, the term 'Value Judgement' to cover both the attribution of goodness (the simply positive form of the value judgement) and also the attribution of degree of goodness. But I wish also to use the term 'value' in a more restricted sense, 'value' corresponding to 'degree of goodness' as assigned in the comparative form of the value judgement. That is to say, to attribute 'goodness' will mean to make a 'simply positive' value judgement; while to attribute 'value' will mean to attribute a 'degree of goodness'. Value will be used in this sense because this usage will the more readily enable us to utilise the work of economists in the theory of value. To avoid confusion over the term 'value judgement', it will I think be sufficient if I retain the term 'value judgement' for the comprehensive purpose indicated in the title of the book, and always refer to 'valuation' when I mean to indicate the attribution of value in the narrow sense (i.e. degree of goodness).

Part I of the book will deal with 'Valuation' and Part II with 'The Attribution of Goodness'. The concept of 'goodness' is, of course, the more fundamental of the two; but the character of the 'value judgement' as a whole will be better understood if we begin with 'valuation' rather than with the 'attribution of goodness'.

PART I
VALUATION

Chapter One

VALUATION AND ECONOMIC THEORY

1. 'VALUE' IN ECONOMICS

THE sense in which we understand the 'value judgement', and particularly the sense in which we propose to use the term 'valuation' (the choice between alternatives, both of which are regarded as good, when objective circumstances enforce such a choice), becomes very significant when we consider the use of the term 'value' in economics. In our sense, and in the economist's sense, 'valuation' implies conditions of 'scarcity'. It is true that Professor Macfie has recently suggested that 'economising' has no essential reference to scarcity[1] and we shall have to consider this point[2]; but for the present it will be proper to take the generally accepted view of 'economy' and 'economics'. 'Economics is the study of the influence of scarcity on human conduct in circumstances where men have freedom of choice in allocating scarce resources between competing wants'.[3] As this definition or description of economics is intended to cover the three main conceptions of exchange, scarcity and choice, we may take it that a reference to 'exchange' is implicit in the reference to 'allocation of scarce resources'. This is brought out explicitly by Little,[4] who regards economics as concerned with 'the things and services which the individual consumes or enjoys, and which could be exchanged for money, together with the amount and kind of work which the individual does'.

The generally accepted view of economics, then, regards it as concerned with a field very closely related to, if not exactly the same as, what we have called the field of the comparative value judgement, or 'valuation'. The principal difference would seem

---

[1] 'What kind of experience is Economising?', in *Ethics*, Vol. LX, No. 1, Oct. 1949.   [2] See below pp. 55-7.
[3] A. K. Cairncross, *Introduction to Economics*, p. 7.
[4] *A Critique of Welfare Economics*, p. 6.

to be that the economist's interest in valuation is primarily an interest in the way choice operates in creating the order of exchange, while we are primarily concerned with valuation as an activity in the individual mind. What significance this difference of interest has, and how far it affects the relevance of economics to our problem, will be discussed later. For the moment the most important thing is to show why we have thought it helpful to use the term 'valuation' for the comparative value judgement.

In economics, anything exchanged for money, or capable of being stated in a monetary equivalent, is said to have a 'price'; and 'price' is usually regarded as synonymous with 'value' (in the economist's sense). How have 'price' and 'value' come to be thus generally identified?

Older economists used the term 'value' in a much broader, popular sense. Anything wanted, needed or demanded could be said to be valuable. But, adopting this broad meaning for the term, it became clear that there are two different orders of value which can vary surprisingly in their relations with each other. These were distinguished as 'value-in-use' and 'value-in-exchange'. Thus, with regard to 'value-in-use', it will be generally agreed that, if a person had to choose between having no water for a week and seeing no theatrical performance for a week, he would unhesitatingly choose the water. Its value-in-use to him would unquestionably be greater. And yet the 'price' we pay in this country for, say, four gallons of water may be measured by the fraction of a penny, while to attend a theatre performance may cost ten shillings. Why this paradoxical relation of value-in-use to value-in-exchange? The explanation may be more easily given if we take two commodities like water and gold. In respect of man's fundamental needs, water has a higher value-in-use than gold; and it is perfectly conceivable that in certain circumstances the value-in-exchange of four gallons of water might be equal to or higher than, one ounce of gold. But this would depend on how plentiful the water was in comparison with gold. In this country no one would normally consider exchanging even half an ounce of gold for four gallons of water. Water is so plentiful that there are very few occasions on which we could be confronted by the choice: either no water, or surrender an ounce of gold.

Thus, while value-in-use depends on the qualitative character of a thing in relation to want or need, value-in-exchange is relative in a much more complicated way. It is relative to the quantity of the thing in relation to total amount of want or need, and also to the relative scarcity of the thing as compared with other scarce things wanted or needed. If the quantity available were exactly equal to or in excess of demand ('demand' here meaning 'expressed need or want' and not merely the 'effective demand' of the economist to be discussed later), and were so distributed that each person could secure as much as he wanted without the assistance of anyone else, then the thing would have no value-in-exchange at all, however much value-in-use it might have. If, however, it is less than adequate to demand, or if the quantity is so distributed that a person cannot get as much as he wants without the co-operation of someone else, the thing will have a value-in-exchange.

This, very crudely, is the old distinction between value-in-use and value-in-exchange. It will be observed that value-in-exchange is synonymous with 'price'. It is the ratio in accordance with which things are exchanged for each other.

But since the economist is primarily concerned with 'values' in so far as they form the basis of exchange, there has been a natural tendency to shorten the term 'value-in-exchange' to the simple term 'value'. 'Value' thus normally means exchange-ratio or price. For the older term 'value-in-use' it was the custom to substitute the word 'utility', but the point is not immediately relevant. We are merely concerned with the use of the term 'value' and the bearing of this usage on our own problem of the nature of valuation. Value for the economist always implies scarcity. A thing has value when it has a place in an order of things which are in demand, but where the quantities available are scarce and the situation therefore enforces on the persons concerned a choice between alternatives, both of which are in fact demanded. It is the choice situation, manifesting itself in the realm of exchange, which gives rise to value or price in the economist's sense. Plainly then, although we are not specially concerned with the manifestations of valuation in exchange, there is a very definite relation between the economic theory of value and the philosophical problem of valuation. It is highly probable that various concepts developed in systematic economic theory will be of assistance to us in the philosophical field.[1]

2. THE LAWS OF SUPPLY AND DEMAND AND THEIR POSTULATES

The department of economics of special interest to us will clearly be, not any of the detailed practical applications, but the general theory of supply and demand. We need not even go into the complexities of the general theory itself. It will be sufficient for our purposes to take what are called the main 'laws of supply and demand' and then bring out the main assumptions underlying the formulation of these laws. With regard to the laws, they are stated by Sir Hubert Henderson in the following terms:

I. When, at the price ruling, demand exceeds supply, the price tends to rise. Conversely when supply exceeds demand the price tends to fall.

[1] It is perhaps necessary to explain that by 'economics', throughout the whole of the following chapters on the theory of valuation, I mean what may be called 'pure or positive economic theory'. It appears that the attention of many contemporary economists is directed to the problem of devising or discovering 'criteria' or 'norms' for the valuation of social policies, and that there is a tendency to contract out of the discussion of the basic problems—somewhat philosophical and psychological—in valuational theory which are dealt with in the 'general theory of value' by economists of the latter part of the nineteenth and the earlier part of the twentieth century. That is to say, while older economists paid a great deal of attention to the attempt to discover and formulate a pure theory of 'the laws of valuation and choice', as these operate in the mind of the individual, the enormous growth of social planning in our day has tended to move the emphasis towards the search for 'norms for the valuation of economic policies'. It is this latter problem which, one understands, is central to what is called 'welfare economics'. The controversies which have arisen over 'welfare economics' do not, it seems, necessarily challenge the basic assumptions of the older economists' 'laws of valuation and choice'; they appear to be concerned with the question whether 'pure economics' can discover 'norms for policy valuation' on a purely scientific basis. (See Little, *Critique of Welfare Economics* and Miss Honor Brotman's paper on 'The Concept of Welfare in Economics' in *Proc. Arist. Soc.*, Sup. Vol. XXVII.) For purposes of a philosophical theory of the value judgement, it is the older discussions of the 'laws of valuation and choice'—as found, e.g. in Marshall, Smart and Wicksteed—which are of special importance; and 'economics' is understood in that very limited sense throughout the present work.

II. A rise in price tends, sooner or later, to decrease demand and to increase supply. Conversely a fall in price tends, sooner or later, to increase demand and to decrease supply.

III. Price tends to the level at which demand is equal to supply.

Henderson adds: 'These three laws are the cornerstone of economic theory. They are the framework into which all analysis of special, detailed problems must be fitted'.[1]

(1) *The Laws as Laws of Exchange*

It may seem unnecessary to repeat that economics is concerned with the realm of exchange; but the point is of importance when we are trying to understand the concepts employed—supply, demand and price—and to elicit the main postulates underlying the laws. We know that 'price' is equivalent to 'exchange-value', and we have already used the terms 'demand' and 'supply' as roughly equivalent to 'need or want expressed' and 'things qualitatively suitable and available for meeting demand in this sense'. But it is clearly not 'demand' and 'supply' in these general senses that the laws are about. It is simply not true, for instance, that if my demand for wood exceeds my supply, the price will tend to rise. Hence if we assume the laws to be true or approximately true statements, then the terms must be understood in senses which are consistent with the truth of the laws.

The meanings of the terms 'supply' and 'demand' are governed by the concept of 'price', which occurs in all the laws.

Supply: This cannot simply mean a quantity of things which are qualitatively suitable to meet demand and are physically available. They must of course be physically available; but to be 'supply', in the sense of the laws, they will be available only on certain conditions prescribed by a person possessing them. They are available 'at the ruling price' or 'at a price'. The 'making available' is an act of transfer from Supplier to Demander on condition of the reception of the price. Suppose I have a stock of wood physically available; then there is 'supply' in the general sense of the term. But there is not necessarily 'supply' in the sense of the term as used in these laws. There is supply only if I am

---

[1] *Supply and Demand*, pp. 18-19.

prepared to transfer the wood (or some of it) to a Demander in return for his transferring to me a certain sum of money (or equivalent of this sum). This may be called 'Effective Supply' to distinguish it from 'supply' in the general sense of 'physically available'. Anything said about 'effective supply' clearly refers to an exchange transaction, and to an exchange transaction alone. In other words, the term has no meaning except in the order of exchange.

Demand: Similarly, this cannot mean 'demand' in the general sense as equivalent to expressed need or want or desire. We are talking of 'demand at a ruling or given price'. In other words, we mean 'an expression of need or want *supported by a certain amount of purchasing power*' equivalent to the 'price'. Let us call demand in this sense 'Effective Demand'. Effective demand, like effective supply, has no meaning whatsoever except in a system of exchange.

Price: It necessarily follows from all this that the term 'price', as used in the laws, has no meaning apart from a system of exchange. The term can be, and is, used in other senses, e.g.

> Gigantic mice
> Lord Bumble bred;
> His life the price:
> On him they fed.

Price here means a 'forfeit' or 'penalty' or perhaps 'a natural consequence'. But, in our laws of supply and demand, it means something different. It means the 'ratio in which things are exchanged'. Thus if pears, apples, oranges and pennies exchange in the ratio: 1 pear, 3 apples, 2 oranges, 6 pennies; then the price of a pear stated in terms of apples is 3, in terms of oranges 2, and in terms of pennies 6.

Obviously, then, the 'price' at which we have effective supply is necessarily identical with the 'price' at which we have effective demand, and *vice versa*. It is the ratio in which things actually exchange. If Supplier says 'My price for a pear is 7d', and Demander says 'My price for a pear is 5d'; then there is no price. S and D are merely 'stating' or 'naming' prices in the sense of proposing what they think the price should be. There is neither effective supply from S nor effective demand from D until the proposals have been altered so as to coincide with each other, and thus, for the first time, create a price or ratio of exchange.

If, then, 'price' is meaningless apart from exchange (meaningless, i.e. in the sense used in our laws of supply and demand), it follows that if we identify 'price' and 'value', 'value' in this sense cannot possibly mean the same thing as the 'value' which an individual sets on a thing when he gives it a place in an 'order of degrees of goodness'. We are not objecting to the economist's equation of value and price; nor are we saying that it is wholly irrelevant to the 'value' a person gives to a thing when placing it in an order of choice. We are merely drawing attention to the fact that the 'order of values' in the sense of the 'order of prices' is necessarily something quite different from the 'order of values' in the sense of the 'valuational order in the individual mind'.

(2) *The Postulates of the Laws*

The insistence that 'demand', 'supply' and 'price', as used in the formulation of the laws of supply and demand, have no meaning apart from the realm of exchange may seem to be an unnecessary insistence on the obvious. The fact may be obvious, but the insistence is not unnecessary, for we find that these concepts are distinguished, in this respect, from the *fundamental postulates* of the laws. 'Demand' and 'supply' (as equivalent to 'effective' demand and supply) and 'price' refer to what we may call a public order of values. But the postulates with which we are now about to deal are postulates, not about relations of exchange, but about the individual minds participating in exchange. The postulates are assumed to be valid whether the individual stands in economic relations with his fellows or not, and indeed to be the psychological basis of all economic relations. Further, they assume that there is an 'order of values' within the mind of the individual which is, in its essential nature, something quite different from the 'public order of values' stated in terms of price or exchange ratio.

These assumptions and postulates apply indifferently to Supplier and Demander. Or rather, they apply to persons in their capacity as demanders (in the general sense of demand and not in the sense of effective demand), but assume that every Supplier (in the sense of effective supply) is *ipso facto* a Demander (in the sense of effective demand and *therefore* also in the sense of demand in the general sense). Effective supply is supply at a price agreed between supplier and demander. Hence the Supplier is always a demander of what is paid as the agreed price. Hence, as every party to an economic transaction may be considered as a demander, we can set out the main postulates of the laws of supply and demand by concentrating on the demander.

(a) *The Postulate of the Personal Gainful Motive*

These laws will not hold unless all the persons engaged in the process of exchange are engaged in the personal pursuit of maximum gain. If they are not, then there is no possible reason for saying that rise and fall of demand will affect price levels and *vice versa*.

Consider the first law. 'If, at the price ruling, effective demand exceeds effective supply, price will tend to rise.' This means that, if there is an operative ratio of 1 pear to 6 pennies; and if, on this ratio, there is a greater demand for pears than the number available; then the ratio will tend to alter towards a greater number of pennies per pear. Why? It can only be if someone—or some group—wants the ratio to rise; for 'available' means available 'at a price'. It is clearly the suppliers who want the price to rise. They assume that they are not getting the maximum possible return in the circumstances. They assume that, with so many wanting pears, there are likely to be many persons who would be willing to give more rather than do without. The suppliers will therefore tend to feel their way towards the highest possible price consistent with their total interest. That is to say, they will tend to demand more and more up to the point at which they consider that effective demand will just clear their stock, or clear the bulk of it at a price which will more than compensate for not selling the whole at a slightly lower price. The suppliers of pears want the maximum possible gain from the exchange.

On the other hand, the demanders of pears want the lowest

possible ratio of pennies to pears. Hence, if the ratio is 1 pear to 6 pennies, and if there is not enough effective demand to clear the substantial part of the stock, the supplier tends to give way to the demander's view of the desirable price. The supplier does this, not because the demander is rendered happier thereby, but because, in the unfortunate situation, that is the way to reduce supplier's loss as far as possible.

We can illustrate the same general point in another way. Suppose there is no actually agreed price, and one has to be fixed. Suppose that the initial proposals of supplier and demander are made by the method of the sealed tender. In that case there are three possibilities. First, the supplier and demander might by accident hit on exactly the same ratio; secondly, the supplier might demand a higher ratio of pennies to pears than the demander offered; thirdly, the demander's offer might be higher than the supplier's demand.

In the first of these cases, there would be no further discussion. The ratio would be agreed. S and D would be willing to do business.

In the second case, business could not be done on the original proposals. If agreement were finally to be reached, it would be by S trying to get D to move as near to S's original proposal as possible, and D trying to get S to move towards D's original proposal.

In the third case, again, business could not be done on the original proposals; but in this case, S would attempt to keep D as near as possible to D's original proposal, and D would try to keep S as near S's original proposal as possible.

In short, the motive for the exchange is gain; S's motive is S's gain, and D's motive is D's gain.

We must, however, limit our statement of the postulate to this positive motive. It is true that we are considering a competitive situation in which any increase in S's gain means a diminution in D's gain, and *vice versa*. It is perfectly true that both are aware of this fact. But this does not permit us to say that S's motive is 'the maximum gain for S and the minimum gain for D'. The motive is 'the maximum gain for S' with the known and accepted consequence (which is not, nevertheless, part of the motive) that this will entail minimum gain for D. Unless we keep clearly in mind the distinction between S's motive and what he knows will be a necessary consequence of the successful pursuit of his end, we shall fall into serious errors in our interpretation of the economic relation.

(b) *The Postulate of Economy*

The postulate that the 'principle of economy' is operative in exchange could probably be brought out in connexion with the first law if we took rather more complicated examples. But this postulate is more obviously present in the second law. 'A rise in price tends to decrease effective demand.' The supplier who tends to step up his price proposals when effective demand exceeds effective supply is perfectly well aware that this will render some present effective demand ineffective. The point here is not simply that some of the demanders will decline to pay more, but that they will 'go out of the market' rather than pay more, even if they do in fact have the necessary funds to pay the higher price. Why should they go out of this particular market? It is because every demander evaluates the various ways in which his resources could be employed. While he may be prepared to pay 6d for a pear plus 3d for an orange, he may consider it better, if pears rise to 7d, to buy two oranges and one or two apples.

Similarly, a person who could produce pears, but is not willing to do so when the price is 6d, may be willing when the price is 7d or 8d. Why? Because he considers that, at the old price, his resources could be more profitably employed, while at the new price pear production will give the best return for costs incurred.

We should reach the same conclusion by considering all the situations to which the law applies. What this law reveals, on reflection, is that, while demanders want prices to sink to zero, and while suppliers want them to rise to infinity, the actual range within which they can rise and fall, without destroying the possibility of exchange, is relatively limited. Suppliers of x ($=$demanders of y) and demanders of x ($=$suppliers of y) are all economising their resources, distributing them so as to satisfy as far as possible various demands. It is the attempt to avoid waste of scarce resources (the attempt to economise) which is brought to light when we consider the effects of rising and falling prices on diminution and increase of effective demand and supply. Each person concerned is engaged, it is postulated, in the search for the maximum realisation of an all-round ideal of life which we call 'the pursuit of happiness'.

(c) The Postulate of Valuation

From what has been said, it is obvious that there is a third postulate. Not only is exchange undertaken in a personal effort for gain, and conducted under the guidance of the principle of economy, but it is also conducted in a situation which enforces a choice on all persons entering into the economic relationship. Choice here is choice in the sense explained in our early account of the value judgement, distinguishing it from the moral, efficiency and aesthetic judgements. We pay a 'price' for what we get in exchange. We surrender something which has a value to us. It has a value, if not directly as itself qualitatively capable of meeting some need or want of ours, at least indirectly in that it could have been exchanged for something else had it not been utilised by being exchanged for what we now receive. In any particular exchange situation, the circumstances confront us with the necessity of renouncing (renouncing as meaning either 'surrendering' or 'not receiving') one of the alternatives x and y, both of which we want. That this is the same as saying we are confronted by a situation in which we are forced to evaluate the alternatives is clear when it is remembered that effective demand and supply are demand and supply at a price. The words 'at a price' imply that the supplier or the demander has weighed up what he may get in exchange against the proposals as to what he should surrender, and at a given point has decided that it is better to retain what he has than to part with it for what is offered. In short, we are dealing with the 'comparative value judgement' or 'valuation' in the sense explained. Valuation is thus a postulate of our laws of supply and demand.

D

It should be particularly noted that this valuation is postulated as antecedent to the determination of price. It is when the valuations of both supplier and demander make possible the fixing of an exchange ratio that we have price (exchange ratio). The exchange ratio may be below the maximum that the demander would have been prepared to accept, and above the minimum that the supplier would have been prepared to accept, if necessary; but, if demander's offer were to fall to a certain level, supplier's valuation would operate as a check on any further fall consistent with the possibility of exchange. Similarly, with regard to the limits imposed on the rise in supplier's terms. The valuations made by the parties to an exchange must be antecedent to the determination of price, for these valuations determine the limits within which price must fall.

It is apparent, therefore, that we are dealing with two quite different 'comparative orders of values'. One of these is the order of value when 'value' is taken as synonymous with 'price'. The other is the order of value constructed in each individual mind which sets the lower or the upper limit within which price must fall. The former is a 'public order of values'. The latter is an 'order of value (or a valuational order) within the individual mind'. The former is one of the things about which economics is primarily concerned to theorise. The latter is a postulate the economist makes in his theorising. This is not to say that the economist does not offer some sort of theory about the process of valuation which occurs in the individual mind. Most economists say something about it, and many economists say a great deal which is of the first importance in relation to the philosophical problem. But their reason for offering some sort of theory of valuation is that they are aware that they postulate the process of valuation in what they say about the 'public order of values', and naturally feel that the nature of the postulate has to be explained at least in outline. We shall return to this point on a future occasion. For the present it is sufficient to say that the activity of valuation is the third essential postulate of the laws of supply and demand which are 'the framework into which all analysis of special, detailed problems must be fitted'.

3. The Postulates of Economics and 'The Economic Man'

If we reflect for a moment on these three postulates of the laws of supply and demand, the inevitable inference appears to be that what we are postulating is 'the economic man' of ill fame. We postulate that the parties to an exchange are each personally endeavouring to maximise gain (the 'egoism' of the 'economic man'), that they are guided by the principle of economy (the 'purely rational behaviour' of the 'economic man'), and that each party is acting on a valuation in an enforced choice situation (the 'competitive character' of the 'economic man').

Now, if we try to think out the meaning of 'the economic man', it is evident that our postulates do not and cannot refer to him. They refer to the total man in an economic relation, which is an entirely different thing. The 'economic man', as a rationally directed competitive egoist, is neither more nor less than Hobbes' man 'in the state of nature before the foundation of civil society' —an individual who knows nothing of juridical rules guiding his behaviour in relation to his fellows, and is incapable of acting otherwise than in the pursuit of self-interest, employing his rational faculties to acquire 'power after power' in order to secure not merely present satisfaction, but also the means of satisfaction for all needs over the foreseeable future, and thus engaged in 'a war of all against all'. If we are right in saying that the conception of the 'economic man' is really the equivalent of Hobbes' man in the state of nature, then it is utterly impossible that this should be the kind of person envisaged in the three postulates of the laws of supply and demand; for the general assumption of the laws is that men engaged in economic exchange are living within, and not outside of, a juridical order, and that exchange on the economic level presupposes that all are observing the rights of their fellows. That is to say, we are assuming, not Hobbes' state of nature, but an organised civil society composed of eminently law-abiding citizens.

This is clear from the very conceptions of (effective) demand and supply and price. Price is an *agreed* ratio of exchange. Supply is not supply at all in the sense of our laws of supply and demand, except 'at a price'. This means that it is a stock of things possessed by one person which is available for transfer to another (the demander) on conditions which are agreeable to the present possessor. We do not have economic exchange if the demander collects his friends and violently dispossesses the supplier. That is not an economic relationship. We have exchange (in the economic sense) when the demander does not possess himself of supplier's goods until supplier confers the right in terms of an agreed ratio of exchange. The economic relation with which the laws of demand and supply are concerned is therefore one which has no meaning except as a relation between persons who are already 'respecters of mutual rights and duties', members of an established society operating within the framework of a juridical order. Hence whatever its postulates may mean, they cannot possibly mean the postulation of 'the economic man'.

What the postulates signify will be clearer if we speak, not of the economic man, but of the economic relation in which man may stand to his fellows, and consider whether this relation implies any view of man which from any other point of view—say the moral or the psychological—is regarded as certainly or probably false. Our third postulate, namely the postulate that valuation in choice situations is a necessary condition of economic exchange will not, presumably, be questioned. There is no other view of man which would find difficulty in accepting this. The difficulties apparently arise in connexion with the first and second postulates which seem to suggest an egoistic attitude and that man's actions are governed entirely by reason. Many moral theorists would object to the first suggestion, and presumably all psychologists would object to the second. We shall consider these two points in that order.

(1) *The Economic Relation and the Idea of the Good*

The economic relation is but one of many relations in which men stand to each other within the total social order. It cannot, as we have just seen, exist alone. It can however be distinguished from other relations; and perhaps its nature will become sufficiently clear if we distinguish it from two others which we may call the 'fellowship' and the 'juridical' relation, respectively.

The Fellowship Relation: The name given to this relation does not much matter so long as we understand the kind of relation which is meant. It is the relation in which individuals stand to each other when they are pursuing a genuinely common good. A common good is an end which is pursued by a number of persons in collaboration, each pursuing it, not only because he himself wants it to be realised, but also because he knows that those collaborating with him want it to be realised. Thus, if *A* thinks *x* good, and pursues it quite irrespective of whether *B* thinks it good, there is obviously no common good. Or if *A* thinks it good, and at the same time thinks that its realisation would be good for *B*, we cannot say that there is necessarily a conception of common good operating. Thus, if *A* thinks *x* good for *A* and for *B*, and pursues it because of this; and if *B* thinks *x* good for *B* and for *A*, and pursues it because of this; we are not necessarily dealing with a common good *x*. Before we can say that we are dealing with a common good, in the proper sense of the term, *A* must think *x* good for *A* and *B*, *B* must think *x* good for *B* and *A*, *A* must know that *B* thinks so, *B* must know that *A* thinks so, and the knowledge that both desire the realisation of *x* must be part of the motive which determines each of them to pursue it. Possibly a simple but adequate illustration of the fellowship relation, when individuals are pursuing a common good, may be found in a choir. Smith and White are both members, tenor and bass. In this respect they regard themselves (and not merely their vocal organs) as 'instruments for the realisation of a common purpose' or common good which is the making of grave, sweet melody. As members of the fellowship they are not thinking of a right-duty relationship in which they stand to each other (although there is this relationship also), but of making their respective contributions to a common end for the production of which they have a joint responsibility.

The Juridical Relation: Smith and White are also neighbours living in adjoining houses. Smith has a passion for fruit. White has a small orchard, some of the best fruit-trees growing temptingly near the wall dividing the two properties. But Smith respects the property rights of White and refrains from touching the apples and plums. He limits the pursuit of the ends he considers good out of respect to White's rights, i.e. from a sense of duty. However, some time earlier Smith and White have made an agreement—an economic agreement, as they both consider it —that, when the fruit is ready, White will sell Smith x stone of apples at y shillings the stone. When the crop is ready for market, White finds that the prevailing conditions show that his bargain with Smith was a bad one from the economic point of view. He could have got more than double the price in the open market. But the contract has vested a certain right in Smith, and White does not hesitate about fulfilling his obligation. He carries out what is in fact a bad bargain for him, one which he would never have made had he been able to anticipate what the conditions would be. Here Smith and White are standing in juridical relations with each other, thinking in terms of their mutual rights and duties—White's real rights as owner of the orchard, and Smith's personal rights against White in consequence of the contract.

The Economic Relation: The economist, as such, is not interested in either the fellowship or the juridical relation between White and Smith. It is true that the economic relation presupposes the existence of juridicial relations at least; and it is true that, when a business deal is put through, it establishes a new juridical relation which we call the right and obligation arising from contract. But the subject-matter of economics is the process of making the business deal, and not the juridical relations which it presupposes or those in which it results.

The economic relation is of the following kind: Let us say that Smith is anxious to found a Home for destitute children. White is not interested; he has got his own preoccupations, being anxious to send an orphaned nephew to the university to take a medical degree, a project in which Smith is politely interested, but in which he feels no call to render assistance. Smith and White may, nevertheless, co-operate in the realisation of each other's ends. White is a builder; and, in the ordinary course of business, he submits a tender and secures the contract for the building of Smith's Home. In return, he is paid a sum of money by Smith; and this money actually makes it possible for him to send his nephew to the university. Smith and White here stand in an economic relationship. They are not interested in each other's ends (the ends relevant to this relationship); they do not (in this respect) have any common end; they do not (in this respect) have any rights and duties until they have made the economic agreement; and yet they do assist each other in essential ways to realise each other's ends (the building of the Home and the education of the nephew). They help each other by exchanging services and money on a business footing.

What is the bearing of this account of the economic relation on the question of 'egoism'? What is certainly true is that each party to the economic exchange is actuated by the motive of maximum gain for himself, not for the other party. But by 'gain' we mean a realisation of what he personally considers to be good. Maximum gain is the greatest possible realisation in the circumstances of some end or ends which is or are part of the content of his total personal conception of good. But, quite obviously, many of the things which a person considers good are not pursued for selfish or egoistic reasons. We cannot—as some of the older economists supposed—adopt a theory of egoism, hedonistic or otherwise. The fact that the economic relation presupposes the existence of juridical relations makes egoism quite untenable as a psychological theory for the economist to assume. What the economist is really assuming is not that the parties to the exchange are egoists, but that they are each engaged in the pursuit of a total conception of good, utilising scarce resources, and that the particular end each is at the moment pursuing is not also an end to the other. The total conception of good, as entertained by Smith, will include all sorts of ends, some of them common ends which he shares with White, some common ends which he shares with other persons, and some of his ends will be best stated in terms of the performance of personal or social obligations. But, in anyone's total conception of good, there will always be some end which is not also an end to (i.e. not also a common end with) another person who is yet in a position to help the former. When

there is a mutual 'uninterestedness' along with a mutual ability
to assist, and when such assistance can be geared to the promotion
of the ends which are not common ends to the two parties in
question, and when there is no existing obligation to render such
assistance, that is when the economic relation is likely to arise.

Thus, in the case supposed, Smith's desire to found the Home
is anything but egoistic; and the same may be said of White's
desire to send his nephew to the university. Both of the ends are
'other regarding'; and we may assume that the former is a common good cherished by Smith and some others including the
children who will benefit, and that the latter is a common good
cherished by White and his nephew. The point is simply that
the building of the Home and the nephew's education are not
common goods to Smith and White. Of course Smith may have
'ulterior motives'; he may be angling for public approbation and
a title. White may also have the 'ulterior motive' of retiring and
living on his nephew's earnings. But such egoistic motives, if
they exist at all, will have to be established by the appropriate
evidence. That the motives are egoistic could not be deduced
from the fact that Smith and White are, in this case, bargaining
for gain as against each other; nor, if we could establish ulterior
motives, would it help us in the least to understand the transaction
between Smith and White. All we need assume is that each is
conserving scarce resources in the pursuit of a total conception of
good, and that neither will 'waste' resources on the production
of an end not included in his conception of the good.

To put the general point as concisely as possible:

When A is pursuing an end x (which may in fact be a common
good for A, C and D), and B is pursuing an end y (which may in
fact be a common good for B, C and D), and neither x nor y is a
common good to A and B, and neither A nor B has a duty to
assist in the production of y or x respectively; and when, nevertheless, A and B do render each other assistance such as to make
possible the attainment of x and y; then here we have the establishment of the economic relation. It is not egoism, but the
absence of common good in the relevant respect, which is assumed.

(2) *The Assumption of Purely Rational Behaviour*

The second objection to the postulates was that the place of rational calculation in human behaviour is exaggerated to the point of distortion.

The answer to this objection is that to assume, for purposes of theoretical analysis, that the person entering into an economic relation is acting with a coldly perfect rationality is the only assumption which could properly be made. This does not mean that we assume men to be abstractly rational creatures never at the mercy of their emotions. We do not make any such assumption when we study logic and attempt to understand the nature of thinking and the process of inference; but in logic we do assume that we are dealing with men in respect of their rational nature, and therefore we study the operations of reason as such. Similarly, in attempting to understand how men 'assess' or 'estimate' the ways in which things will contribute to their total conception of what is good, and how they 'compare' degrees of goodness, we are studying the application of reason to the situations in which that conception of the good is being sought. Smith knows that buildings are not created by wishful thinking. He has to employ resources at his command to get the building created; and these resources (his money) are also useful for realising many of his ends besides that represented by the Home. He has, therefore, to assess the significance of the tender submitted by White, relatively to the tenders submitted by other builders, in the light of the principle of 'economy'; that is to say, he has to consider whether, by paying White's price for the work, he will not only realise the end represented by the Home, but will also have more power (money in this case) to realise the other ends comprised in his total conception of the good than he would have if he accepted some other tender. Taking into account the reputations for reliability, etc., etc., of all the tenderers, if White submits a figure of £40,000, and other figures range from £40,500 upwards, the principle of economy indicates that White's should be accepted. This is to range the various tenders in a 'valuational order', and it is quite patent that the operation of arranging them is rational.

It is the intricacies of this rational operation in its objective social manifestations in the market which are studied by economics, while the subjective character of the operation itself is the subject-matter of the theory of valuation.

4. Provisional Conclusions

In our Introduction, we began by distinguishing two possible approaches to the theory of goodness or value, one being the approach more commonly adopted by contemporary philosophers, an inquiry as to the 'nature of goodness', the other being an investigation of the 'nature of the value judgement'. It was intimated that we should follow the latter approach.

It was then necessary to define, as accurately as could be done in an introductory chapter, the nature of the value judgement, distinguishing it from other forms of judgement liable to be confused with it. As a preparatory step we noted the two forms of the value judgement itself—the simply positive 'attribution of goodness', and the comparative 'attribution of degrees of goodness'; and we found that the comparative form of the value judgement often provides a clearer test than does the simply positive form for distinguishing between the value judgement and other kinds of judgement. We were able to show that the value judgement is essentially different from the moral, efficiency and aesthetic judgements.

Concentrating, then, on the comparative form, we saw that it is really the expression of choice when objective circumstances enforce a choice between alternatives both of which are thought good. For the attribution of 'degree of goodness' in this sense we decided to use the term 'valuation', and we also decided that it would be expedient to treat first of valuation (attribution of degree of goodness), and subsequently deal with the attribution of goodness itself, even though the conception of goodness is more fundamental than that of degree of goodness.

It was apparent that our problem of valuation has some close relationship with the theory of value as developed by economists; and, on inquiring what this relationship could be, we found that

the general laws of supply and demand, as formulated by the
economist, make three basic assumptions or postulates—the personal gainful motive, the principle of economy, and the act of
valuation—all of which postulates, though made for the purpose
of explaining exchange between individuals, are postulates about
the operations of the human mind which do not depend upon
the fact of interpersonal relations, but would operate even if an
individual were living in isolation.

We then considered possible objections to these postulates on
the ground of alleged ethical or psychological impossibility, and
endeavoured to show that, properly understood, the postulates
are eminently reasonable. What the economist's laws of supply
and demand postulate is not 'an economic man' as traditionally
understood, but an ordinary, normal human being who, in choice
situations, evaluates the ends he considers 'good' by placing them
in an order of 'degree of goodness', so as to distribute his scarce
resources, in accordance with the principle of economy, in 'the
effort after personal gain' (i.e. in the pursuit of the 'totality' of his
personal or individual conception of the good). This does not
imply that none of the ends included in this totality can be
completely benevolent in character, or that none of them will be
ends jointly pursued with other persons, or that none of them
will be pursued as honouring obligations. The 'effort after gain'
or 'search for total happiness' will embrace the pursuit of ends of
all these kinds. We call it the 'effort after personal gain' only
because the relative valuation of such ends must be within a
single, unitary self-consciousness.

But this process of valuation is of special interest to the economist only in so far as it expresses itself in a social setting, resulting
in individuals affording assistance to each other in the pursuit of
their ends, when such assistance is *not* motivated by benevolence,
not motivated by the conception of common good, and *not* motivated by any sense of obligation, as between the persons so assist-
ing each other. It is this kind of collaboration which constitutes
the 'economic order', an aspect of the total social order which,
both for theoretical and for practical purposes, is distinguishable
from other aspects, such, for instance, as the juridical aspect.

The philosopher is not specially concerned with the study of the economic order in this sense. But he is very much concerned with the postulates which the economist makes in attempting to explain the nature of the economic order; for these postulates are postulates about the individual mind; and what the economist is doing in making them, and in erecting a general theory of value upon their foundations, becomes pretty clear on reflection. He is providing the essential basis, and a fair amount of the superstructure, of a theory of the comparative value judgement.

This being so, it seems safe to assume that, if we are to carry out, in the philosophical field, the analysis of the principles which manifest themselves in the economic order, and have been studied there more systematically than anywhere else, some of the most important clues for the philosopher will be found in reflecting on the nature of the concepts used in economic analysis, and on the relation of these concepts to each other. Our next step, therefore, will be to examine these concepts and see how far they can be employed in elucidating the nature of the comparative value judgement.

5. THE CONCEPTS OF VALUATIONAL THEORY

The concepts which have been used in formulating and discussing the postulates of the laws of supply and demand, and the nature of the economic relation, are the following: demander, demand, supplier, supply, price, cost, purchasing power, economy.

Not all of these concepts, however, will be relevant to the theory of valuation. Some of them can have meaning only in connexion with the realm of exchange, i.e. in connexion with those phenomena which arise when the valuations taking place in different individual minds interact with each other. Of the concepts which apply only within the realm of exchange, 'price' is the most obvious. As we have seen, one of the postulates of the laws of supply and demand is that the process of valuation in the minds of individuals is antecedent to the determination of price (the exchange ratio). Hence valuation must be capable of explanation without employing the concept of price.

If we exclude price, we must also exclude the concepts of demand and supply as these are understood in the statement of the laws of supply and demand. In the statement of the laws, it will be remembered, 'demand' can mean only 'effective demand' and 'supply' only 'effective supply'. That is to say, the laws can be regarded as significant only if demand and supply are understood as demand and supply at a given price. It is this demand (or supply) at a given price which we have called effective demand (or supply); and since effective demand and effective supply can be defined only in relation to the concept of price, it is clear that these concepts must be as irrelevant as is that of price to a theory of valuation. But we also noted that 'demand' and 'supply' may be understood in a more general sense; and these more general concepts are both relevant to the theory of valuation, for they do not depend for their significance upon the realm of exchange. An individual living in isolation from his fellows could have demands, in the general sense, and could be in a situation where supply, in a general sense, was available to meet demand.

There is one further term which may be set aside as irrelevant to a theory of valuation, namely the conception of the supplier. A supplier is a person, A, who makes available certain goods or services to another individual, B; and, when we talk of a supplier, we are always thinking (when speaking economically) of one who is prepared to make things available only at a price. The conception of the supplier is bound up with that of effective supply, not that of supply in the general sense. Robinson Crusoe could have a supply of timber, nuts and game available, without there being any question of a 'supplier' (in the economic as distinguished from the theological sense).

It would appear, however, that, when we have excluded the concepts of price, effective demand, effective supply and supplier, all the other concepts which we have used are relevant to the theory of valuation. These are (1) Demander, (2) Demand, in the general sense, (3) Supply, in the general sense, (4) Purchasing power, (5) Cost, and (6) Economy. We shall try to explain and define these concepts.[1]

[1] Economists may find some difficulty over some of the following definitions,

(1) *Demander*. Anything which is valued must, of necessity, occupy a place in a valuational order. Since a valuational order is an order of choice or preference, this implies that the order is contained wholly within the one unitary consciousness. And since 'value' means 'degree of goodness', the unitary consciousness assumed in the idea of value is a consciousness which attributes goodness to things. It is this unitary conscious subject which we mean when we speak of a demander. A 'demander' is thus 'a self-conscious subject attributing goodness to various things, and choosing rationally between alternatives to which he attributes varying degrees of goodness with a view to the realisation of his total personal conception of "good".'

(2) *Demand* (in the general sense). This concept is not so easy to define. We speak of a 'demand for something', or of an 'object of demand'. What do we mean by the 'object' here? The answer to this question seems, at first sight, simple. We demand such things as 'tea', 'bags of corn', 'money' and so forth; and these, we may say, are the objects of demand. This implies that the object of demand is always some actually existing thing. But we also speak of a demand for 'services'. Are services, at the time when they are demanded, things which actually exist? The question is not whether services can ever be said to exist in the sense in which tea can exist. Assuming that services can be said to exist at the time when they are actually being performed, do they necessarily exist in this sense when they are demanded? Indeed, the same question can be raised with regard to tea and corn. When bags of corn are offered for sale in the market, the bags of corn are in

particularly the definitions of 'Demand', 'Supply' and 'Purchasing Power'. If they do, it is probably because they find it hard to dissociate these terms from the conception of the process of exchange. The terms 'value', 'demand', 'supply' and some others have been taken over from common usage and have been defined or adapted by economists as technical concepts and have therefore had their meanings restricted (in economic usage). My definitions are for purposes of the theory of the value judgement. For this reason, my definitions of 'demand', 'supply' and 'purchasing power' cannot be precisely the same as those adopted or implied in, for instance, the formulations of the laws of supply and demand. 'Demand' and 'supply' in the economist's sense ('effective demand' or 'demand at a price') would have meaning for Unilever but none whatsoever for Robinson Crusoe, because Robinson is not operating within an order of exchange, entering into economic relations with other persons. 'Demand' and 'supply' for a theory of valuation must be significant for Unilever and for Robinson Crusoe.

existence and are presumably objects of demand. But we can also talk of corn which does not exist as the 'object of demand'. It is the demand for (non-existent) corn which makes the farmer plough and sow in the spring. The object of demand may thus, apparently, be either an existent or a non-existent thing.

But when we look closer at the conception of demand, we see that there is a difficulty in speaking of any actually existing thing as an object of demand. When two competitors demand 'the same bag of corn', what each of them is really aiming at, or demanding, is the possession of the bag for himself to the exclusion of his rival. From this it is clear that we are apt to use the term 'object of demand' in two quite different senses. In one sense, the competitor is demanding what actually exists (the 'object of demand' being an existing bag of corn); but in another sense, the competitor is demanding what does not exist (his 'object of demand' being the possession of the bag).

This ambiguity in the use of the term 'object of demand' does not, I think, greatly worry the economist. The economist can speak significantly about the demand for corn, meaning sometimes the corn in the market, and sometimes the corn which the farmer hopes will be produced as a result of his collaboration with the forces of nature; and the fact that corn, in the first case, is an 'existing object' and, in the other case, the 'content of an end' which the farmer has in view, makes no real difference to the argument of the economist, generally speaking. But when the philosopher is dealing with the theory of valuation, the distinction becomes important, because the 'objects of demand' which we evaluate against each other cannot be things which actually exist. If they did exist, no choice would be involved. Both would be 'there'. Thus, when you 'choose' between 'a bag of corn' and 'a sum of money', both the corn and the money are present; but the 'alternatives' between which you choose are 'your possession of the corn' and 'your possession of the money'. These are the alternatives one of which has to be renounced if the other is to be realised, and the essence of alternatives for choice is that they are possible future, but not actually present, existents.

It is, therefore, in connexion with the theory of valuation, and not for the more general purposes of economics, that the distinction between the two senses of 'object of demand' becomes important.

The most sensible course to follow, it seems to me, is to recognise that, normally, when the economist talks of the object of demand, he is using the term 'object' in the wide sense to cover both the things which are physically existent and also those states of affairs, such as possession of physical things, which do not exist at the time when they are demanded; and to recognise also that, for the theory of valuation, these two senses of 'object' must be clearly distinguished. In the strict sense of the term 'demand', we can never demand that which already is. We can demand only that which does not exist. Demand always, and necessarily, has a future reference. It is a conative disposition directed towards the acquiring, creation, maintenance or destruction of some state of affairs. To indicate this is essential in any definition of 'demand'.

We can, I think, get over the difficulty by using the two terms 'object' and 'content' to mark the distinction between the two senses of 'object'. Henceforth, when we speak of the 'object of demand', the reference will be to things actually in existence—commodities such as pounds of tea, bags of corn in the marketplace, and services so far as these may be said to be in actual existence; and, when we speak of the 'content of demand', the reference will be to that which is, in the strict sense, demanded—the acquiring of tea or corn or services, the production or maintenance of a certain state of affairs. The content of demand will always, therefore, be an 'end' of some kind, and 'objective of conation'. When it is not necessary, for purposes of our argument, to distinguish between 'object' and 'content' of demand, we shall speak simply of a 'thing' being demanded or valued.

Using our terms in this sense, and bearing in mind that what is demanded, in the strict sense, is always the 'content' and never the 'object' of demand, we must obviously define the concept of demand by reference to its content, not by reference to its object. The following definition appears to be appropriate: 'Demand is a conative disposition, the content or end of which is the creation, maintenance or destruction of some state of affairs.'

(3) *Supply* (in the general sense). This may be defined as 'the total quantity of a thing actually available at any given time, some at least of which is actually, and of which the remainder is potentially, an object of demand'. The various parts of this definition require some explanation.

Firstly, supply in this general sense, has no necessary connexion with economic exchange, although it has a necessary connexion with the conception of demand in the general sense.

Secondly, it is to be noted that supply is an 'object', not 'content', of actual or potential demand. What is in supply is something which actually exists. If we attempted to define supply in terms of content of demand, supply would be an 'end' which we had a conative disposition to realise. It would therefore be an element integral to demand itself. If this were the case, we could not possibly speak of supply as exceeding or falling short of demand. Corn in Robinson Crusoe's store-room is corn in supply. The trees actually growing on his island are timber in supply. It is the distinction between that which exists, on the one hand, and that the existence of which we have as an end, on the other, which makes it possible to say that the former (supply) may be greater than, equal to, or less than the latter (demand).

Thirdly, not all of the thing in supply need be actually an object of demand, but some of it must be. Supply and demand are correlative terms in the sense that the one cannot be understood except in relation to the other. But they are not correlative in the sense that supply and demand must be strictly co-extensive in relation to the same thing. If the whole of supply were necessarily an object of demand, then it would be impossible to speak of supply as exceeding demand; for any quantity not actually in demand would, for that very reason, not be supply; nor would it be possible to speak of supply as falling short of demand, since what was not in supply would, for that very reason, not be in demand. It is because supply may be greater than, equal to, or less than demand that it is possible to speak of valuation; for valuation only arises when we have to choose between the expenditure of our resources on alternatives both of which are in demand.

E

But while some of the supply need be only potentially in demand, some at least of it must be actually in demand. If the terms were not correlative in this limited sense, then supply would mean exactly the same as 'existence'. We should speak of anything actually existing as being in supply, even if we supposed that it had no conceivable relation to what any person wants. Man is so acquisitive that we hardly dare set limits to the things he may want; and he is so versatile that it would be rash to say of anything that he will never find a use for it; but, normally, we should not speak of atmospheric dust as being in supply. It exists, but it is not the sort of thing which is in demand.

Fourthly, what is in supply must be actually available. We may say that since people do actually demand some coal, some sand and some water, then coals at Newcastle, sand in the Sahara and rain at Applecross constitute supply. But whether they can really be considered as part of the supply of coals, sand and water depends upon whether they are actually available to the person or persons whose demands are under consideration. The water of Applecross is not really available to the inhabitant of North Africa. The sand of the Sahara is not really available to the Esquimau sugar merchant in the Arctic circle. Availability is a relative term, and whether we consider anything available to a given person depends on empirical circumstances. But the conception of availability must be applicable in any given case in which it is appropriate to speak of a thing as being in supply.

Supply, then, is the total quantity of a thing actually available at any given time, some of which at least is actually, and of which the remainder is potentially, an object of demand.

(4) *Purchasing Power* is 'that which, being in possession of a demander, is necessarily employed, by its operation, consumption or transference, in realising the content of a demand'. It is essentially acquisitive power which will be expended in the course of satisfying demand. We usually think of purchasing power in terms of money; but money is merely a special form which, because of its great importance, tends to appropriate to itself the generic name. The exercise of bodily strength or the shooting of an arrow to bring down game are instances of the effective employ-

ment of purchasing power. The exercise of a right is the exercise of purchasing power. To take other instances, there is no difference in principle between paying a fee in money for professional service, and enticing, with a handful of oats, a skittish pony to come and be harnessed. We assume, of course, that the professional fee, the oats, the arrow and the bodily energy are being 'expended', and are therefore not available to the person for employment on some further occasion to realise the content of some other demand. Thus a 'throwing spear' assumed to be recoverable after each throw is not purchasing power in the sense defined. It is a 'means'. It is the 'service' of the spear which would be the purchasing power expended on any given occasion.

Purchasing power, therefore, does not mark off a class of things which are quite distinct from objects of demand. The same thing —gold or water or cattle or a particular service—may be both an object of demand and also an item in purchasing power. It is an item in purchasing power in so far as it performs a certain function—whatever else it may be or do—namely the function of realising the content of some demand by being itself expended.

(5) *Cost*. In popular usage, 'cost' and 'price' are often equated. 'What is the price of this suit?' 'It costs 25 guineas.' But presumably even in popular usage there is a slight difference of emphasis. When the tailor says, 'It costs (or will cost you) 25 guineas', he has probably a faint twinge of sympathy for you. This is more evident in a case where, for instance, the engine of a car has been damaged by frost, and the mechanic says to the unfortunate owner, 'That will cost you £60'. He is probably thinking, not only of the price of a new engine-block, in the strict sense of price (the exchange ratio), but also of the sacrifice to be made if a new one is to be acquired. It is this conception of something 'devoted', 'expended' or 'sacrificed' which is essential in the economist's conception of cost. Thus, while 'price' is 'the ratio in which things exchange', 'cost' is, e.g. the total of commodities and services consumed in the production and conveyance of something to the market. And while, according to the theory, costs of production and prices in exchange tend towards equality, cost and price of the same article may be very different. The cost

of production may be considerably less (or in particular cases considerably more) than the price fetched in exchange.

But, even for the economist, the concept of cost is by no means a simple one. Consider the following statement: 'The cost of producing any commodity is fundamentally the cost of *detaining* productive resources so as to make their services available to the industry producing the commodity *rather than* to some other industry. Now the cost of retaining resources is equal to the value of these resources for other purposes, plus the cost of transferring them from their existing employment to the most attractive alternative employment. Cost, in other words, measures the pull of competing attractions. If the cost of any factor is not covered, that factor will move to some other industry, and the value of what it could produce in that industry is its cost in its present use. Cost, therefore, must always be considered in terms of alternatives. Cost measures what we could produce instead—what we forgo by using productive resources for one purpose rather than for another. Alternatively, it measures what we could save by not using the resources at all'.[1]

The view here stated is not entirely free from ambiguities. For instance, one wants to look carefully at the word 'measures' when it is said that 'cost measures the pull of competing attractions', or that 'cost measures what we forgo by using resources for one purpose rather than another'. The general line of the argument suggests that, instead of saying 'cost measures', we ought to say 'cost is'. But these linguistic points can best be dealt with once we realise what the fundamental view is. The view is that 'cost' does not mean, in the last analysis, the resources expended in producing something, but the amount of demand *A* which is left unsatisfied when resources are employed towards the satisfaction of demand *B*.

To make this point clear we may distinguish between two different senses in which the term 'cost' could be used; and, in order that the distinction may be most easily apprehended, we shall not make use of monetary conceptions. Suppose that I want to make a bookcase, and that I am at present in possession of a table, the necessary tools, screws, etc. If I cut up the table in order

---

[1] A. K. Cairncross, *Introduction to Economics*, p. 189.

to make the bookcase, it could be said that the 'cost' of the bookcase is the wood of the table, screws, glue, etc., wear and tear of tools, and the time and energy utilised. Cost in this sense would be equivalent to the resources expended in making the bookcase. Cost would, in fact, be the amount of purchasing power (as purchasing power has been defined above) required to meet the demand for the bookcase. It is plain that cost in this sense is not the same as the conception of price, for it does not depend upon the existence of exchange. There could be cost in this sense for Robinson Crusoe. Let us call this the conception of 'productive cost'. The term is perhaps a little unfortunate since it may be confused with the economist's 'costs of production'. There is obviously a close relation between the economist's 'costs of production' and what we are here calling 'productive cost'; but the two are not exactly the same. Productive cost (in our sense) is something which could exist for an individual living in isolation.

But we could use the term 'cost' in a rather different sense. We could say that the cost of making the bookcase is not the total amount of resources expended in making the bookcase, but the demand or amount of demand which is left unsatisfied by using those resources for making the bookcase. In this sense, cost necessarily implies competing demands, while it does not necessarily imply competing demands when cost is used in the sense of productive cost. Thus, there will only be a cost in the second sense (i.e. the sense other than 'productive') if I demand, not only the possession of a bookcase, but also the continued possession of the table and, as between these alternatives, choose the table rather than the bookcase. The cost (in the second sense) of having the table is 'the doing without the bookcase'; and the cost of having the bookcase is 'the doing without the table'. Let us call this 'opportunity cost'. Opportunity cost[1] may be defined,

[1] I was, I confess, in some difficulty over selecting terms which would emphasise the nature of my problem and yet not be too objectionable to the economist. 'Opportunity cost' I owe to Professor A. L. Macfie, and it will be obvious from the subsequent argument that this is the kind of 'cost' which is important from the point of view of valuation. I am not specially happy about 'productive' but can think of nothing better. The distinction between 'opportunity' and 'productive' here seems to correspond very closely to Dr L. M. Fraser's distinction between 'displacement' and 'embodied' costs (*Economic Thought and Language*, p.

then, as 'the unrealised content of a demand which could just have been realised by utilising in its favour the purchasing power actually utilised towards the realisation of the content of an alternative demand'. It is clearly the conception of 'opportunity cost' which Cairncross has primarily in mind in the passage quoted above. It is this conception of cost which we shall find to be of fundamental importance for the theory of valuation.

(6) *Economy*. Economy is the name we give to that principle which makes a demander direct his purchasing power towards the realisation of his total conception of good. Economy is thus, broadly speaking, the same as 'the greatest happiness principle' of J. S. Mill, or the conception of 'blessedness', to use Carlyle's term. It does not refer to 'the greatest happiness of the greatest number' but to the greatest happiness of the individual person concerned. As already explained, this does not imply an egoistic theory of human nature; for, amongst the 'ends' forming the content of a person's conception of happiness or total good, many will be 'other-regarding'. The greatest happiness principle, in this connexion, simply means the principle of the co-ordination of an individual's ends (whatever those ends may happen to be) in a coherent system.

Since the Utilitarians were very confused over this whole issue, perhaps it would be less misleading to compare the principle of economy with Kant's conception of the Assertoric Imperative; that is to say, the principle governing our selection of detailed ends in the prudential pursuit of that which we all do, as a matter of fact, seek (happiness), as distinguished from the Problematic Imperative (concerned with technical rules of skill), or the Categorical Imperative (which governs our judgement as to what we ought, as a matter of duty, to do or seek).

This conception of the principle of economy will not, I conceive, be unfamiliar to economists; but it may seem strange to others. 'Economy', in ordinary usage, means the careful adminis-

92); but it appeared to me that 'embodied' does not cover all that should be covered in what we are contrasting with 'opportunity'. We have to think, not merely of materials embodied in products or even of wear and tear of instruments, but also of what is expended by being given in exchange, if we are to cover all the things which are 'productive' of the satisfaction of demand.

tration of scarce resources; and this may appear to have little connexion with the conception of 'the summum bonum' or 'blessedness'. But the connexion is very real. The conception of economy, as here explained, seems appropriate precisely because, in the ordinary sense, it does mean the careful administration of scarce resources. We conserve resources because each of us is a subject with a unitary self-consciousness, because (as Kant might have said in this connexion) we are subjects to whose rational nature the 'unity of apperception' necessarily belongs. The individual comes to every situation with more in mind than the ostensible alternatives between which he has to choose. There is, in the background of his thought, the sense of 'all the rest' of the things which are in actual or potential demand by him. It is this awareness which makes him practice economy in the ordinary sense of the word.

Thus, without the operation of the principle of economy it would be quite impossible to explain why, in conditions of 'perfect competition', prices for the same sort of commodity tend to be the same for all buyers, irrespective of the varying amounts which different individuals would be prepared, if necessary, to pay. While an individual 'will, if necessary, pay x rather than go without', the 'if necessary' is an essential qualification. If, at price x-minus-y, effective demand is not greater than effective supply, then the necessity will not arise. The person in question will therefore conserve y, simply because he is impelled by the principle of economy to husband resources for 'all the rest' of his actual and potential demands. The principle of economy operates because we have the ability to hold together, in the one unitary consciousness, the conception of a totality of diverse demands and to utilise all available resources for the greatest possible realisation of this totality.

The foregoing account of the principle of economy has very much in common with the conception of economy as expressed by Professor A. L. Macfie.[1] There is, however, a difference of some importance. Macfie[2] takes the view that, in emphasising

---

[1] 'What Kind of Experience is Economising?', in *Ethics*, Vol. LX, No. 1, Oct. 1949.   [2] See, especially, pp. 21-2.

'scarcity conditions' in connexion with the notion of economy, we are in danger of obscuring the nature of the principle of economy itself. In his view, 'economy and efficiency are progressive stages of the one process'.[1] Again, 'Scarcity of means is not the defining character of economy . . . For instance, the economising of a good craftsman is present whether means are scarce or not'.[2] So far as I am able to follow Macfie's argument, it seems to me that he has not made out a case for the wider use of the term 'economy', and that the generally accepted view, which ties up the concept of economy with conditions of scarcity, is the correct one. If we omit to stipulate conditions of scarcity, then we are not dealing with the comparative value judgement at all. It is perfectly true that the 'efficient' selection of means or materials implies the operation of the psychical principle which is also expressed in economising. It is perfectly true that this principle is also expressed in the creation of beautiful things. In all three cases, the co-ordination of an individual's activities is inexplicable unless we assume the activity of a unitary consciousness. But to say that economy is therefore the same as efficiency is to ignore the essential distinction between the efficiency and the value judgement.[3] Efficiency relates to the functional appropriateness to a desired end. To achieve an end efficiently we have to 'select' our means and materials, however plentiful these means and materials may be; but we do not necessarily have to make any 'choice' in the proper sense. On the other hand, we only 'evaluate' means and materials when a choice is necessary—enforced upon us by objective conditions which require the surrender of one thing if the other is to be secured, both the alternatives being considered 'good' (both being demanded) by us. Since valuation is something quite different from making efficiency or aesthetic judgements, and since the unity of self-consciousness expresses itself in a very special way in this form of conative activity, we require some special term to signify the operation of the unity of self-consciousness in valuational or choice situations. If we do not use the term 'economy' to signify this, we must invent some other term. On the whole, it seems preferable to retain the

[1] P. 21.   [2] P. 22.   [3] See pp. 12-20 above.

traditional term, for this term does, after all, indicate the essential relation between the study of 'economics' and the theory of the value judgement.

Economy, then, may be defined as 'the psychical principle which impels a demander, in any choice situation, to employ and conserve purchasing power towards the maximum realisation of his total conception of good'.

We have now defined (somewhat differently, it is true) those six concepts—demander, demand, supply, purchasing power, cost and economy—used in economic theory which will be of most assistance to us in our analysis of the comparative value judgement.

Chapter Two

VALUATION AND OPPORTUNITY COST

In this and the four following chapters we shall try to explain the main principles governing valuational activity. It will be recollected that when we speak of 'valuation' or 'valuational activity' as distinguished from the 'value judgement in general', the reference is to the comparative value judgement. That is to say, the reference is to the judgement that one thing is better than another, and not to the judgement that one thing is good and another bad. We shall, in other words, be speaking of the attribution of degrees of goodness, and not of the simple attribution of goodness or badness.

In explaining the nature of valuation in this sense we shall use illustrations sometimes from the valuations which a man makes when he is a member of a social group, and sometimes from valuations which we may reasonably suppose him to make when he is living in isolation. It may be considered that, since we are now concerned with the operations of the individual mind, examples of the former type will be out of place. Their use, however, can be fully vindicated. It would be very strange if our theory were completely irrelevant to a man's valuations in those situations which account for perhaps nine-tenths of his life.

If we exclude them from consideration, then reliable data will be very scanty; and we shall be tempted to argue on the basis of imaginative situations—a procedure which easily degenerates into treating as 'facts' a collection of fictions foisted on 'the plain man' and used as 'evidence' in support of our theory. So far as possible, we wish to keep in touch with what systematic inquiry has revealed to be generally admitted facts, and to use these both to illustrate and to test the theories we propound. It is, of course, necessary at times to make use of imaginative situations, in order to abstract the individual from all those conditions which are irrelevant to the specific problem which we are studying; and when we use concrete situations which involve a social setting, we must always be ready to defend any inferences drawn by translating our conclusions into terms which do not involve a social setting. We cannot translate a particular valuation into terms of a non-social setting if the conditions to which it is a response are essentially social; but we should be able to state in non-social terms the principle which is operating, and to illustrate its character by reference to a situation from which the social reference has been excluded.

With these preliminary remarks, we turn to the subject of the present chapter. The method I propose to adopt is to state my main points in a series of 'propositions', and to explain and comment upon these propositions as they are given. In some cases the requisite commentary will be very brief; in other cases it will be rather more elaborate.

PROPOSITION I

Valuation is always relative or 'comparative', never absolute or 'simply positive'.

This first proposition is merely the formal statement of an initial postulate which has to be accepted in view of the distinction between 'value' and 'goodness'. The point will, by now, be familiar to the reader. Since valuation is an act enforced upon us by an objective situation which requires that, of two or more demands which we entertain, one must remain unsatisfied, a situation therefore which requires us to place those things in an order of choice; and since the value of a thing is the place assigned to it in such an order, then the value of x is indicative of its relative place in an order. The predication of 'goodness' may be simply positive, but the predication of value (valuation) must always be comparative. x is 'good'; but x has 'more (or less) or higher (or lower) value' than y.

PROPOSITION II

Value is attributed to the non-existent, never to the existent.

This proposition could be deduced from what has already been said. We evaluate alternatives when a choice is enforced. The alternatives are alternative contents (not alternative objects) of demand. The content of a demand is always an 'end', or the 'objective of the conative disposition'.[1] Hence what we evaluate is always a state of affairs to be brought into existence, never a thing or state of affairs which now exists. Value is therefore attributed to the non-existent, never to the existent.

However dear to the heart of the philosopher such formal arguments may be, they generally arouse a healthy suspicion in the mind of the practical man. Some further discussion of the matter is therefore desirable in order to establish a proposition which is of great importance for all our subsequent argument.

Let us, then, consider valuations which are, apparently, valuations of existing things. If there are sheep and bags of grain on Robinson Crusoe's wrecked ship, let us suppose that, in estimating what he can take ashore, he can find room for either a sheep or a bag of grain, but not for both; and that he believes that this first trip will be the only one he will be able to make between ship and shore. He has to choose between the sheep and the bag. Now surely here, it may be said, he is valuing existing things—the sheep against the bag of grain.

It is perfectly true that the sheep and the bag exist. They exist aboard the ship. But Robinson's choice is between the sheep or the bag as existing ashore—clearly two states of affairs which are both potential but neither of which is actual. The point of our proposition would seem less paradoxical if we bore in mind the distinction drawn, in the definition of 'demand', between the 'object' of demand and the 'content' of demand. It is the 'contents' and not the 'objects' which we evaluate against each other.

The point at issue may be illustrated again by altering somewhat the nature of the alternatives. Suppose that, having decided in favour of the bag of grain, and having brought it ashore, Robinson

---

[1] See definition of the concept 'demand', pp. 46-9 above.

finds that he can make one more trip to the wreck, and that this time he brings back a sheep. Later, let us say, when there is no possibility of securing more grain, he finds that his feeding stuff for the sheep will not last for the year, and that, if the sheep is to be kept alive, he must use the bag of grain for its food. He is again faced by a choice. The potential states of affairs which he had previously evaluated against each other, when they were both merely potential, are now actual; and it may be considered that what he now has to evaluate is not two non-existent but two existent states of affairs—the bag ashore and the sheep ashore. But that is not the situation now confronting him. What he has to choose between is the continued existence of the one rather than the other, the continued existence of the sheep or the continued existence and utilisation for other purposes of the bag of grain. The choice is between two potentialities and not two things which are actual; there is always a future reference in the act of choice, and therefore the things evaluated against each other are future states of affairs, not actual states of affairs.

Illustrations could be selected from many situations. If I have a stock of wood sufficient to make a bookcase or a table, but not both, the choice is between non-existents, the potential bookcase and the potential table. If I have an actually existing table, and am considering whether to make a bookcase out of it, the things evaluated against each other are not an existing table and a potential bookcase, but the potential continuance of the table and the creation of the bookcase—again two non-existents. It does not matter what kind of example we select for consideration. When we consider carefully what it is that we are evaluating, we find that what we place in the valuational order, the alternatives between which we choose, are potential states of affairs, contents of demand carrying a future reference, and not actual existents.

PROPOSITION III

Value is measured in terms of 'opportunity cost'.

The discussion of this proposition will have to be rather more elaborate.

One might naturally suppose that we are here resurrecting the older 'cost of production' theory of value; but there is no connexion between that theory and what we are here asserting. The 'cost of production' theory of value was a theory of 'price', a theory as to how price either is or ought to be determined. We, however, are not concerned with the conception of price at all. The 'public order of value', relevant to the realm of exchange, is the only order of value for which the conception of price is significant; and we are concerned with the activity of valuation which takes place in the individual mind, an activity which—according to the postulates underlying the general laws of supply and demand —is antecedent to any price-fixing operation.

Having disposed of this possible misunderstanding as to the question we are dealing with, we turn to the main point—the relation of 'cost' to 'value' for the individual. In a passage already quoted, we find Professor Cairncross asserting that 'the cost of detaining resources (for one purpose) is equal to the value of these resources for other purposes'.[1] If 'cost' and 'value' are thus equal, and if the equality is not merely fortuitous or inexplicable, we should be able to explain one of the terms by reference to the other. The general implication of the whole passage which was quoted is that it is cost which measures value. The cost of producing anything means the sacrifice entailed in producing that thing; and the sacrifice is the unrealised amount of an alternative demand which could have been realised by the resources utilised for that which is being 'costed'. The cost of satisfying demand A is the amount x of dissatisfaction involved for demand B. This amount of dissatisfaction is equivalent to the amount of unrealised content of demand; and since the maximum realisation of the contents of the totality of demands is the fundamental motive to valuation in a choice situation, it seems clear that it is some comparison of the amounts of dissatisfaction involved which determines our assessment of the values of alternative expenditures of resources.

Admittedly, this view of the relation of costs to valuation raises some difficult questions. We hope to deal with these as the argu-

[1] See p. 52 above.

ment proceeds. All we need claim at the moment is that to regard 'opportunity costs' as determining valuations is, *prima facie*, the obvious hypothesis to adopt. When we work out the full implications of this view we shall, I think, find that it is the only hypothesis which will fit in with an all-round intelligible theory of valuation.

Now it will be noted that it is 'opportunity cost' and not 'productive cost'[1] which our proposition asserts to be the measure of value; and the remainder of our remarks in connexion with Proposition III will be concerned with this question. We shall argue that productive cost, as such, can have no bearing on valuation, while opportunity cost has an essential relation to valuation.

Firstly, with regard to productive cost and its irrelevance to our valuations: let us begin with the conception of cost in its most common signification. If I purchase a house for £2000, we may say that 'the house cost me £2000'; and in this case we are employing the notion of productive cost. The £2000 does not, of course, 'produce' the house in the sense of increasing the already existing supply of housing; but that point does not seem to be of any importance for the argument. What I set a value on is never an existing thing, but a future state of affairs, 'a content of demand'; and so 'productive cost' (see definition) can be used to signify whatever I must expend in the way of purchasing power in order to realise the content of my demand.

Using productive cost in this sense, it is apparent that '£2000' indicates productive cost only in the sense that it expresses this in terms of a conventional medium of exchange. The £2000 may really stand for heritable and moveable property which I am transferring in order to secure the house. If we consider this property transferred as the productive cost, this will enable us to see more clearly why productive cost, as such, does not influence valuation.

Suppose that the £2000 is the proceeds from the sale of my old country house (A), car (C) and small yacht (Y): we may say that the productive cost of the new town house (B) is $A + C + Y$; for it is by the expenditure or utilisation of these as purchasing power that I am able to realise the content of my demand—the demand

[1] As defined on p. 53 above.

for B. But what makes $A + C + Y$ purchasing *power* with respect to possession of B? Purchasing power may take the form of crude material operation, but that is not what we mean in the present case. $A + C + Y$ constitute purchasing power in relation to B only because they are themselves demanded by the person or persons able and prepared (on condition of the transfer) to put me in possession of B.

The significant point, however, is that, while their being purchasing power implies their being demanded by someone else, no demand for them on my part is implied; and it is my valuations which are to be analysed, not the valuations of the other person or persons. Thus, what is purchasing power for me—that which constitutes productive cost in the realisation of something demanded by me—may not be itself something demanded by me. For example, it is perfectly conceivable that I have become so disgusted with a country life that my house and everything associated with it—the car and yacht included—are to me objects of utter distaste. I should be prepared to abandon them forthwith or present them to anyone as a free gift. I want to live in town; and the sooner I get rid of my country possessions the better. It just happens that there is a person who does want them; and that, he will give me what I do want, namely a house in town. That is to say, while B is definitely an object of demand to me, A, C and Y are not objects of demand to me. They have to me no 'goodness' and therefore no 'degree of goodness'. Hence, in exchanging $A + C + Y$ for B, while it is perfectly true that I cannot have both, it is equally true and far more relevant that I do not, in point of fact, want both. I want only B. I am not being confronted by a choice situation with these as alternatives; and since no choice is enforced there is no valuation of $A + C + Y$ against B. B may, of course, be evaluated against something else; but the point is that it is not being evaluated against $A + C + Y$. If B is *not* being evaluated against *something*, then it will have no value in the sense of degree of goodness; and yet it will have the 'productive cost' $A + C + Y$. Productive cost, therefore, has no necessary relation to the value placed on a thing.[1]

[1] The argument of the text does, of course, siover-mplify the position once we

Let us take another illustration. Robinson Crusoe, let us say, has to expend 4 units of Time plus 4 units of Energy to get a pail of water to his house. The $4T$ plus $4E$ are the productive costs. But they will not be related to any value which he sets on getting the pail of water *unless* the $4T$ plus $4E$ are themselves objects of demand competing with the demand for water. If he has in fact so much time and energy on his hands that he is thoroughly bored, he may welcome an excuse for getting rid of the energy and passing the time. He may go and collect water just for the fun of the thing. Or, wanting the water, he may be delighted to go and fetch it without any thought about the time and energy expended. In such cases, the productive costs involved can have no relation to any value he sets on the possession of the water; for no choice is involved which requires him to renounce the content of one demand in order to secure the other.

If, then, we understand 'productive cost' as here defined, if it means the amount of purchasing power (of whatever kind) actually expended in realising the content of demand, then the conception of purchasing power does not imply that it is itself necessarily something in demand. Hence productive cost, as such, has no influence whatsoever upon the value of the thing realised through the incurring of this cost.

Secondly, we have to explain why opportunity cost is said to have a necessary relation to value.

While productive cost, as such, has no such relation, that which constitutes productive cost may in fact, and normally does, constitute also an object of demand to the person who utilises it as

think in terms of exchange. In so far as $A + C + Y$ are demanded by someone prepared to give B or £2000 for them, then since I do in fact demand many things besides B, and am unlikely to have more money than I know what to do with, $A + C + Y$ will be in 'derived demand' by me (even if, in themselves, I detest them) as productive of £2000 which will be in derived demand by me for securing B or things which I demand other than B.

But this more realistic account of the situation does not affect the principal point of the argument, except perhaps to reinforce it. Assuming no direct demand for $A + C + Y$, then they are in demand by me only for their 'surrender value' in securing B or something else. That is to say, any value I place on $A + C + Y$ belongs to them because of the value set on B or other things their surrender will secure. So far, then, from productive cost, as such, giving value to B, the position could be that the value placed on B gives any value possessed by the thing which constitutes the productive cost.

F

purchasing power. Thus, supposing that the owner of the country house, car and yacht would like to have these as well as the house in town, here we have a demand for $A + C + Y$ in competition with the demand for B. A choice is thus enforced, and the contents of the competing demands are accordingly evaluated against each other. In placing B higher in the valuational order (if this is in fact the order adopted), the person concerned will realise the content of the demand for B only at the cost of renouncing the content of the demand for $A + C + Y$. The denial or frustration of this latter demand is the opportunity cost of the satisfaction of the demand for B. Hence it is clear that the opportunity cost of anything has some necessary connexion with the value placed upon it.

What this connexion is, precisely, we shall be able to understand if we recall the definition of opportunity cost. It is 'the unrealised content of a demand which could just have been realised by utilising in its favour the purchasing power actually utilised towards the realisation of the content of an alternative demand'. Thus, if $A + C + Y$ and B are both objects of demand, the content of the first of these will be 'the continued possession and use of the country house, car and yacht', while the content of the second will be 'the acquiring of the town house'. If the country house, car and yacht are sold in order to purchase the town house, then the power which could have been utilised to satisfy the first has in fact been utilised to satisfy the second. The opportunity cost of satisfying the second demand is therefore the 'unrealised content of demand for $A + C + Y$ which could just have been realised by utilising for it the power actually utilised for satisfaction of the demand for B'.

We may take a different example which does not involve any element of the exchange relationship between different persons (for it will be remembered that we are primarily concerned, not with the process of exchange in society, but with the process of valuation in the individual mind). Robinson Crusoe has a demand for an additional $1\frac{1}{2}$ pails of water; and to satisfy this demand he will have to use $8T$ plus $7E$. He has also an urgent demand to get his stooked corn under cover before the threatening rain descends. He has to choose between using his immediate time and energy to fetch water or to get his crop under cover. If he chooses to deal with the corn, the 'productive cost' will be the total T plus E (and any other factors such as wear and tear of implements) necessary for getting the corn under cover. But, assuming that there was no demand other than the demand for water competing with the demand to secure the crop, the 'opportunity cost' will be the unsatisfied demand for $1\frac{1}{2}$ pails of water.

Or again, if I have a certain quantity of wood sufficient to make either a bookcase or a table, but not both; and if I want both; then I am faced by the necessity of choosing. If I choose the bookcase, the productive cost is the wood, screws, wear and tear of tools, polish, etc.; but the opportunity cost is the unsatisfied demand for the table. If I have a table, and have to choose between retaining it as a table and turning it into a bookcase; and if I choose to retain it as a table, there is no productive cost (though of course there was a productive cost when the table was made); but there is an opportunity cost—the unsatisfied demand for the bookcase. If, on the contrary, I choose to turn it into a bookcase, the productive cost will consist of the materials, tool-wear, etc.; and the opportunity cost will be the unsatisfied demand for the continued possession and use of the table.

To summarise our conclusions; Productive cost, as such, can never have any relevance to the value of that of which it is the productive cost. Opportunity cost has a necessary relation to the value of that of which it is the opportunity cost; for it is that content of demand which is renounced when, confronted by the necessity of choosing between alternatives, a demander chooses one and renounces the other.

PROPOSITION IV

Value is measured in terms of anticipated, not actually incurred, cost.

This proposition follows necessarily from Propositions II and III. If value is measured in terms of cost, not price; if that cost is opportunity cost, not productive cost; and if that to which we attribute value is the non-existent, not the existent; then the value of the thing must be measured in terms of anticipated, not actual, cost. What does not yet exist cannot have any actual cost; we can only anticipate or forecast what its cost will be. It can have an actual cost only when it has itself been realised.

I shall not spend time in elaborating this, for it is as plain as anything can be that, if Propositions II and III be accepted, Proposition IV must also be accepted.

But, while no one will seriously question the necessary connexion between these propositions, perhaps some will seriously question the trend of the argument as a whole. It may be felt that Propositions II-IV, taken together, are leading to conclusions so foreign to our ordinary ways of thinking that something must have gone wrong with the argument somewhere. It will be convenient, then, to take this opportunity of considering a general objection to the trend of our argument. Perhaps the objection which will occur to most readers will be this: People do think that they place values on existent things such as tables, bags of corn, houses, cars, pails of water. And they do think that what these things have cost to produce has something, if not necessarily everything, to do with the values placed on them. The argument seems to run counter to commonsense belief on both of these points; hence it is probably invalid.

It will be noted that there are two possible lines of attack on our position. One may attack the conclusion that value has nothing to do with actual cost; but if this attack is pressed successfully, it will also have overturned our conclusion that we do not value the existent, since only the existent (or that which has actually existed) can have an actual cost. Or one may attack the conclusion that we do not value the existent; but here, again, the attack will also necessarily be directed against the view that value has nothing to do with actual cost, since the cost of the existent is actual and not merely anticipated. It does not really matter very much, therefore, which line of attack is adopted, for the final result will be the same in either case. Since, therefore, we have already, in Proposition II, dealt with the question of value in relation to the existent and non-existent, it will be more profitable to consider here the question of anticipated and actual costs.

The objection may be put briefly in the following form: it is quite clear that we do value things partly at least because of the costs incurred in their production. We place a higher value on expensively produced handmade shoes than on the factory product. We place more value on a thing secured after great toil and privation than we should have placed on it if it had come easily. Thus we all understand what is meant when we are urged to 'stand fast in the defence of our constitutional liberties bought at so great a price by our forefathers'. The cost which has been paid, and the recollection of this cost, while not wholly determining the value of the product, do enormously affect the value of the product in our eyes.

I agree that there is a point of great importance which is here being emphasised. The question is: What precisely is the point, and how is it related to the problem of valuation?

Let us consider what appears to be a straightforward case of actual cost affecting value. Suppose that Robinson Crusoe, at considerable labour, collects timber and other materials from the wreck, with the intention of building a substantial house, and then decides to utilise the greater part of them to build a boat. His house will, in consequence, be a rather poorer affair partly composed of locally produced materials. The productive cost of the boat is the sum-total of the materials, time, energy, wear and tear of tools; the opportunity cost (neglecting any other demand left unsatisfied by the boat-building operations) will be the amount of demand left unsatisfied by the difference between the more primitive hut and the substantial house.

No doubt, once the boat is completed, Robinson will launch it with due ceremony; in moving round his island he will derive an enhanced pleasure from the thought of all that went to its building; he will often stand admiring its fine lines (perhaps crude to the professional eye). All that it 'cost' will, apparently, add to its 'value' in his eyes.

But, now, it seems to me that the fundamental ground of this approval must be the conviction that the boat, as completed, does substantially, and to all intents and purposes, meet the demand which its construction was designed to meet, and that this demand has not itself withered away in the interval. Granted that this fundamental ground of approval is present, then there is a sense in which we may say that 'contemplation of costs (productive and opportunity)' can intensify the approval. But we can say this only in a very loose sense; for this enhancement of approval comes, not from contemplating the costs or sacrifice involved, but from contemplating the fact that the boat is a visible memorial to positive achievement, skill, endurance and other qualities exhibited in face of difficulty and the sacrifices involved.

That it is not contemplation of cost, but contemplation of the memorial to achievement despite cost involved, which enhances the approval will be evident if we consider what happens if the fundamental ground of approval is not present. If, having completed the boat, Robinson finds that he cannot launch it, or that, once in the water, it is so defective as to be entirely unsuitable for his purposes—that it does not in any substantial respect satisfy his demand—then, not only will he disapprove of it, but the contemplation of what it cost will actually enhance the disapproval. He will then think of it, not as a memorial to achievement despite costs involved, but as a useless article which has cost a great deal. He will be exasperated when he thinks of all the time and material which have been wasted to create this useless thing. When our efforts have failed, when we feel cheated in our expectations, we often hurl from us with violence that which has cost much, when we should only drop with a mild expression of distaste that which has cost but little. It seems that, if the final product does substantially meet the demand it was meant to satisfy, the approval of it is reinforced by the thought of the positive virtues it symbolises— the persistence in the task despite the costs involved. If it fails to meet the demand, we contemplate not so much the virtues it symbolises as the cost which now appears as 'waste'. It is because the virtues are not significant apart from the circumstances which called them forth that, on a superficial inspection of our psychical state, we get the impression that contemplation of the 'cost incurred' is enhancing the approval with which we regard the product.

But, whether this be a correct interpretation of our attitude or not, the attitude itself is clearly concerned with the attribution of 'goodness' to the boat, and not with the attribution of a degree of goodness compared to the degree of goodness of something else, the two things being presented as alternatives in an enforced choice. When Robinson is sailing round his island and reflecting on all that went to the building of his boat, he is not evaluating it. He is savouring to the full its goodness for him.

Circumstances can arise, however, when a valuation may be enforced. If, one evening, he sees a ship far out at sea, knows that he cannot possibly get out in his boat to intercept the ship, but does think that, if he makes a bonfire of it, the attention of the ship will be attracted and his immediate rescue effected; then he is faced by the choice between the satisfaction of two demands. On the one hand, there is the complex of demands which the existence and possession of the boat now satisfies—journeys of modest exploration, fishing, the boat as a memorial to achievement in the face of odds; and, on the other hand, there is the demand for immediate rescue. The boat can be utilised with the view to satisfying either demand, but not both. He has to choose between preserving it for the one demand and destroying it for the other.

When he is thus faced by a genuine valuational problem, to what extent do the costs—productive or opportunity—of the boat's creation affect the process of valuation? It seems to me that they do not affect it in the very least. The things he evaluates against each other are, on the one side, the activities to which the boat is instrumental, plus the continued existence of a memorial to the creative effort of making it, and, on the other side, the being taken back at once to civilised society. No doubt the thought of burning the boat may arouse such a sense of 'desecration' that this will be decisive in making him place the content of the demand for rescue lower in the valuational order than the complex of demands which the continued existence of the boat will serve; but it is the anticipated opportunity cost of satisfying either of the competing demands which is relevant to the valuation, and not any past cost of building the boat. The question is whether what he takes to be the probable opportunity cost of being rescued (namely the denial of all future satisfaction to the

demands for exploration, fishing and endurance of his memorial)
should be incurred rather than the probable opportunity cost of
engaging in these varied activities (namely the denial of the demand for contact with his fellow-men). The boat is a form of
purchasing power; its utilisation for the satisfaction of either demand will be the anticipated productive cost of satisfying that
demand, and its utilisation for satisfying one set of demands will
entail an opportunity cost which is the amount of 'un-satisfaction'
involved with respect to the other set of demands. But the boat
itself is not being evaluated. The things being evaluated against
each other are the two demands, or two sets of demands, between
which he has to choose; and since the boat is not being evaluated,
then the actual cost—opportunity or productive—of the making
of the boat cannot enter into the valuation now being made; for
that cost was the cost of making the boat, and is not in any sense
the actual or the anticipated cost of being rescued or of continuing
various activities about and around the island.

If we reflect carefully upon the various occasions on which
actual cost seems to influence the value or even the goodness
which we attribute to anything, we see that, in the case of valuation in the proper sense, the actual cost of any actually existent
thing does not enter into consideration; and that, in the case of
goodness, it is not the cost which is significant but the maintenance
of something which symbolises or commemorates positive endeavour and creative effort in which we have persisted despite the
costs involved. As has already been indicated, the effect of contemplating costs can be vastly different according as we approve
or disapprove of the product for the sake of which they have
been incurred. If anything satisfies some profound demand, and
is accordingly profoundly approved, then the contemplation of
it will extend approval over all the positive factors which have
contributed to its existence, provided that they are not disapproved
on some other ground. It is not the sacrifice (the cost) which is
approved, but that which (even at this sacrifice) was done.

It is perfectly true that we can evaluate as well as approve
memorials to achievement. We can and do evaluate the maintenance of institutions and more concrete symbols representative of

national struggle, such as the flag, constitutional monarchy, certain formalities over the election and installation of the Speaker of the House of Commons, the sacraments celebrated in religious worship, the tomb of the unknown warrior; but we only evaluate (as distinguished from attributing goodness to) these things when we have to choose between them and some alternative; and when such choice is enforced, as, for instance, when we have to choose between an obviously good technical piece of town planning and the preservation of some historic building or other feature, the arguments advanced *pro* and *con* make it quite clear that the valuation is forward-looking, not backward-looking. If we analyse the arguments which we advance for the preservation of apparently 'useless' things such as the scarcely habitable residences of famous men, old ships renowned in battle or exploration, or academic dress and ceremonial, we shall probably be very surprised at the fundamentally 'utilitarian' character of our arguments. We find that we are evaluating their preservation as perpetual stimulants to the preservation and enrichment of social traditions and ideals. We are trying to do for our own and future generations what Pericles sought to do in the funeral oration. Without such forward-looking there would never be any interest in the sacrifices and achievements of the past, or at any rate there would never be any valuation of the preservation of their memorials as against other competing demands. Even if we should approve of them, approval is not enough to constitute valuation. We evaluate only when we are faced by the necessity of making a choice; and when faced by such choice, it is the content of the competing demands to which we attend, evaluating them against each other by reference to their respective anticipated opportunity costs.

PROPOSITION V

The order of value is the inverse of the order of estimated opportunity costs.

Since things are evaluated relatively to each other in terms of estimated opportunity costs, then if we know that the cost of x is

estimated as higher than the cost of y, we know at the same time
that the person making the estimate will place y higher than x on
his valuational scale. He will choose y in preference to x. If the
descending order of estimated opportunity costs is A, B, C, D,
then the descending order of values will be D, C, B, A.

The substantial proof of this proposition will only be made out
in the course of the argument in the next two chapters; for the
proposition will be necessarily true of all valuational orders only
on two conditions. *Firstly*, the truth of the proposition implies
that all things evaluated against each other carry a reference to a
'common demand'; and, *secondly*, it implies that degrees of satisfaction of this common demand can be expressed quantitatively
in terms of more and less. To establish these two conditions will
require a lengthy argument which, for the moment, we postpone.
Our immediate purpose will be to show that the proposition is
not, on the face of it, wholly unreasonable, and that it does follow
if the two conditions just mentioned are granted.

To show the *prima facie* reasonableness of the proposition, let
us begin with two fairly simple examples, admittedly highly
artificial.

Suppose—this is our first example—that I have more time and
energy at my disposal than I know what to do with, then no
opportunity cost relating to time and energy will be involved in
going to fetch a pail of water. But if time and energy are scarce
enough to make me consider whether I shall use them in fetching
water or in some other pursuit, opportunity cost will be involved.
If, in these latter circumstances, I am able to choose between four
wells, A taking 15, B 13, C 11 and D 10 minutes for the return
journey, and assuming that the quality of the water is exactly the
same in all the wells, then the estimated opportunity costs of the
four different pailfuls will be in the descending order A, B, C, D.
On the principle of economy I shall certainly prefer to save time
and energy for the contents of demand competing with the demand for water, and so I shall put the pailfuls in the descending
order of value, D, C, B, A.

Suppose—our second example—that I have a pint of milk, am
not thirsty, and am unlikely to become so before the milk turns

sour, but that I am, on the other hand, very hungry; then no opportunity cost will be involved in exchanging the milk for bread. But if I am both thirsty and hungry, I shall look very carefully at any proposal to exchange bread for milk. If four men each offer me $\frac{1}{4}$ loaf, but each asks for a different quantity of milk in exchange, A $\frac{5}{8}$, B $\frac{1}{2}$, C $\frac{3}{8}$, D $\frac{1}{4}$ pint, I shall reverse this order of estimated costs in making up my order of value. The offers will be put in the descending order of value, D, C, B, A.

To the intelligent reader who has not thought a great deal about this problem, all this must appear to be extraordinarily naive theorising, founding a sweeping generalisation upon a conclusion drawn from quite artificial examples. The supposition was that I have to choose one of four things all of which are exactly alike, but the opportunity costs of which will be different—say, one of four pieces of bread in return for different quantities of milk. Of course, in such a case, I shall choose the one which costs least. But consider a different situation. Suppose that one person offers $\frac{1}{4}$ loaf for $\frac{1}{2}$ pint of milk and another offers an apple for $\frac{1}{2}$ pint of milk; does this mean that, because the costs are the same, I shall be completely indifferent whether I have the bread or the apple? Shall I value them equally because the costs are to be equal? Or, if the $\frac{1}{4}$ loaf is offered for $\frac{1}{2}$ pint, and the apple for $\frac{1}{4}$ pint, does it necessarily follow that, because the apple costs less, I shall choose it rather than the bread?

The commonsense answer—and surely the true answer—is that it is perfectly conceivable that I may still take the bread even if it is to cost more milk. If this be true, how can one maintain that values are the inverse of estimated costs? It is evident that there is a failure, in this objection, to distinguish between 'productive' and 'opportunity' costs; but this retort will not take us far until we go more deeply into the nature of opportunity cost and its implications.

To give the effective reply it will be necessary to introduce the conception of 'common demand'. I do not ask the reader to accept uncritically the validity of this conception; I merely ask him to suppose that it may be valid, and to follow out the implications of this supposition in dealing with the problem as here presented to us. This being understood, we may accept the commonsense view that, even if the cost in milk is higher for the bread than for the apple, the bread may nevertheless be chosen; and still hold that the order of value is the inverse of the order of costs. The explanation will take the following form: The cost represented by the sacrifice of milk is not the total estimated opportunity cost; there is another element of opportunity cost, namely the extent to which an apple will satisfy demand less than ¼ loaf will satisfy it.

Thus—to take first the problem in its simpler form where the 'milk cost' was in both cases assumed to be ½ pint—bread and apple are different ways of meeting a 'common demand' for 'food'; and an individual on a particular occasion may feel that ¼ loaf will satisfy this demand for food to a greater extent than will an apple. Hence the selection of the apple will cost more (in terms of unsatisfied demand) than the selection of the bread; the opportunity cost represented by the milk being in each case the loss of ½ pint, it is clear that the descending order of opportunity costs will be represented by apple + milk, bread + milk. And so the descending order of value will be bread + milk, apple + milk.

To take the problem in its more complex form, we have to consider how our proposition stands in relation to the situation when the apple costs only ¼ pint and the ¼ loaf costs ½ pint, and the person concerned still chooses the bread in preference to the apple. We are assuming, for purposes of argument, that the apple and the bread can be compared against each other as satisfying, in different degrees, the 'common demand' for 'food', the apple giving less satisfaction than the bread. The position, then, is:

Bread costs less in terms of 'food'; bread costs more in terms of 'drink'. We must therefore assert that, if the bread + milk combination is given a higher value than the apple + milk combination, this must be because the satisfaction provided by ¼ pint of milk (the extra milk going with the apple) is less than the satisfaction provided by the difference between ¼ loaf and one apple. To put this in a different way: If the ¼ loaf would satisfy the demand for 'food' to an amount x greater than an apple would satisfy the demand for 'food', then x must be a greater satisfaction of demand than could be derived from $\frac{1}{4}$ pint of milk. Hence the combination 'apple + $\frac{3}{4}$ pint milk' will leave more demand unsatisfied (i.e. will stand higher in the order of opportunity costs) than the combination '$\frac{1}{4}$ loaf + $\frac{1}{2}$ pint milk'; and therefore it will stand lower in the order of values.

Here, not only are we measuring quantitatively against each other the satisfactions of the demand for 'food' provided by apple and by bread respectively, but we are also measuring quantitatively against each other the satisfactions of the 'food' demand and the 'drink' demand. How can we measure against each other demands so different as those for food and drink? Only if we assume that they are, in their turn, merely diverse expressions of a still more general 'common demand', namely the demand for 'sustenance'. It is obvious, therefore, that the whole argument which we are advancing in support of our proposition (that the value order is the inverse of the anticipated opportunity costs order) depends on the postulates, *firstly*, of some 'common demand' to which all the things evaluated against each other are related, and, *secondly*, that their opportunity costs can be measured quantitatively against each other in terms of satisfaction of this common demand.

We are postulating, in other words, that the things evaluated against each other are in some sense in 'composite supply' with respect to the 'common demand'. Things are in 'composite supply' when they are, to some degree, substitutes for each other in providing satisfaction for the same demand.[1]

Having pursued the implications of our proposition so far, let us consider whether the trend of the argument is sufficiently reasonable to warrant proceeding with it in more detail. Is it in any sense reasonable to suggest that bread, apples and milk are 'substitutes' for each other in satisfying some 'common demand'? It seems certain that, to some extent, they can be regarded as substitutes, because if we progressively vary the quantity of milk in the combination of bread + milk which was initially placed higher on the valuational scale, there comes a point at which that combination will be regarded as less valuable than the apple + milk combination.

[1] See below, pp. 133-40.

Thus, suppose the seller of the $\frac{1}{4}$ loaf, observing that the prospective buyer is very anxious to get it, demands more and more
milk for the same quantity of bread, rising from $\frac{1}{2}$ pint to $\frac{5}{8}$, then
to $\frac{3}{4}$, then to $\frac{7}{8}$ pint. At some point the owner of the milk will
call off the bargaining, and say: 'I'll give so much, and no more.
If that does not satisfy you, then I'll be better off with the apple
and my $\frac{3}{4}$ pint.' Or if the bread owner, instead of demanding
more and more milk for the same amount of bread, offers less and
less bread—quarter, eighth, sixteenth, quarter of a slice, a crust—
for the same amount of milk; at some point the milk owner will
say: 'Keep your bread; I'm for the apple and my $\frac{3}{4}$ pint.' The
bread, milk and apple are all capable of being regarded, not as
objects of distinct isolated demands, but as objects of a comprehensive demand for sustenance, and as, within limits, substitutes
for each other in different combinations. The place which 'bread'
or 'apple' or 'milk' takes in the valuational order will depend
upon the quantity in question and the combination in which it
stands; for it is total combinations which will be evaluated against
each other. That combination which leaves least of the common
demand unsatisfied will have the greatest value.

We may conclude, then, that the trend of the argument is not
too unreasonable or too far removed from ordinary experience
to warrant its development in more detail. Still, we are making
very bold assumptions. We have only been able to advance a case
for our proposition on the assumption that things evaluated
against each other are in 'composite supply' relative to some
'common demand', and that combinations of these things are
comparable with respect to the 'amount' of the common demand
which they satisfy. Hence, if we claim that the proposition under
consideration is valid with regard to every valuational order
without exception, we must be prepared to widen the scope of
the discussion. We shall have to show that what is obviously
operative with respect to things in 'composite supply' is merely
one expression of a principle universally operative. We shall have
to show, *firstly*, that all things evaluated against each other carry
a reference to a 'common demand'; and, *secondly*, that the degree
of satisfaction of this common demand can intelligibly be ex-

pressed in quantitative terms of 'more and less'. The first of these points is much the more difficult to deal with and will occupy the whole of the argument in Chapters III and IV.[1] The second point will be dealt with more briefly in Chapter V.

[1] The argument of the two following chapters on the subject of 'common demand' is an attempt to work out the principles underlying the general theory of value and valuation in 'pure or positive economic theory' and has not been influenced by present-day controversies on 'welfare economics'. But if I correctly understand one of the main issues in these controversies to be the question whether pure economics can, without making or assuming any value judgement, provide practically useful criteria for the valuation of public economic policy, then it seems to me that the theory of the 'common demand' is highly relevant and shows that the answer must be in the negative.

Those who are not familiar with the literature on the subject may find the issue presented very clearly in Mr Corbett's contribution to the symposium on 'The Concept of Welfare in Economics' in *Proc. Arist. Soc.*, Sup. Vol. XXVII. As against Hicks and others who apparently suppose that pure economic science can devise criteria or norms for valuation, Mr Corbett argues that such norms, being standards of behaviour to which we wish people to conform, cannot be scientifically deduced. The necessary foundation of any criterion of valuation, says Mr Corbett, is a 'programme'—the making explicit of some 'end' which the economic system is to realise, and with reference to which alternative policies must be evaluated.

On this point his argument seems to me to be entirely sound. He does, it is true, go further than this; for he apparently thinks that 'pure or scientific economic theory' cannot exist; and I am not able to follow him so far. I think that there can be and is pure economic theory (e.g. the general theory of value and valuation), formulating the laws and principles in accordance with which the choices of rational agents are made; and such pure economic theory does not make or presuppose value judgements as premisses from which it works to conclusions. It presupposes value judgements only in the sense of accepting these as the data —the material—about which it theorises and draws conclusions.

But this being said, I am fully in agreement with Mr Corbett's view that, when we come to the question of criteria or norms *for* valuation (as distinguished from the laws and principles *of* valuation which are elucidated by pure economics), it is not possible to formulate such norms without incorporating some value judgement or value judgements as a premiss or premisses in the argument. This must be so if the argument of the next two chapters is valid. If a 'common demand' is postulated in every valuational order—if we cannot evaluate *A* against *B* without postulating a common demand *C* to which both are relative, then, since the content of any demand is an 'end' or something accepted as 'good', quite clearly there can be no norm or criterion for the valuation of policy *A* against policy *B* independently of the value judgement that *C* is good.

Chapter Three

VALUATION AND COMMON DEMAND

IN this and the following chapter we shall try to establish the first of the two conditions without which Proposition V cannot be maintained. We have to consider whether the comparison of two or more things with respect to their value (or degree of goodness) implies a 'common demand' to which they are all relative. The proposition now to be established is:

PROPOSITION VI

Every valuational order postulates a common demand with reference to which the opportunity costs of the things placed in that order are estimated.

I. PRELIMINARY OBSERVATIONS

Two preliminary points may be made to indicate what, if this proposition be established, will be its relevance to two other questions arising in connexion with a theory of valuation.

Firstly, we have to note carefully the limited nature of what is asserted in the proposition itself. It does not state that, if two things can be valued, they necessarily imply some demand common to them both. It is only if they are valued *against each other* (that is to say if they are within the same valuational order) that they imply a common demand. Actually they may be in different valuation orders, and the proposition says nothing about things which are in different orders. Thus, if one individual *A* values *x* and another individual *B* values *y*, *x* and *y* cannot (in this respect) belong to the same valuational order; for, as we have already seen,[1] a valuational order in the strict sense (as distinguished from what may be called the 'public order of values' expressed in terms of price) must be contained within the limits of the consciousness of a single individual. But this is not the only con-

[1] See definition of 'Demander', p. 46.

sideration to be borne in mind; for different valuational orders may exist within the same consciousness. Whether there are in fact different orders within the one consciousness we shall discuss later[1]; but we are not entitled to assume offhand that there are not such different orders. Hence, when we say that the same individual values both x and y, we are not entitled to infer (if our proposition be established) that x and y are therefore relative to a common demand; for x and y may belong to different valuational orders in the mind of the person in question. All that the proposition is concerned to affirm is that, if things are evaluated in relation to each other (are members of the same order), then they postulate a common demand.

Secondly, we have to note an important implication if the proposition be established. If this proposition is true, then it will be impossible to accept the view, once held by Ross,[2] that two things —e.g. virtue and pleasure—are comparable but not commensurable in value. In saying that virtue and pleasure are comparable in degree of goodness or value, Ross meant that we can put the two things on a common valuational scale to the extent of saying that virtue has more or higher value than pleasure. In saying that they are not commensurable, he meant that virtue starts at a point on this scale which pleasure, no matter how great, can never reach; so that no amount of pleasure, however great, can ever exceed or even equal in value any amount of virtue, however small. I am not concerned to discuss this view but merely to indicate, by contrast, what will follow if our proposition is true. The implication will be that, if two things are comparable in value, then they will necessarily also be commensurable; and they will therefore be liable, in certain circumstances, to have their places in the valuational order reversed. It will not follow that Ross was wrong in saying that virtue and pleasure are comparable in value; it will not follow that he was wrong in saying that they are not commensurable in value; but it will follow that he was wrong in saying both that they are comparable and also that they are not commensurable. Comparability and commensurability will be

---

1 See discussion of 'Joint Supply', pp. 140-50.
2 R. *and* G., Chapter VI on 'Degrees of Goodness'.

bound up together. If two things are in the same order, holding 'comparative' places as 'higher' and 'lower' in respect of their opportunity costs relative to a common demand, then it is always theoretically possible that the decreasing opportunity costs of the one can, at some point, become less than the increasing opportunity costs of the other, and thus reverse their respective places in the valuational order, in the same way as decreasing and increasing costs of apple and bread may, at some point, reverse their initial relation within the valuational order.[1]

2. COMMON DEMAND AND DIMINISHING UTILITY

Having made these two preliminary points, we proceed to the

[1] This is to make what is, I think, substantially the same point as Ross himself makes in *Foundations of Ethics*, p. 275. In commenting on his own earlier view that the three intrinsically good things are virtue, knowledge and pleasure, he now argues that pleasure cannot be good in the same sense as virtue and knowledge are good; for, if it were, then pleasure could, under certain circumstances, have a higher value than virtue; and he cannot accept such a conclusion. His later view, apparently, is that virtue and pleasure cannot be compared at all in the matter of their respective values. But in seeking to avoid the difficulties inherent in his earlier view (that virtue and pleasure are comparable but not commensurable) Ross appears to be entangled in difficulties equally serious. If choice is, as the basic assumptions of economics would seem to imply, the overt expression of valuation, and if valuation is always comparative, Ross's revised view seems to imply that we can never make an intelligent or conscious choice between seeking pleasure and doing our duty. If the relation between valuation and choice is as it seems to me to be, and if it is possible to believe our duty to be one thing and yet choose to do something different, it would appear that, in realising the untenability of his earlier view, Ross should have frankly accepted the commensurability of pleasure and virtue and not denied their comparability. (See pp. 188-95 below for a fuller discussion of this point.)

These comments on Ross's doctrine depend, of course, upon my view (as explained on pp. 8-11) that the value judgement and the moral judgement are quite distinct in character. Assuming the correctness of this distinction, it is easy to avoid Ross's difficulty. It is easy to see that there is a difference between asking 'Would it be good (or better) to do x rather than y?' and 'Ought I (is it my duty) to do x rather than y?'. I might perfectly rationally answer the first question in the negative and the second in the affirmative. If I do so answer, this does not imply that I cease to believe x to be what I ought to do. It merely means that, in this particular case, I choose to seek my pleasure rather than to do what I believe to be my duty. Whether I choose (place a higher value on) x or y depends on my rational assessment of their respective contributions to my total personal conception of what is good. Whether I regard x as my duty depends on my rational assessment of its significance in an inter-personal order of equities. I may or may not be the kind of person who normally places a high degree of value upon the doing of duty because it is a duty.

substantive discussion of the proposition itself: every valuational order postulates a 'common demand'. As already indicated, this conception of 'common demand' is the notion of a comprehensive demand of the valuing subject of which the different demands whose contents are evaluated against each other are but different expressions. If, for example, we can evaluate the consumption of apple, bread and milk against each other, this is only because the demands for apple, bread and milk are qualitatively different expressions of the 'common demand' for 'sustenance'.

Now we should expect that, if a common demand in this sense is necessarily implied in the comparative value judgement, this point would emerge quite clearly in the course of the economist's analysis of demand and valuation. But if we seek for the support of economic theory here, we come at once upon a formidable difficulty. The economist, apparently, gets on perfectly well without the assumption of common demand, and appears to regard it as entering into the picture only in exceptional cases—cases which he regards as of little importance for the theory of valuation in general. The usual statement of the position in the text-books[1] suggests that valuation normally takes place in accordance with the law of diminishing utility: 'The marginal utility of a commodity to anyone diminishes with every increase in the amount which he already has.' Hence, 'the larger the number of cigarettes that we smoke, the less is the marginal utility of cigarettes, and the less, therefore, is the value that we set on an extra cigarette'.[2] There is here no suggestion of anything like the assumption of a common demand.

On this 'older' doctrine, the possibility of a common demand's influence on valuation is not, indeed, excluded. If we have some comprehensive objective (common demand) which we are trying to realise, the orthodox theory seems to be that it is 'increasing' and not 'decreasing' utility which operates. Thus (according to the theory), the valuations which a man normally places upon successive pints of beer will follow the law of diminishing utility; but if he has some definite objective (e.g. to make a complete

[1] See, e.g. the brief statement of the 'older' doctrine in Cairncross, *Introduction*, p. 165.
[2] Cairncross, *Introduction*, pp. 161-2.

tour of all the local public houses in two hours), the law of increasing utility will apply, since each pint consumed will bring him nearer to the attainment of his goal—nearer to the achievement of the 'demand set' which he is pursuing. But it seems to be generally accepted that the really important valuational analysis is concerned with valuation which follows the law of diminishing utility. This is quite inconsistent with our proposition; for our proposition states that every valuation, without exception, postulates the conception of 'goal', 'set', or 'common demand'.

As the problem here raised calls for lengthy and intricate analysis, perhaps the reader will be assisted in following the argument if I indicate now the general course it will take.

I want to make it quite explicit at the outset that I entirely accept the conception of 'marginal utility' as the clue to the process of valuation. But having said this, my argument will be directed to show that this conception does not imply, and is indeed inconsistent with, a 'law of diminishing utility', for the following reasons:

Firstly, the orthodox formulation of this 'law' is based on a confusion between the conceptions of 'utility' and 'returns', and falsely presupposes that successive 'units of satisfaction' of the *same* demand can be compared in value or utility relatively to each other. *Secondly,* if we try to reformulate the 'law' so as to make explicit the essential reference to different *competing* demands, we find that we cannot get any law of 'diminishing' (or 'increasing') utility; for, *thirdly,* an analysis of the meaning of 'marginal utility' shows that to speak of 'diminishing marginal utility' is to use words without meaning; and, *fourthly,* we find that no units of satisfaction of competing demands can be evaluated against each other *except* marginal units of utility. *Fifthly,* although we must for these reasons reject the notion of a 'law of diminishing utility' operative in valuation, we discover that there is a 'law of equilibrium' which can be stated with fair precision; and it is with the conception of equilibrium that the conception of marginal utility is necessarily associated. *Sixthly,* the conception of equilibrium—of proportionate satisfaction of qualitatively different demands—implies that these competing demands are necessarily complementary subordinate expressions of a more comprehensive 'common demand'.

This being the scope of the argument in the present chapter, it will be convenient to begin by dealing with the relation of the Law of Diminishing Returns to the 'Law of Diminishing Utility'.

3. The Law of Diminishing Returns

The law of diminishing returns was initially observed to operate, I understand, in agricultural production. It was observed that, with respect to a given piece of land, there is a point of maximum efficiency in the application of labour and capital for the production of a given crop. When this point has been reached, any addition of labour or capital, or both, will result in decreasing proportionate return of crop. Thus, if we have a field of a given size and quality of soil, and if the expenditure of 10 units of labour and 7 units of capital will produce a crop of 50 units, we may find that, by further applications of units of either labour or capital, we get, for a time, proportionately greater returns in crop; but we shall certainly find that, at some point, the most efficient 'mixture' of land, labour and capital will be reached, and that any further addition of units of the one factor will result in the phenomena of 'diminishing returns'. It may be that, the land factor remaining the same, and the capital application remaining constant at 7 units, the application of an 11th unit of labour (1 unit more than the original 10) will yield an additional 5 crop-units per acre, the application of a 12th labour unit yield an additional 7 crop-units, the 13th labour unit an additional 8 crop-units, the 14th labour unit an additional 7 crop-units, the 15th labour unit an additional 6 crop-units. In this case it is patent that, land and capital applications remaining constant, we have 'increasing returns' up to 13 units of labour, and 'decreasing returns' beyond that point.

This is not the place in which to elaborate the conceptions of increasing and diminishing returns. It is sufficient for our purpose to present the conceptions in bold outline without all the explanations and qualifications with which they are naturally presented in the text-books. It is sufficient to say that these well-authenticated facts about the application of the 'factors of production'—land, labour and capital—are of such importance as to justify the conception of the 'Law of Diminishing Returns' which may be formulated thus: 'Successive applications of labour and capital to a given area of land must ultimately, other things remaining the same, yield a less than proportionate increase in produce.'

We may accept the view that this law operates also in human life. The following instances may be open to criticism, but we may, for the sake of argument, regard them as legitimate examples. In any repetitive activity—running, chopping wood, and so forth—we seem to be putting forth as much 'will effort' when we are tired as when we are fresh to the job, with gradually diminishing effective results. If we persist long enough, we find that, 'with the greatest effort of will', the results may be exceedingly feeble. Again, if we go hungry to a meal, we begin to eat with zest, appetite gradually weakens, and it may reach zero if the food lasts long enough. With successive glasses of water or beer, the pleasure derived from drinking gradually diminishes. The law of diminishing returns seems to apply throughout the physical and psychical orders. It applies presumably to the efficient use of skills and virtues, and to all qualities of character, just as much as it does to the application of 'doses' of land, labour and capital. Personally, I am doubtful whether this sweeping statement can really be justified; but I am prepared to accept it, so as to put the case to be answered as strongly as possible.

Now when we consider this law of diminishing returns, we see that it is valid—and indeed intelligible—only on certain conditions. We can attach a meaning to it only on the supposition that the things about which we are speaking can be discussed in terms of a cardinal numerical system. We cannot say that successive doses of labour, other things remaining equal, will yield a progressively less proportionate return in crop, unless we can speak of units of labour and units of crop. We are speaking not merely of 'more' labour, but of 7 rather than 6, or 8 rather than 7, labour units; and similarly for our returns in crop. Again, if we assert that the law of diminishing returns[1] applies to the production of pleasure through drinking beer, we must be assuming, not only that the beer can be measured in pints, but also that the pleasure can be measured in appropriate units. While this may not be the case with regard to pleasure, I am prepared to be accommodating and allow the assumption to pass muster.

But granting all this, what bearing could the law of diminishing returns have on the problem of valuation? If we say that the first pint of beer will produce 10 units of pleasure, the second 11 units, the third 10 units, the fourth 9 units, and so forth; or if we say that the 12th labour unit yields an additional 7 crop-units, the 13th an additional 8 crop-units, the 14th an additional 7 crop-units, and the 15th an additional 6 crop-units; are we not stating a law of increasing 'productive costs' of pleasure and crop respectively? The law of diminishing returns (this will, I think, be agreed to by all economists) can be stated alternatively as the 'law of increasing costs'. Costs, obviously, mean what we have called productive costs, not opportunity costs; and productive costs, as such, we have also seen,[2] have nothing to do with valuation. The law of diminishing returns is a law of the objective order which, when we become aware of it, we take into account in valuing alternatives set before us, just as we take the law of gravity and all other objective conditions into account, in so far as we are aware of them. But these objective conditions (including the law of diminishing returns) are the conditions and laws which set the alternatives and constitute the 'choice situation' confronting us—the situation which enforces valuation upon us and sets the alternatives between which we have to choose. The law of diminish-

---

[1] The economist who suspects that the word 'returns' here is being wrongly used, and that it is 'utility' which is really meant, is asked to reserve judgement on the point until he has considered the discussion of the *meaning* of 'utility' and 'returns' on pp. 88-95 below. If the argument contained in that discussion be substantially correct, then it is the word 'returns', not 'utility', which is appropriate in the present context. It is true that 'the law of diminishing returns' is normally—and perhaps exclusively—used with regard to the situation where we increase the amount of one or two of 'the three factors of production'. But while that may well be true of 'the law of diminishing returns', the conception of 'returns' has a more general significance; and if there is any 'law' applicable to the *production* of pleasure through beer-drinking, it is a law of 'returns', not a law of 'utility'.   [2] Pp. 61-7, and 69-73.

ing returns is one of the factors creating the situation in which we value. It is not a law of valuation.

4. THE 'LAW OF DIMINISHING UTILITY'

When we pass from the law of diminishing returns to the law of diminishing utility we are dealing with a very different matter. But unfortunately the law of diminishing utility is sometimes stated as though it were a particular form or particular application of the law of diminishing returns. Thus Wicksteed[1] refers to it as the law of 'diminishing psychical returns'. This is a serious error which affects the whole of his subsequent exposition of the phenomena of diminishing utility.

(1) *Utility*

(a) *Its Meaning*

So far as contemporary economists use the term 'utility', it bears a very different meaning from its obvious, original meaning. Ordinarily, if we say that X has utility we mean that X is 'useful' for, or is a 'means' to, the production of something. A knife has utility or is useful for producing slices of bread by cutting them from a loaf. It was in this plain sense that Bentham used the term in his ethical theory. He argued (or assumed) that pleasure is the only thing ultimately desired, and that actions are right or wrong so far as they do or do not produce a surplus of pleasure over pain. His conception of moral rightness and wrongness is thus 'utilitarian', in the sense that it is the utility or usefulness of actions in producing pleasure which determines their moral quality in the last resort. On such a theory it would be neither proper nor intelligible to speak of pleasure itself as having utility. Utility would attach to 'means', not to 'ends' (unless those ends were themselves also means). Utility could thus be defined as 'the capacity or power of a thing or action to produce something else'.

But since Bentham's school attained to a certain fame—or notoriety—on account of its doctrine that pleasure is the one ultimate end of action, 'utilitarianism' tended to be associated with

[1] *Commonsense of Political Economy*, Bk. I, Chap. II.

the doctrine of hedonism. It was easy to fall into the habit of talking of a 'purely utilitarian' end as equivalent to 'pleasure' or 'happiness'; and 'utility' thus became vaguely associated with the alleged end of all human action rather than with the conception of productive means.

It so happened that nineteenth-century economists were, for a considerable period, strongly influenced by the psychological doctrines of the Benthamite school, and they adopted the term 'utility'. But they had some trouble in giving it a technical meaning. Their difficulties were not lessened when Bentham's ethical and psychological position became out-moded. In the long run, the economists adopted a technical meaning for 'utility' which has no essential connexion with its original meaning. Marshall, for instance,[1] wishes to exclude not only all ethical but also all prudential implications of the term, and regards 'utility' as simply correlative to 'desire' or 'want'. To say that a thing has utility means, for him, that it is desired or wanted. What is wanted may be 'morally' right or wrong, or 'prudentially' wise or foolish; but such considerations are irrelevant. In ascribing utility, all that is meant is that the thing is desired (and it may be desired either as a means or as an end). It will be noted, incidentally, that to define utility in this way leaves quite open the old question whether pleasure (or anything else) is the ultimate end. The definition is quite neutral on the question of what *has* utility.

The present position seems to be that, so far as economists continue to use the term, they explicitly accept the Marshallian correlation. 'Utility' means 'desiredness' or 'demandedness (in the sense of general, not effective, demand)'.[2]

---

[1] *Principles of Economics*, 8th edition, p. 92.
[2] See, e.g. Little, p. 19, and Cairncross, p. 166. I have been trying to state here the sense in which economists *say* the term 'utility' is now used; and this is the sense in which I shall use it throughout the following argument. But it may seriously be doubted whether all economists—even all who profess to use the term as so defined—keep consistently to this definition and accept its strict implications. Thus when we are told that 'the *utility* or *welfare* the individual gets is dependent on the goods he buys', or when *utility* is equated with *satisfaction* (these uses of the term are noted in a very interesting paper by Miss Brotman, *Proc. Arist. Soc.*, Sup. Vol. XXVII, p. 184) it seems clear that 'utility' does not mean 'desiredness' or 'demandedness' in things but something (welfare or satisfaction) produced by our having secured the things demanded. In this

If, then, utility means desiredness, we may say that, in the
modern sense, when utility is predicated of anything, this signifies
neither more nor less than that the thing is desired or demanded
by someone. The thing has utility for me if I demand it, and
none for you if you do not.

(b) *Utility and Returns*

If this is what utility means, then patently the conception of
'utility' is something very different from that of 'returns'. What
do we mean by a 'return'? We mean a particular effect produced
by certain causal or productive factors. Thus the return on a
certain piece of land to which x units of capital and y units of
labour have been applied will be z bushels of corn. When we call
z bushels of corn a 'return', we are thinking of that commodity
as having resulted from the operation of the factors. But when
we say that the same z bushels of corn has 'utility' we are simply
saying that the commodity in question is demanded by or has
desirableness for someone. The commodity could be a return without having utility (without anyone wanting it); and it could have
utility without being a return (in the sense of being a product of
deliberately applied factors).

The distinction between the conception of a thing as a 'return'
and that of the same thing as having 'utility' is obvious in the
case just mentioned. But when we are dealing with psychical
states, rather than with material commodities, confusion is apt to
arise. Suppose that I drink a pint of beer in the expectation of
deriving pleasure from this activity. Since I desire the pleasure,
the pleasure has 'utility' (desiredness). If the drinking of the beer
does in fact produce the pleasure, then the pleasure is a 'return' of
(something produced by or resulting from) the beer-drinking.
In this case the pleasure has 'utility' and is a 'return'; but it has
utility because it is demanded; and it is a 'return' because beer-

---

case, therefore, 'utility' means neither 'usefulness for producing a result' as in its
original Benthamite sense, nor 'demandedness' in something, as in the modern
definition, but 'that which is (or may be?) *produced* by choice amongst competing
demands'. If 'utility' is sometimes used in this last sense we need not be surprised
to find the conceptions of 'diminishing utility' and 'diminishing returns' sometimes
confused with each other.

drinking has produced it. It has utility only as a content of demand (a non-existent thing). It is a return only as an actually existing product.

Since the conceptions of 'utility' and 'return' are so very different, and are yet so liable to be confused with each other when we are dealing with psychical states (say pleasures of beer-drinking) rather than with material objects (say bushels of corn), it is extremely important that we should not allow the conception of the law of diminishing returns to mislead us in our attempts to formulate the law of diminishing utility. Indeed we must consider carefully whether we can draw from the operation of the law of diminishing returns any inference whatsoever as to the way in which utility diminishes or increases.

Suppose, for instance, that, having produced a certain pleasure by drinking a pint of beer, I go on drinking; and let us further suppose that each successive pint produces a lesser amount of pleasure than did the immediately preceding pint, then here we have the phenomena of diminishing returns. The drinking of each additional pint produces, let us suppose, a proportionately less return in terms of pleasure; just as, after a certain point, each successive unit of labour applied may produce a proportionately less return (land and capital remaining constant) in terms of corn.

The question is whether, granting the operation of a law of diminishing returns to beer-drinking in terms of pleasure, we can draw any inferences from this with regard to 'utility'. To answer this question we must be clear, not only as to what we mean by 'utility' and 'returns', but also as to the utility about which we are inquiring. It is postulated that I desire the pleasure. It is also postulated, by necessary implication, that I desire the indispensable means, namely the beer-drinking. We are therefore postulating that both the pleasure (end) and the beer-drinking (means) have utility (desiredness). Which of these two utilities do we have in mind when we ask whether the operation of the law of diminishing returns (diminishing returns to the successive pints in terms of pleasure) has any implications for the 'utility'? Do we mean the utilities of the successive states of pleasure, or do we mean the utilities of the successive drinks of beer?

Suppose that the question relates to the utilities of the states of pleasure. The question then presumably is: Do the utilities diminish as the returns diminish; or, in other words, does the desiredness of the state of pleasure diminish directly as the amount of pleasure diminishes with each successive pint? If the first pint gives 10 units of pleasure, the second pint 9, and so forth, does it follow that the demand for or desiredness of the 9 units is less than the demand for the 10 units? If one pleasure is less intense than another, does it follow that I desire the lesser pleasure less than I desire the greater?

To assert that this does follow would be to assert an indirect (though not a direct) correlation of 'returns' and 'utilities'. The correlation would be indirect, because the thing whose returns were diminishing would not be the same as the thing whose utility was diminishing. In the case supposed, it is the *returns to beer-drinking* which would be diminishing, but it is the *utilities of the pleasures* which would be diminishing. Now what grounds do we have for asserting that diminishing returns to the 'means' have, as a necessary consequence, diminishing utility in the 'end'? I think it is in fact true that, under the conditions in which we are normally placed, namely conditions requiring the distribution of scarce resources over competing ends, the onset of diminishing returns to the means tends to produce diminishing utility with respect to the end. But it will be noted that there is an essential qualification here: this tendency operates when we have to distribute scarce resources over competing ends. It does not in the least follow that, if a single end could be taken in isolation from all competing ends, diminishing returns to the means to that end would necessarily produce diminishing utility in that end. Indeed the most obvious line of argument to take would be to say that this is precisely what does not happen. The argument would be: If the first pint produces a return of 10 units of pleasure, and the second pint a return of 9 units; and if, nevertheless, a person is prepared to expend the same amount, namely one pint of beer, on the later 9 as on the earlier 10 units; then it follows that the desiredness of the 9 is exactly equal to that of the 10, and therefore the desiredness of each unit of the 9 is proportionately greater than that of each unit of the 10. Hence the operation of the law of diminishing returns to the means is necessarily correlated with increasing utility (increasing desiredness) with respect to the end.

But however ingenious such an argument might be as an exercise in dialectics, it is worthless as a serious contribution to the theory of valuation. It assumes that there can be some sort of correlation between 'utility' and 'returns', and that the two are commensurable, when we are dealing, not with the marginal utilities of objects of competing demands, but merely with successive satisfactions of the same demand. We know that, as a matter of fact, when demands are in competition for scarce resources, diminishing returns to the means do tend to produce diminishing utility in the end to which those are the relevant means. This is hard to reconcile with the apparently impeccable logical argument that, when we take a single demand out of relation to competing demands, diminishing returns are necessarily bound up with increasing utility. The general inference to be drawn is that we are almost certainly asking a nonsensical question when we ask whether the utility of an end, considered in abstraction from all competing ends, diminishes, increases or remains the same, as the returns to the means diminish. I think the question is indeed based on false assumptions. But if it is not, then the answer does seem to be the paradoxical one that, in such a case, diminishing returns are correlative to increasing utility.

Hence, whatever view we take, we are bound to reject the suggestion that the law of diminishing utility is a form of the law of diminishing returns. If the question whether the utility of an end, taken in isolation, decreases or increases as the returns to the means diminish is nonsensical, there is no answer. If it is a real and pertinent question, the answer appears to be emphatically that the utility increases.

Of course it may be thought that we can get a more significant correlation between 'returns' and 'utility' if we speak of the psychical states produced, not in terms of pleasures but in terms of satisfactions. But in that case we should have to say what is meant by 'satisfaction'. And, assuming an acceptable definition of satisfaction to have been reached, it would be necessary to explain what exactly is supposed to be 'diminishing' as the 'returns' to the beer-drinking are diminishing. In terms of what do we state the 'returns'—in terms of pleasure or in terms of satisfaction? And as these 'returns' (of pleasure or of satisfaction) diminish, is the argument that the 'satisfaction' diminishes, or is the argument that the 'utility of satisfaction' diminishes? If we say that 'the utility of satisfaction' diminishes, then we simply invite a demonstration (on the lines already given with regard to the 'utility of pleasure') that the utility of satisfaction must, on the contrary, increase. If we say that it is not the utility of satisfaction, but 'satisfaction' itself which diminishes, then we have abandoned all pretence of showing that utility diminishes directly as returns diminish.

So far we have been considering the suggestion that utility (desiredness) in the successive increments of the 'end' (pleasure or satisfaction) diminishes directly with diminishing returns to the means. But it has to be remembered that, the end having utility (desiredness), the indispensable means must also have utility (desiredness). It may therefore be suggested that the correlation between returns and utility is to be found in the relation of the *returns to the means* and the *utility of the means* themselves. For instance, the suggestion may be that, as the successive pints of beer bring proportionately less returns in terms of pleasure, so the desiredness of pints of beer will become correspondingly less. Now it may well be that this does in fact happen when there are *other* demands competing with the demand for pleasure from beer-drinking. But granting that, when there are these other competing demands, diminishing returns to beer-drinking will be accompanied or followed by decrease in utility (desiredness) of beer-drinking, we cannot infer that this diminishing utility of beer-drinking would also accompany or follow diminishing returns to beer-drinking if the beer-drinking and pleasure produced by it were taken in complete abstraction from a situation where we were confronted by the necessity of distributing scarce resources between competing demands. Quite obviously the utility (desiredness) of the means (beer-drinking) will be directly correlated with the utility (desiredness) of the end (pleasure) to which they are means. Hence to find any correlation between the *utility of the means* and the *returns to the means* we shall have to find this correlation *via* the utility of the end; and as we have already seen, this correlation of the utility of the end and the returns to the means is something which we cannot achieve so long as we take the end in abstraction from competing ends. It would be an entirely different matter if we were to look at the problem in the context of competing ends. In such a context we could very reasonably argue that, when we find diminishing returns setting in with respect to the production of end *A*, this will alter the utility or desiredness of the means as applied to the production of *A* rather than to the production of end *B*. But to adopt this line of investigation is to alter the whole character of our problem, and to abandon all attempt to correlate diminishing returns and diminishing utility within the compass of a single means-end situation, i.e. by considering only the relation of means to a single end abstracted from all relation to one or more competing ends.

Now what has all this fine-spun argumentation been about? What is the point of it? Simply this: We are emphasising the difference between the conception of 'diminishing returns' and that of 'diminishing utility'. They are radically different conceptions. We have shown that diminishing returns, as such, have no necessary implications for diminishing utility. It is therefore quite improper and wholly misleading to speak of the law of diminishing utility as though it were a law of diminishing returns— 'diminishing psychical returns'.

(2) *Two Interpretations of the 'Law of Diminishing Utility'*

But it may still be asked whether such elaborate criticism is necessary with regard to what may have been a mere verbal indiscretion on Wicksteed's part. Does the name he gives to this law affect in any way the soundness of his substantial account of what should properly be called the law of diminishing utility?

I think that we are dealing here not merely with a verbal indiscretion but with an error of substance into which Wicksteed and other economists have fallen, an error which has misled them in developing their theory of valuation. They argue as though the law of diminishing utility were concerned primarily with the relative utilities of successive increments of a commodity utilised in satisfaction of the same general demand; and while they do not wholly or consistently take this interpretation of the law, the fact that they often do so, and indeed formulate the law itself as though this were its essential meaning, has unfortunate results.

The law of diminishing utility is usually formulated in some such terms as these:

The marginal utility of a commodity to anyone diminishes with every increase in the amount he has.

We shall have to elucidate, in a later part of the argument, the meaning of 'marginal utility'; but for the moment we may attend primarily to a more general question, namely the broad interpretation of the meaning of this law. There are two main interpretations which, for the sake of convenience, we may call the 'unilateral' and the 'bilateral' theories of diminishing utility.

The unilateral interpretation of the law is the view that the law of diminishing utility is concerned with the utilities of successive units of a commodity relatively to each other, the general demand which they satisfy being taken simply by itself out of all relation to competing demands. For instance, if we say that the third pint of beer will have less utility than the second, the fourth than the third, and so on, and assume that this is the fundamental point made in the formulation of the law, then we are adopting the 'unilateral' theory.

The bilateral interpretation is that the law is concerned with the relative utilities of successive units of different commodities (or, it might be, the same commodity) to which different competing demands are directed. For instance, if we suppose that a person has demands for both beer and ham-sandwiches; and say that, when he has already secured one pint and one sandwich, the utility of each additional pint, relatively to the utility of an additional sandwich (or *vice versa*), will progressively diminish; and if we assume that this is the fundamental point of the law; then we are adopting the 'bilateral' theory. Possibly it might equally well be called the 'multilateral' theory; but the term 'bilateral' brings out sufficiently the essential point.

The difference between these two interpretations of the law is quite fundamental; but those who confuse the conceptions of 'diminishing utility' and 'diminishing returns' are apt to switch back and forth between the unilateral and the bilateral interpretations, to the detriment of their theories of valuation.

(3) The 'Orthodox' Formulation

To which of these two theories do modern economists generally subscribe? If we consider typical statements of what economics is about (e.g. 'the allocation of scarce resources to the satisfaction of competing wants'), it would appear that the questions with which the economist is concerned are those to which the bilateral theory would be most relevant. This is not to say that the unilateral theory, if it could be made really intelligible, would necessarily be irrelevant to the problems of economics. One might be able to hold that the law of diminishing utility operates with respect to the units successively applied in satisfaction of every single demand considered in isolation from other demands; and that the economist is concerned with the interaction of demands each of which is independently governed by this law.

But while this is a possible view, assuming that the unilateral theory can itself be intelligibly presented (though our argument will be that it cannot), the natural presumption is that, from the very nature of the problems of economics, it is the bilateral theory which the economist really intends to present. The probability that this initial presumption is correct is strengthened by reading, say, Wicksteed's extremely lucid exposition of the problems of valuation confronting the housewife in her household administration,[1] and noting that it is the theory to explain her mode of tackling these problems which he proceeds to expound in the theory of 'diminishing psychical returns' and 'marginal uses' of resources.

But while the typical statement of the nature of the problems of economics suggests the bilateral theory of diminishing utility, the typical or 'orthodox' formulation of the law of diminishing utility suggests that it is the unilateral theory which is, in fact,

[1] Pp. 18 ff.

H

being propounded. We shall see that Wicksteed himself tends, on the whole, to express it in unilateral terms—'Second helps are never as good as first'; 'The second pound of tea has less utility than the first'. Marshall[1] formulates the law in unilateral terms. Henderson[2] does so also; and his explanatory discussion of the law strongly suggests that his view is primarily the unilateral one.

(4) Criticism of 'Orthodox' Formulation

What we have now to consider is whether the unilateral theory —and this, in effect, is the theory adopted in the orthodox formulation of the law of diminishing utility when taken at its face value —can withstand examination, and whether it can have any relevance to the problems of valuation. I shall contend that it is wholly irrelevant to the problem of valuation, and that it only appears to be relevant because, through illogical processes of reasoning, it appears to yield conclusions which it cannot, from its very nature, yield.

Valuation—the choice of 'this' in preference to 'that'—occurs in situations where the objective conditions enforce upon us the necessity of relinquishing A (B) if we are to secure B (A), it being postulated that we demand or desire both A and B. Since valuation or choice is precisely the same thing as attributing a higher value to one thing than to the other, or regarding one as better than the other, it necessarily follows that we cannot significantly say that A is better than B unless A and B can be real alternatives in a choice situation. To say, for instance, that second helps are never so good as first helps—meaning that we set a higher value on first helps—necessarily implies that we are able (and the following argument will show that we are not able) to think of these as genuine alternatives in a choice situation.

But if we are not able to think of these as alternatives—if it is utterly impossible for successive increments of a commodity devoted to the same demand to be alternatives in a choice situation—then it is utterly impossible for one of them to be given a higher or lower value than the other. They can have no comparative values with respect to each other. And if we cannot say

---

[1] *Principles* (8th edition), p. 93. [2] *Supply and Demand*, pp. 42-3.

that one has a higher value than the other, then we cannot say that one has more utility than the other, for utility means desired-ness or demandedness; and to say that there is more utility (de-mandedness) in A than in B would be to say that A has a higher place than B in a valuational order. Consequently, if it is impos-sible for successive units of a commodity utilised for the same demand (say successive helpings of pudding or successive cigar-ettes) to be alternatives to each other in a choice situation, then it is impossible for them to diminish in utility relatively to each other. That is to say, the unilateral theory of diminishing utility will be completely devoid of significance and can have no bearing on the problems of economic theory or the philosophical problem of valuation.

The following argument will endeavour to show that it is indeed impossible for the successive increments of any commodity to be alternatives with respect to each other in a choice situation, and that any appearance of such a possibility (and consequently any suggestion that they can or must follow a law of diminishing utility) is a mere illusion generated by illogical thinking.

It will be convenient, for purposes of our argument, to take a somewhat lengthy passage from Wicksteed,[1] and critically ex-amine the main contention embodied in it.

Suppose the usual consumption of potatoes in a family is about 4 lb a day (2 stone a week), and sound old potatoes are about ½d the lb. If new potatoes are 2d the housewife may determine to buy 2 lb that week, for a treat, reckoning that they will go once round on Sunday, the second dish to be of old potatoes as usual, or if that takes too much trouble the second dish to be dispensed with. If they are 1½d a lb she may buy 4 lb and have all new potatoes on Sunday, or one dish on Sunday and one on some other day in the week; or she may buy enough for the birthday dinner of one of the children. But when new potatoes come down to a penny she will buy no more old potatoes at all. It is not likely that she will buy new potatoes to the extent of 4 lb a day, as she did the old. They are still too expensive a form of food for that. She will perhaps buy 3 lb a day for 3d (instead of 4 lb for 2d as before), and this will involve some readjustment of expenditure on other articles of food, and perhaps in other branches of expenditure as well. But without following out these complex reactions we may at once

[1] Pp. 39-40.

grasp the fact to which we must now apply our closest attention, that the place which a pound of new potatoes takes on the marketer's scale of preferences is not fixed. For if at 2d she buys 2 lb but not 3 lb, this shows that she prefers the second pound per week to 2d, but prefers 2d to the third pound per week; and *therefore a third pound stands lower than a second on her scale of preferences.* If at 1½d she buys 4 lb but not 5 lb, it shows that she prefers the fourth pound to 1½d, but prefers 1½d to the fifth pound.—that is to say, that the fourth pound stands above and the fifth pound stands below 1½d on her scale of preferences. . . . There is, of course, nothing inconsistent, anomalous, or mysterious in this. *Each successive pound takes a lower place on the scale of preference than the one before it,* because the want to which it ministers is less urgent. (My italics.)

Wicksteed's argument is presented with such clarity and detail that the passage quoted is admirably suited to indicate both the true and the false doctrines which he expounds. What he is arguing in the later part of the passage is (*a*) that, if the housewife is prepared to buy 2 lb but not 3 lb of potatoes at 2d per lb, this shows that she prefers a second lb to 2d, and that she prefers 2d to a third lb—which is true; and (*b*) that *therefore* a third lb stands lower than a second lb on her scale of preferences—which is false and impossible.

Superficially, it would seem that the statement in (*b*) must be true. If a person prefers *A* to *B*, and *B* to *C*, it is ridiculous to suggest that he does not prefer *A* to *C*, *provided* that *B* means the same thing when placed as an alternative to *C* as it means when placed as an alternative to *A*, and that *A* and *C* can be alternatives genuinely open to the person in question. But neither of these two conditions is satisfied in the choice situations as presented by Wicksteed. 2d as an alternative to the third lb does not, and cannot, mean the same thing as 2d as an alternative to the second lb; and the second and third lb cannot be genuine alternatives to the housewife.

To deal, first, with the latter point: Alternatives are things between which you have to choose. You may have one, but only at the cost of doing without the other. Now a 'second lb' and a '2d' can be alternatives to each other: a 'third lb' and a '2d' can be alternatives to each other: but a 'second lb' and a 'third lb' cannot possibly be alternatives to each other. Therefore they cannot be placed in the same valuational order or order of choice. They cannot be genuine alternatives for the following elementary reasons: You cannot choose the 'second' rather than the 'third', for, until you are already in possession of the 'second', the 'third' is not a possible item of choice. You cannot choose the 'third' rather than the 'second', because, if the 'third' is a possible alternative, then being already in possession of the 'second' is a factor in the choice situation confronting you, and not one of the alternatives between which you must now choose. The situation before you is that you are in possession of the 'second', and that you have two alternatives open (neither of which can actually be in your possession since they are both alternatives for choice); you may have *either* a 'third' *or* a '(what?)'. What do we insert here after the 'or' as a genuine alternative to the 'third'? It cannot be the 'second'. It cannot be 'no more'; for 'no more' would be the *absence* of an alternative—Hobson's choice. A genuine alternative must have a positive content. This content of an alternative to a 'third' lb of potatoes cannot be any lb or number of lb of potatoes (for any number less than three would already be possessed, and therefore be part of the choice situation; and any number greater than three must include the third, and therefore cannot be alternative to the third). The alternative to the 'third' must therefore be the content of a demand for something other than any lb of potatoes. When we express a preference, or accord one thing a higher point than another in a valuational order, the alternatives or things valued against each other must be the contents of qualitatively different competing demands.

What has misled Wicksteed into the impossible position of maintaining that the 'third' lb of potatoes has a lower place on the scale of preferences than the 'second' lb? This brings us to the consideration of the other proviso which his choice situation would require to (and does not) satisfy. We said that if a person prefers A to B, and B to C, we must infer that he prefers A to C, provided that B means the same thing in both cases. Wicksteed argues that because the housewife prefers a 'second' lb of potatoes to '2d', and '2d' to a 'third' lb, we must infer that she prefers a 'second' lb to a 'third' lb. The fallacy in the argument is largely due to the fact that he uses the conception of money in at least two different senses. Initially, '2d' is itself a thing valued—a content of demand placed below or above a lb of potatoes on a valuational scale, the housewife choosing between the alternatives 'a second lb' and '2d', and again between the alternatives 'a third lb' and '2d'. But almost immediately he switches over to the conception of '2d' as a mark on a scale on which we place alternatives, rather than as one of the alternatives placed on that valuational scale, the 'third' lb falling below and the 'second' lb falling above that mark. Now, even granting that money can be considered in these two ways—as one of the alternatives valued by the individual, and as a measure of values in the 'public order of values'—it is quite illegitimate to switch back and forth between these two conceptions in the same chain of reasoning. Had Wicksteed conformed to the rules of logically consistent reasoning he would have found it impossible to reach the conclusions he professes to demonstrate.

Let us take '2d', in the sense in which he employs it initially, as a content of demand which is an alternative to a lb of potatoes. If we think of '2d' in this way, it is at once evident that the '2d' which is an alternative to the 'second' lb cannot possibly be the same as the '2d' which is an alternative to the 'third' lb; for, if the person chooses (as is assumed) the 'second' lb rather than '2d', then he must have surrendered *this* '2d' in exchange for the 'second' lb; and any '2d' which is an alternative to the 'third' lb must be a different '2d'. Hence we cannot represent the position by saying that the housewife prefers A to B, and B to C; for the 'B' which is an alternative to A is not the same as the 'B' which is an alternative to C. The position is that the housewife prefers A_2 to B_x, and then in the new choice situation prefers B_{x-1} to A_3. Even if A_2 and A_3 were possible alternatives (which they are not), we could not infer from these two valuations which she has made how A_2 and A_3 stand to each other, for there is no evidence as to how A_2 stands in relation to B_{x-1}, or how A_3 stands in relation to B_x.

It does not assist us here to say that our valuations of 'twopences' will necessarily follow the same law of diminishing utility as governs our valuations of 'pounds of potatoes'; for the impossibility of evaluating an nth against an mth '2d' is just as evident as is the impossibility of evaluating a 'third' lb of potatoes against a 'second' lb. In any case, Wicksteed only reaches his conclusion—that the 'third' has a lower value than the 'second' lb of potatoes—by assuming that the '2d' does *not* follow the law of diminishing utility; for it is on the assumption that '2d' has a fixed place (or is a fixed mark) on a valuational scale that he infers that the 'third' must have a lower value than the 'second' lb.

The fact of the matter is that, in the case as presented by Wicksteed, we are dealing with two quite separate and distinct valuational orders arising from two distinct choice situations.

The *first* choice situation is: You have 1 lb of potatoes and X twopences; and potatoes and twopences exchange at the rate of 1 lb for 2d. In this situation which of the alternatives do you choose: (a) to retain the 1 lb and the X twopences, or (b) to exchange a 2d for a 'second' lb? It is assumed that the person in this choice situation has chosen (b).

Then, and only then, will the *second* choice situation arise: You have now, by your last choice, altered the position somewhat. You have 2 lb and X − 1 twopences, although potatoes and twopences still exchange at the same rate. Which of the alternatives do you now choose: (a) to retain the 2 lb and X − 1 twopences, or (b) to exchange a 'second' 2d for a 'third' lb? It is assumed that the person in this choice situation chooses (a).

What Wicksteed does is to treat these two separate and distinct choice situations and valuational orders as though they were one choice situation and valuational order with the descending order of preferences: 1. 'Second' lb

2. '2d'

3. 'Third' lb.

This is a serious error. We are not dealing with one, but with two distinct valuational orders.[1] If, however, we allow the as-

---

[1] It is a question for consideration whether the whole conception of the 'indifference curve' adopted by economists is not vitiated by the same error as we find in Wicksteed—the attempt to plot a whole series of choices made in

sumption that we have here a comprehensive single valuational order, may we not still object that Wicksteed has drawn the wrong conclusion? May we not say that, since each successive twopence will have a lower value than the preceding twopence, the descending order of preferences is:

1. 'Second' 2d
2. 1 lb of potatoes
3. 'First' 2d?

This is to take the value of 1 lb of potatoes as fixed or as a mark on a valuational scale on which we indicate the diminishing utility of twopences; and the conclusion is as sound (or unsound) in the one case as in the other.

To put in a general way our criticisms of Wicksteed's exposition of the general law of diminishing utility or diminishing psychical returns: Wicksteed attempts to explain the operation of this law in accordance with a 'unilateral' theory of diminishing utility, and there are three fallacies in his argument.

Firstly, it is assumed that one can have a single valuational order covering different choice situations. This is not the case. A valuational order is the order of choice in any given objective situation such as to present the person concerned with alternatives, both of which he demands at that time and in that situation, but only one of which he can have. There may be different valuational orders in the mind of the same individual; but, so far as they are different, we cannot say that something in one of these orders has a higher or lower value than something in another such order; we cannot say this for the simple reason that the two things are not alternatives presented in a genuine choice situation.

Secondly, Wicksteed is attempting to show, by his various examples, that in any given case each successive unit of a commodity employed for the satisfaction of a demand 'takes a lower place on the scale of preferences than the one before it, because the want to which it administers is less urgent'[1]; but in order to

separate choice situations, and then to argue that the person is 'indifferent' as between the choices plotted on the curve. We can only be 'indifferent' as between alternatives in the same order—which such choices are not.

[1] P. 40.

make out his case in any particular situation, he postulates that this *must not* hold in at least one case. Thus, to prove that it holds with regard to pounds of potatoes when the alternatives are pounds of potatoes and twopences, it is necessary to assume that it must *not* hold with regard to twopences; and to prove that it holds with regard to twopences, it is necessary to assume that it must *not* hold with regard to pounds of potatoes. To prove that the law of diminishing utility (in this unilateral sense of the 'law') *is* 'universally operative', we must begin by postulating that it *isn't*: we must begin by postulating that the utility of twopences remains constant for the successive twopences (or alternatively that the utility of pounds of potatoes remains constant for the successive pounds of potatoes). It is therefore just as reasonable to emphasise the assumption, and draw the conclusion that 'utility remains constant however many successive units you add', as to emphasise the aspect of the argument after the assumption has been made, and draw the conclusion that 'utility diminishes with every successive additional unit'.

Thirdly, in so far as Wicksteed speaks about the 'second' and 'third' pounds, but not of the 'first' and 'second' twopences, and apparently regards the 'twopence' as the same twopence in both cases, he has quite changed the meaning of 'twopence' within the limits of a single sentence in his argument. ' . . . she prefers the second pound per week to 2d but prefers 2d to the third pound per week; and therefore a third pound stands lower than a second on her scale of preferences.' In the first part of this sentence we are dealing with two different twopences which are the alternatives to the second and third pounds respectively; but in the second part of the sentence it is assumed that we are dealing with the same twopence, which must be taken therefore as a point on a scale above and below which the 'second' and 'third' pounds fall.

But if he wishes to use the conception of money as a scale on which to indicate preferences, then the foundations of the whole argument are destroyed. Initially, twopence is regarded as a commodity in demand, one of the alternatives to be placed in an order of preference. If, however, it is a mark on a scale in terms

of which we are assumed to be able to locate preferences in relation to each other, it cannot also be one of the things preference
for which is indicated on that scale. In other words, it cannot be
both a mark on a valuational scale and also a commodity in
demand offered as an alternative to a pound of potatoes. If twopence is a mark on a scale, what is the alternative to the pound of
potatoes—either the second or the third? Apparently none. If no
alternatives, no choice; and therefore no preferences to place on
the scale.

How very serious these confusions are is shown by Wicksteed's
subsequent argument. The entirely fallacious 'demonstration' that
the successive units of a commodity employed to satisfy a single
demand (say for potatoes, or for tea, or for anything else), that
demand being considered quite out of relation to any other competing demand, is assumed to be valid. Money is henceforth
taken as a scale in terms of which the utility or value of these
successive units can be stated, and Wicksteed proceeds to a most
elaborate explanation of rates of declining utility and the curious
conception of 'surplus value'.

But it is not within the province of this work to pursue this
question into the details of Wicksteed's argument. He may well
be dealing in an illuminating manner with points which are of
genuine concern to the economist. The fact that the basis of a
general theory is logically unsound need not prevent the theory
from being fruitful and enlightening with regard to some of the
particular issues with which it deals. But, so far as the philosopher
is concerned, it is the general theory, as touching the nature and
principles of valuation, which is important; and I think it has been
shown that Wicksteed's theory is, in this respect, fundamentally
unsound. On no interpretation of it can we say that he has shown
that the principle of diminishing utility is relevant to the successive
units employed in satisfying a single demand, that demand being
considered out of relation to some competing demand.

(5) The 'Bilateral' Theory

To all the foregoing criticism it might be replied that, if what
has here been called the 'unilateral' theory of diminishing utility

commands the assent of economists generally, then external criticism by a philosopher can hardly carry much weight. The 'defects' are likely to be due to misunderstanding on the part of the critic rather than to the reasoning of the economists who have built up the theory. It is, of course, necessary for the critic to realise the *prima facie* reasonableness of such a reply; but there are two considerations on the other side. The first is that the theory covers ground which is not exclusively the province of the economist. We are dealing with one of those issues which link up the work of economists, psychologists and moral philosophers. It may well be (and I think it is) true that the major contribution to the solution of problems in this field has been made by economists; but this does not affect the point that the solutions offered have a psychological and philosophical content which may stand in need of revision, a revision which could remove defects on the philosophical level and thus help, indirectly at least, in the clarification of the theory of marginal utility for purposes of economics itself.

The second consideration is that economists themselves have not been satisfied with the doctrine we have been criticising. They do not express their objections in the form in which I have stated them. They do not differentiate between the 'unilateral' and the 'bilateral' theory of diminishing utility. But they do make, in their own terms, substantially the same objection as I have made. Thus Cairncross, after setting out briefly what I have called the 'orthodox' unilateral theory of diminishing utility,[1] turns to what he calls an 'alternative version'.[2]

The theory of marginal utility, even when it is stated in a simplified form, is difficult for students to understand. . . . The theory of marginal utility was worked out at a time when most economists were utilitarians (hence the muddle of economics with ethics) and believed that utility was something quantitative. They spoke of a quantity of utility as they might have spoken of a pound of cheese. But it would be as reasonable to speak of a quantity of temperature. The fact is that we can only measure the intensity of one demand in terms of the intensity of another, and that, behind the screen of 'utility', is exactly what the theory does—or should do.

If we remove the screen, what kind of theory are we left with? In its

[1] Pp. 160-6.   [2] P. 16.

essentials the new theory is very much like the old. But it lays emphasis on the word 'preference' instead of on the word 'utility'. Where we talked of 'marginal utility' we now talk of 'marginal preference'; and where we drew curves of marginal utility we now draw 'indifference curves'.

While this passage criticises the older theory from a point of view rather different from the one I have adopted, it makes the same general point, inasmuch as it stresses the fact that we can compare relative strength of demand (comparative desiredness or utility) only when we have different competing demands. In fact it rejects the unilateral theory of diminishing utility.

Since there is this broad general agreement between the approach of contemporary economists and the line to be taken by my own argument, it is a matter of minor importance whether we do or do not continue to speak of 'utility' rather than of 'preference', provided that we are quite clear as to the meaning of our terms. For purposes of the present argument it will be safer to retain the older term, particularly as the conception of utility has been defined, and since we are, after all, concerned with the 'law of diminishing utility'. There would, indeed, be a certain disadvantage in changing over to the terminology of 'marginal preferences' and the 'indifference curve', for the theory of the indifference curve itself is not free from difficulties and has been subjected to a critical review by Little[1] who would substitute a

[1] *Welfare Economics*, Chap II. Little's criticism of the indifference-curve analysis is rather different from the one which I should myself have offered if the question had to be discussed here. Fortunately the main line of the argument does not require such discussion. It may be noted in passing, however, that Little's substitute theory of a 'behaviour line system' is itself somewhat curious. He thinks that he can deduce a system of behaviour lines which, when diagrammatically represented, would be like the smooth convex curves of the 'indifference curve' analysis. His deductions are apparently made from the three 'definitions' and three 'axioms' set out at the beginning of the Appendix to Chapter II. But it seems pretty obvious that his behaviour lines could not possibly be deduced from the definitions and axioms. We need consider only the first definition, 'A collection of goods is said to be larger than another collection if there is more of one kind, and no less of any kind . . .', along with axiom I, 'A consumer chooses a larger collection of goods rather than a smaller collection', and axiom III, 'Every possible collection of goods is chosen in one and only one price-income situation.' It will be seen, on looking at his argument, that (given the above definition of 'larger than') axioms I and III are logically incompatible with each other.

'behaviour line' for an 'indifference curve' analysis. To avoid becoming entangled in controversies on very technical economic issues, some of which may even be founded on misunderstandings, it will be safer for us to stick to the conception 'utility'.

Our objection to the orthodox formulation of the 'law of diminishing utility' was that it cannot possibly be a law of valuation. It is apparently conceived on the analogy of the law of diminishing returns and expressed in a 'unilateral' form. Now there *may* be a *psychological* law governing our desiring such that, if successive units of resources applied to the realisation of some end or purpose show decreasing 'returns' of 'pleasure' or 'satisfaction', the utility (desiredness) of the successive increments of 'pleasure' or 'satisfaction' will also progressively decrease. That is to say, it *may* be that the desiredness of a lesser pleasure is always less than the desiredness of a greater. We have shown above that this is a proposition which it will be extremely difficult to substantiate if it is true that a person is prepared to put out as much of his resources on securing the lesser as he put out on securing the greater; and it has to be borne in mind also that those who formulate this law of 'diminishing utility' also tell us that there is an opposite law of 'increasing utility'. But what precisely would be the sound psychological interpretation of such so-called diminishing and increasing utility it is not our business to discuss. Our point is simply that, even *if* there is a general psychological law of diminishing utility in the sense alleged, this cannot be a

---

The argument, illustrated by inset diagram, is: Suppose a person has an income OC of Y, and that the rate of exchange between X and Y is OC of Y to OD of X. Assume that, in this situation, he chooses the collection marked E. If we then rotate the price-income line on E, so that E is still a possible alternative, to the new position FG, then, according to axiom III, the choice cannot remain at E but must move elsewhere along FG (say to J).

Now it is perfectly true that, according to axiom III, the choice must move from E; but it is equally true that, according to definition I and axiom I, this is what cannot possibly happen. By definition I, no point along FG can represent a 'greater good' than E since movement in either direction entails *less* of X or Y; and, by axiom I, choice is always directed to the 'greater good'. Hence, if the consumer has once chosen E, then he must *always* choose E on *any* price-income line running through E, for there can be no 'greater good' to induce him to move.

law of valuation. We have valuation only when we are choosing between qualitatively different demands in competition for our scarce resources—when we are dealing with the relative utility of x+ 1 *A* and y+ 1 *B*.

If, then, there is any genuine *valuational* law of diminishing utility, this will have to be stated in 'bilateral' terms; and we shall now consider whether any revision of the orthodox formulation will meet the requirements. The orthodox statement is:

The marginal utility of a thing to anyone diminishes with every increase in the amount he already has.

It will be noted that the law is really formulated as a law of diminishing *marginal* utility. Our first task therefore is to consider the notion of 'marginal utility'.

5. MARGINAL UTILITY

(1) *Marginal Utility and the Marginal Unit*

What do we mean by saying, not that 'utility' diminishes and increases, but that 'marginal utility' diminishes and increases? What is the difference between simple 'utility' and 'marginal utility'?

'Marginal utility' might mean a particular kind of utility distinguishable from other kinds of utility; or it might mean utility-in-general attaching to a particular kind of thing. To illustrate the distinction here drawn: we may ask what is meant by 'the royal slice of bread' when the king craves a little bit of butter for the royal slice of bread? Is a slice called a 'royal slice' because it is a particular kind of slice which can, on inspection and comparison with other slices, be distinguished from the latter as having certain 'intrinsic properties' which non-royal slices do not possess? Or is a royal slice 'intrinsically' exactly like any other slice of bread, and distinguished from all other slices only by being placed on the royal table or otherwise 'attached' to the royal person? If by a royal slice we mean a slice intrinsically different from other slices, then we have to identify it by comparing it with other slices. If by a royal slice we mean simply any slice 'attached' to the royal person, then the meaning of a royal slice will be understood when we understand what is meant by 'a slice of bread (in general)' and what is meant by 'a royal person'.

Similarly, if 'marginal utility' means a particular kind of utility, we have to distinguish it from other kinds of utility by noting its differentiating intrinsic properties. But if it means simply the utility (in general) of the 'marginal unit', then we shall understand what marginal utility is if we discover the meaning of the marginal unit, having already discovered the meaning of utility.

As I understand the position, economists mean by 'marginal utility', not a particular kind of utility different from other kinds, but simply the utility attaching to the marginal unit. Thus we are told that 'marginal utility is the utility of "the last unit purchased" ', just as we might be told that 'the royal slice of bread is the slice reserved for the consumption of the king'.

(2) *The Marginal Unit and the Saturation-Point of Demand*

The meaning of 'marginal unit' requires careful discussion. For purposes of our analysis certain distinctions have to be drawn.

In the first place, when we speak of the marginal unit as 'the last unit purchased' it is necessary to distinguish between this conception of 'the last unit purchased' and the conception of 'the saturation-point of demand'. Secondly, it is necessary to distinguish 'the marginal unit with respect to utility' from the 'marginal unit with respect to equilibrium'.

The first of these distinctions—namely the distinction between the marginal unit and the saturation-point of demand—is important because the marginal unit is a conception which is relevant only when we are dealing with the application of scarce resources to meet competing demands, while the conception of the saturation-point of demand is clearly relevant only when we are assuming resources adequate to meet demand in full. When resources are superabundant, or even just adequate to meet all demands, the problem of distribution of these resources over the demands will be purely 'technical' or 'administrative' and not 'economic'. Calculation and judgement will indeed be required. Thus, if I have free access to unlimited supplies, and am proposing a week's trek in the wilds, I shall need to sit down and calculate how much of various things I require to take with me in order to meet in full all the demands likely to arise in the course of the week. These problems are technical or administrative rather than economic, for there is no question of scarcity, no question of opportunity cost for one demand in devoting resources to the satisfaction of another, no question therefore of evaluating the contents of the different demands against each other. Hence there is no place for the conception of the marginal unit, however much I may be preoccupied in calculating what would be the 'last unit' sufficient to meet all demand up to satiation-point.

To take a different illustration: If I am at the tea-table of a house-proud lady, it is possible that I shall be pressed to eat up to, or even beyond, comfortable capacity. When I am nearing the saturation-point of demand for iced cake I may hesitate as to whether I shall have another piece; I may have reached the point of indifference as to whether I have another or not. But the question here is not one of evaluating the additional piece of cake; the question is not whether I prefer an additional piece rather than something else which I shall have to go without if I take the cake. The question is simply whether I want another piece at all, or whether I have had quite enough. I am not considering whether the additional piece has a greater degree of goodness than something else, but merely considering whether an additional piece has, in the situation, any goodness (is an object of demand) at all. These considerations are all concerned with the saturation-point of demand, and not with the marginal unit. Of course I may be faced at the tea-table with a choice situation. I may have had quite enough to eat (have reached the saturation-point of demand for iced cake), and be confronted by the alternatives of enduring the discomfort of eating more or offending the good lady by appearing to scorn her hospitality. But this is not a question about the saturation-point of demand. It is a question as to which of two evils I prefer to avoid when I cannot avoid both—the discomforts of over-eating or the giving of offence to a well-intentioned hostess.

This distinction between the conception of the marginal unit and that of the saturation-point of demand is emphasised here because it becomes important in a later section of the argument.[1]

(3) *Marginal Units of Equilibrium and Utility*

Both equilibrium and utility are involved in questions of valuation in the proper sense, and the two conceptions are therefore liable to be confused with each other when we are discussing the meaning of the marginal unit. In expounding the doctrine of 'margins', economists sometimes say that the 'marginal unit' is the one about which a person is 'practically indifferent' as to whether he gets it or not. Now this may be a very useful, rough practical guide in determining whether a person has reached 'within a shilling or so on either side' the point of equilibrium as to the distribution of his expenditure over a variety of competing demands; but it is entirely inadequate as an exact statement of the doctrine of marginal utility. Marginal utility—we must repeat this point at the risk of boring the reader to distraction—is concerned with *choices* or *preferences*, and not with *indifference* or lack of preference. To say that a person is indifferent as between another unit of A and another unit of B is to say that he is not in a state to make any rational choice between them; while the theory of valuation is a theory to explain the fact of the rational choice of A (B) rather than B (A).

It would appear that this seeking refuge in the conception of 'indifference' is the result of a genuine perception of a real problem about 'marginal units', combined with a lack of resolution in thinking out the problem to the final analysis, and hence the failure to distinguish between the conception of the 'marginal unit with respect to equilibrium', on the one hand, and that of the 'marginal unit with respect to utility', on the other. Perhaps the point may be made most clearly if we reflect upon the statement with which Wicksteed opens his most elaborate (and, from the point of view of the theory of valuation, quite irrelevant) discussion of 'marginal significances'.[2]

It will be necessary to justify the practice of speaking of the marginal significance of a commodity, at such and such a point, as measured

[1] Pp. 119-22.   [2] Pp. 47 ff.

I

indifferently by the value of a small increment or the value of a small decrement. This practice is constantly and rightly followed in books on Economics. . . .

It is not for the present writer to say whether this practice is or is not appropriate for certain purposes of economic theory. Presumably if the economist finds it useful and convenient it is very properly adopted. We are concerned here only with the question whether the practice is appropriate when one is expounding the fundamental doctrine of the margin and marginal utility; and I think that we shall have to answer this question with an emphatic negative.

Let us consider, first, the conception of the 'marginal units of equilibrium'. Let us postulate that a person's full demand for A is for 10 A, and that his full demand for B is for 8 B. (If it be asked whether it is realistic to assume that we could, in fact, have this antecedent knowledge of a person's full demands for A and B, it must be conceded that the postulate is a very questionable one. But this problem will be dealt with presently. For the moment, we shall find it easier to explain the essential character of the units of equilibrium if we are permitted to postulate this advance knowledge of the full demands.) Now if he has only 9 units of resources (R), and each unit of R purchases 1 unit of either A or B, then it is reasonable to infer that he will expend his 9 R on the purchase of 5 A and 4 B, rather than, say, 6 A and 3 B, or rather than 4 A and 5 B. That is to say, he will not be prepared to give up the 5th A for an additional unit of B, or the 4th B for an additional unit of A. In this case, then, the 'marginal units of equilibrium' are the '5th A' and the '4th B'. The marginal units of equilibrium are the 'last chosen units of objects of competing demands in the allocation of scarce resources'.

When we turn to the conception of the 'marginal units of utility (desiredness)', it is obvious that these cannot possibly be equated with the marginal units of equilibrium. Marginal units of equilibrium are *objects* of demand; they are the last units *actually* chosen. But anything which has 'utility' must be a *content*, not an object, of demand. What has utility or desiredness must be something which does not yet exist, but must be the content of some end envisaged. Marginal units of utility, therefore, must be alternative contents of demand between which a choice *has to be made*, not (as in the case of marginal units of equilibrium) the 'last choices' on both sides, A and B, actually made. Thus, supposing that, in the case stated, the person had spent 4 R on 4 A and 4 R on 4 B, and had 1 R left with which he could purchase either a 5th A or a 5th B; then, since he demands 6 more A and 4 more B, a 5th A and a 5th B are both contents of demand to him between which he must now choose, for he cannot have both. If we assume that he is in no doubt whatsoever that he prefers a 4th A to a 6th B (that he would not think of surrendering any of the A already purchased in exchange for more B), and that he is equally clear that he prefers a 4th B to a 6th A (that he will not surrender any B already possessed for more A), then it is obvious that it is the expenditure of his last remaining unit of R which presents the critical problem to him. His 'marginal units of utility (desiredness)' are the 5th A and the 5th B. Hence the 'marginal units of equilibrium' and the 'marginal units of utility' cannot possibly be the same things; for the marginal units of utility are the 5th A and 5th B, while (if the final choice falls on the 5th A, as we have supposed) the marginal units of equilibrium are the 5th A and the 4th B.

But while the marginal units of equilibrium and the marginal units of utility cannot be the same, it appears that there is a necessary relation between them. We call them 'marginal' units in both cases because they are in both cases the 'critical' or 'last' units. The marginal units of utility are the pair of contents of competing demands the choice between which will determine the final allocation of scarce resources over the competing demands. The marginal units of equilibrium are the last units on either side when this allocation has been made. This means that *one* of the alternatives constituting the marginal units of utility must be the content of demand corresponding to *one* of the objects of demand constituting the finally determined units of equilibrium. That is to say: if we ignore the distinction between 'content' and 'object' of demand, we conclude that one of the marginal units of utility must necessarily be the same 'thing' as one of the marginal units of equilibrium. Thus, in the case stated, the 5th A and 5th B are the marginal units of utility, while the 5th A and 4th B are the marginal units of equilibrium.

We are now in a position to define the two conceptions.

The *marginal units of equilibrium* are the last chosen units of objects of competing demands in the allocation of scarce resources.

The *marginal units of utility* (*desiredness*) are the alternative contents of demand presented for choice when the alternative actually chosen will constitute one of the marginal units of equilibrium.

With regard to these definitions there are two points requiring special notice.

Firstly, it may be remarked that neither in the case of the conception of equilibrium nor in the case of the marginal units of utility do we need to make any use of the term 'indifference'. On the contrary, we are dealing the whole time with determinate choices, and not with the inability to make specific choices. The marginal significance of commodities is just *not* 'measured indifferently by the value of a small increment or the value of a small decrement'; for it is on the determinate choice as between such small increment and small decrement that we depend in locating the marginal units of equilibrium. What, then, gives rise to 'the practice constantly followed' of 'speaking of the marginal significance of a commodity, at such and such a point, as measured indifferently by the value of a small increment or the value of a small decrement'?

This question brings us to the *second* point to be noted in connexion with our definitions of marginal equilibrium and marginal utility. Observe that marginal utility is defined by reference to marginal equilibrium, and that, in the definition of the marginal units of equilibrium, we do not define 'the last units chosen' by reference to the conception of 'equilibrium'. On the contrary we define equilibrium by reference to the last units chosen. To explain this procedure we must deal with a point mentioned at the beginning of our consideration of the whole conception of the marginal units of equilibrium.[1] In the first attempt to make this conception clear, we postulated that we could know ante-

[1] P. 114.

cedently the full extent of a person's demands for different things. We put the case, for example, that a person has a total demand for 10 A and 8 B, and then said that, with 9 R to expend on purchasing units of A and B, the marginal units of equilibrium could reasonably be inferred to be the 5th A and 4th B. We considered this a reasonable inference because 5 A : 4 B :: 10 A : 8 B. That is to say, we inferred what 'the last units of A and B chosen' would actually be on the basis of an assumed knowledge of the total demands for A and B, and on the assumption that, with scarce resources, the person concerned would aim at a 'proportionate' satisfaction of the competing demands.

But, now, is it legitimate to suppose that we can know, in advance of a person's actual choices, what his total demands are? The truth of the matter seems to be that we can infer the *relative* extent (and the *full* extent, if this can be inferred at all) of a person's competing demands only by reflection on the choices he actually makes. That is to say, our inferences are not really in the form: Because 10 A and 8 B would give complete satisfaction, *therefore* the 5th A and 4th B will be the marginal units of equilibrium (and hence the 'last units chosen') when a person possesses 9 R. Rather, our inferences are in the form: *Because* the 5th A and 4th B are the 'last chosen units' (this being noted as an empirical fact), and *because* everyone aims at equilibrium or proportionate satisfaction of his competing demands (this being an *a priori* postulate about rational beings), therefore what would fully satisfy demand must be in something like the proportion 5 A : 4 B; it will be 10 A : 8 B, or 15 A : 12 B, or 20 A : 16 B, or something of the kind.

Thus, in a realistic approach to the theory of demand and its satisfaction, we abandon the postulate (adopted initially for clarification of the conception of equilibrium) that we can know the full extent of demand and employ this knowledge in deducing the marginal units of equilibrium. How then do we know what these marginal units are? We identify them by reference to what we do know, namely the 'last choices' which people actually make; and hence we define the marginal units of equilibrium by reference to the conception of the last units chosen.

At the same time, it will be evident that we are still making use of a postulate. We have abandoned the postulate that we can know empirically the full extent of demand; but we have at the same time adopted the *a priori* postulate that every person aims at equilibrium or proportionate satisfaction of his competing demands. This *a priori* postulate is one which is integral to economic theory, although it may appear in forms which imperfectly reveal its true character. But in so far as it is fundamental in economics, we are perfectly safe in adopting it for our present exposition. Its ultimate significance for the theory of valuation will be explained in the last section of the present chapter.[1]

Let us now return to the particular question on which we considered this problem of the definition of the marginal units of equilibrium to have a bearing. The question was: why is it often thought that the marginal significance of a commodity is measured indifferently by the value of a small increment or decrement? The answer to the question seems to be this: We can only infer whether a person has reached the state of equilibrium in the satisfaction of his competing demands by observing his actual choices. As a matter of fact the problem of the distribution of resources is an art, not an applied science; and the situations in which we have to take practical decisions are often highly complex, while the units of purchasing power to be distributed do not necessarily adjust themselves to all the refinements of which we may be aware in our demands. Nor, in the workaday world, can we always give all the consideration which could, theoretically, be given to these refinements of our demands. Our attempts at equilibrium must always, in practice, be merely approximate; and in many cases it is true that we cannot really feel that so much more of A is better than so much more of B, although we may be quite clear that the expenditure should be on either A or B rather than on C. Practically speaking, we are indifferent as between the additional increment to A or the additional increment to B.

But all this concerns the practical application of the principles of valuation in a complex and busy world. That the application should have results which merely approximate in a general way

[1] Pp. 129-32.

to equilibrium is one thing. It is quite another thing when we are attempting to clarify and define the principles which are operative in our practical valuations. It would appear that the use made of the conception of 'indifference as between a small increment and a small decrement' is due to a confusion between the question of practical application of principles and the question of the nature of the principles themselves; and one may suspect that this confusion is largely engendered by the failure, in theoretical analysis, to distinguish between the conception of 'the marginal units of equilibrium' on the one hand, and that of 'the marginal units of utility' on the other. Any failure to draw this distinction is liable to encourage the idea that we are 'indifferent' as between small increments and decrements because, in point of fact, *one* of the marginal units of utility is always necessarily a unit *more* than *one* of the marginal units of equilibrium, and *one* marginal unit of utility must necessarily be the same as *one* marginal unit of equilibrium. If we do not take into account the fact that we are dealing with two different conceptions of the marginal unit, it is easy to infer that the 'area' of marginal significance is an area of 'indifference'.

(4) *Relativity of the 'Last' Unit*

The marginal units of equilibrium were defined by reference to the 'last' chosen units in the distribution of scarce resources over competing demands, and the marginal units of utility were defined by reference to the marginal units of equilibrium. The conceptions of the 'last' alternatives for choice and the 'last' things chosen are therefore fundamental to the notion of a 'marginal unit'. What we have now to show is that the conception of the 'last unit' refers exclusively to the realm of the 'more and less' which is intermediate between the initial stage of satisfying demand and the stage of complete satisfaction, and can *never* be applicable to either of the extremes. The notion of marginal unit does not at all imply that there is no initial stage of satisfaction, or that demand can never be completely satisfied; it is simply not concerned with these absolute lower and upper limits of satisfaction.

Consider, *firstly*, whether the notion of the margin can apply to the initial stage of satisfaction. Suppose we have competing demands for some A and some B, and have 1 R which will purchase 1 unit of either A or B. If we use it to purchase 1 A (or B), then A (or B) is to *some* extent satisfied while B (or A) remains *absolutely* unsatisfied. There can be no suggestion of 'equilibrium' here; and since the whole conception of marginal units depends upon the *a priori* postulate that 'last choices' are determined by the effort towards equilibrium, the notion of marginal units is irrelevant to this situation.

Suppose, again, that we have 2 R. In this case the alternatives between which we must choose are: *either* 2 A (or B) and absolute dissatisfaction for B (or A), *or* 1 A and 1 B. On the first alternative we have the same situation as when there was but 1 R to spend. On the second alternative we have absolute equality in the amount of satisfaction, and not the slightest indication as to whether this is really a state of proportionate equality (equilibrium). The conditions supposed in the choice situation do not permit of equilibrium unless the demands happen to be for exactly equal amounts. The conception of the margin can therefore have no significance.

Obviously, then, the notion of the margin has no relevance to initial satisfaction of demand. It assumes that available resources can be divided into sufficiently small units to make possible a distribution in terms of proportionate equality. It postulates that some of these units have been distributed, and that the problem is as to the 'final' distribution to reach equilibrium.

Consider, *secondly*, whether 'marginal unit' can apply to the 'last' unit in the sense of that unit which, if secured, will *completely* satisfy demand (for the time being at least). To suppose that it can apply here assumes that we can know how much would in fact satisfy demand fully; and that, as we have seen, is a somewhat doubtful proposition. But allowing it for the sake of argument, let us suppose that we have competing demands for 10 A and 8 B, and that we have 17 R. We purchase 9 A and 7 B, and have, consequently, one more unit of R to spend on either a 10th A or an 8th B. Whichever alternative we choose, we shall have one

demand completely satisfied and the other to some extent unsatisfied.

Now if we choose, say, the 10th *A*, what are our 'marginal
units of equilibrium'? Are they the 10th *A* and the 7th *B*? No,
they cannot be; for the simple reason that there is here no equilibrium. We are supposing that we *know* there is an amount of
demand for *B* which is unfulfilled, and that the demand for *A* is
completely satisfied. We are therefore assuming that there is no
equilibrium; for, when two things are demanded in *any* proportion, there can be no talk of equilibrium if one of the demands is
absolutely satisfied and the other lacks satisfaction to *any extent*.

Since, then, a choice which would completely satisfy one of
two competing demands, and leave the other partially unsatisfied,
gives us no pair of marginal units of equilibrium, any choice
resulting in such a distribution cannot be concerned with marginal
units of utility, because the marginal units of utility are the
alternative contents of demand when 'the alternative actually
chosen constitutes one of the marginal units of equilibrium'.

But what, it may be asked, if our choice results in both the
demands being completely satisfied? Have we not here reached
a state of equilibrium? Certainly we have; but in this case we
are not dealing with marginal units at all; for, *ex hypothesi*, we
are not dealing with the problem of allocating *scarce* resources to
the service of competing demands. We have sufficient (even if
no more than just sufficient) to meet all the demands. Hence they
are not competing; hence no choice situation arises in which we
have to choose between alternatives both of which we demand.

To summarise our conclusions on the present topic: The marginal units of equilibrium or utility are not concerned with the
'first' or 'last' units of commodities applied to satisfy demands,
in the sense of units which presuppose a prior state of 'absolute
zero' of satisfaction or conceive of a possible state of 'absolutely
complete satisfaction'. They are concerned only with the intermediate realm in which, assuming that some resources have
already been applied to meet every one of the demands in question,
the remaining resources are in fact so limited that complete satisfaction of all demands is impossible; and, in this intermediate

realm, we attend to the marginal units in the valuational activities by which we allocate or distribute resources to secure and maintain equilibrium in the satisfaction of demand.

6. THE LAW OF EQUILIBRIUM

We are now in a position to answer the question whether the orthodox formulation of the law of diminishing utility can be restated in such a way as to provide a 'law of diminishing utility' which is genuinely a law of our valuational activity.

If what is contemplated is a law which, like the old one, refers to 'diminishing *marginal* utility', the answer to the question is definitely 'No'; for if we reflect on the very notion of 'marginal utility' and all that it implies, it becomes abundantly clear that to talk of 'diminishing marginal utility'—or 'increasing marginal utility', for that matter—is to use words without meaning.

'Marginal utility' signifies 'marginal desiredness' or 'marginal demandedness'—the desiredness or demandedness in the marginal unit. Now the marginal unit here in question cannot be the marginal unit of equilibrium; for that which has demandedness (that which is demanded) is always a 'content of demand', a conceived end to be brought into existence. The marginal unit in question must therefore be the marginal unit of utility. 'Marginal utility' therefore *means* 'the utility of the marginal unit of utility'.

But can the utility of the marginal unit of utility *ever* diminish or increase? No. The marginal units of utility are the 'last' alternatives for choice, one of which (the alternative actually chosen) will become one of the marginal units of equilibrium. It is therefore irrational to speak of the 'utility' of such a unit increasing or diminishing, although it would be perfectly rational (and correct) to speak of the marginal unit of utility *shifting* up or down in the scale of any given demand. Thus, if (with demands for 10 A and 8 B, and with 9 R available) the marginal units of utility are the 5th A and 5th B, there could be a shift of marginal utility to the 7th A and 6th B if R were increased to 12; or there could be a shift to the 3rd A and 3rd B if R were reduced to 5. But this is not an increase or diminution in 'marginal utility'.

It is a shifting of the position of the marginal unit of utility.

What induces this shift in the marginal unit—or rather in the two or more marginal units—is an alteration in the group of competing demands, or an alteration in the resources for which the demands are competing; and this shifting of the units can be far more adequately expressed in terms of the *a priori* postulate of the search for equilibrium than in terms of an alleged law of diminishing utility. We can say:

The marginal units of utility (or, less exactly, marginal utilities) move with every alteration in the grouping of demands or in the amount of resources for which those demands are competing, in accordance with the demander's effort towards an equilibrium of satisfaction.

That is a genuine and a significant 'law of valuation'.

It may be asked, however, whether we cannot at least deepen the significance of this suggested 'law of equilibrium' by restating the law of diminishing utility in some bilateral formula which refers simply to 'utility' as distinguished from 'marginal utility' (it being accepted that the words 'diminishing marginal utility' have no intelligible sense).

Again the answer seems to be 'No'. A bilateral formula would certainly give proper recognition to the fact that the things we are valuing relatively to each other are not successive increments of A or successive increments of B, but an additional A as against an additional B. But the difficulty is that the only units of A and B which *can* be evaluated against each other are the units of *marginal* utility. This point requires some elaboration.

We assume *a priori* that the demander is seeking equilibrium in the satisfaction of his competing demands. We do not know, in fact, what the total amounts of his demands are; and he will be vague about this himself. With regard to some of them, past experience will give a rough idea of their extent, but others will be indeterminate and will only reveal their nature and probable extent as he engages in their pursuit. He will therefore have to proceed partly by methods of 'budgeting' and partly by 'seeing what turns up', and making the necessary adjustments as he goes along. We, being at least as much in the dark as he is, cannot do more than attempt to interpret his choices by the rules of common-sense and our own experience. But we do know *a priori*, so to speak, that guiding his choices is the over-all demand for equilibrium in satisfactions; and when we see that with, say, 9 *R* at his disposal, he chooses 5 *A* and 4 *B*, we know that these are approximately the marginal units of equilibrium for him.

Now can we not go on from this point and say that the 5th *A* and the 4th *B*, just because they are the units of equilibrium, are necessarily of *equal value*? And if we can say this, can we not also say that, relatively to the 4th *B*, the 4th, 3rd, 2nd and 1st *A* would have progressively 'increasing utility', and the 6th, 7th, 8th, 9th and 10th *A* progressively 'diminishing utility'? And can we not formulate this in terms of a law of valuation subsidiary to the 'law of equilibrium'?

Unfortunately, the notion that the marginal units of equilibrium are of equal utility or equal value, while a most convenient assumption for certain purposes, is utterly devoid of significance when we try to give it a place in the exact theory of valuation. They could only be said to be 'equal'—or indeed be compared at all—in value if they could be balanced against each other as possible alternatives for *choice*. But this they cannot be. With 9 *R* at his disposal, the choice situation can never arise in which a person has to consider 'either the 5th *A*, or the 4th *B*'. He can have as alternatives the 5th *A* and the 5th *B*, or the 6th *A* and the 4th *B*; but never the 5th *A* and the 4th *B*. Of course these would be alternatives if *R* were reduced to 8; but then they could no longer be marginal units of equilibrium. Hence, since marginal units of equilibrium can never be alternatives, they can never be compared in value; and therefore there can be no significance in saying that they are of equal value to the demander.

The real interest of the marginal units of equilibrium for theory of valuation is this: If a person chooses 5 *A* and 4 *B* in the conditions stated, we can say with confidence that the 5 *A* plus 4 *B* have for him greater utility than 6 *A* plus 3 *B*, or than 4 *A* plus 5 *B*, or than any other possible combination. The significance of this will be brought out in our next section. For the moment we shall confine ourselves to stating our conclusions on the subject of the

'law of diminishing utility'. For any such law to be significant
in valuational theory it would have to refer either to 'marginal
utility' or to 'utility in general'. With regard to marginal utility
it would be meaningless. With regard to utility in general, it
would be significant only if the utility of units other than marginal
units of utility could be compared. But (as we have seen in
criticising the orthodox formulation) no unit of A can be compared in value or utility with another unit of A; and we have now
seen that no unit of A other than the marginal unit of utility of A
can be compared in utility or value with any unit of B, and no
unit of B other than the corresponding marginal unit of utility of
B can be compared with any unit of A. Hence there can be no
law of diminishing utility in general which is significant for the
theory of valuation.

The only law we can derive from reflection on the conceptions
of utility and marginal utility—for the second of which the
philosopher is profoundly in the debt of the economist—is the
'law of equilibrium'.

7. COMPETING DEMANDS, EQUILIBRIUM AND COMMON DEMAND

(1) *Recapitulation*

Before proceeding to the final stage of our argument it may be
useful to recapitulate the argument up to the present point.

We began by stating the proposition that every valuational
order postulates a 'common demand' with reference to which the
opportunity costs of the things placed in that order are estimated.
To vindicate this statement is fundamental to our whole theory
of valuation. But we found ourselves confronted by a formidable
problem in this connexion. The difficulty was that economists,
who have admittedly contributed most to the theory of valuation,
seem to take a view quite inconsistent with our proposition.
They say that valuation normally operates in accordance with the
law of diminishing utility, that only in special cases does the conception of a 'set' (or 'common demand') affect the process, and
that, in so far as common demand does influence the process of

valuation, the law of diminishing utility seems to be inoperative. Such a view cannot be reconciled with our proposition; for it asserts that the conception of common demand is not postulated in every valuational order.

What we have offered to demonstrate is that such a view misinterprets the significance of marginal utility.

In order to substantiate this position we have had to undertake a lengthy analysis of the 'law of diminishing utility'. In the first place, it was necessary to distinguish it from the law of diminishing returns with which it is liable to be confused. To make this distinction clear, we had to investigate the meaning of 'utility' itself. Utility means desiredness or demandedness. We had then, using 'utility' in this sense, to distinguish two possible interpretations of the law of diminishing utility, namely the unilateral theory and the bilateral theory. The unilateral theory is the one suggested by many economists, not when they are explaining the fundamental subject-matter of economic studies, but when they come to formulate the law of diminishing utility itself. The 'orthodox' formulation, taken at its face value, implies that the law is concerned with the relative utilities of successive units of the same commodity utilised for the satisfaction of a single demand taken in isolation from all other competing demands. In our criticism of this theory, as expounded by Wicksteed in particular, we have shown that it is indefensible, inasmuch as the respective utilities of successive units of the same commodity assigned to the progressive satisfaction of the same demand cannot be weighed against each other, for they cannot be alternatives in a choice situation.

Turning then to the question whether the 'law' can be reformulated as a genuine law of valuation, we had to consider the nature of 'marginal utility'. We found that the doctrine of margins has nothing to do with the question of 'saturation of demand'. That is to say, when we speak of the 'marginal unit' as 'the last unit purchased', we are not thinking of that unit which, when purchased, will completely satisfy (for the time being at least) a given demand. We are thinking of the 'last units' in the sense of the units which we should 'just not be prepared to allocate to

demands other than those to which they have been in fact allocated' in the distribution of our scarce resources. They are the
units which indicate that the 'equilibrium' of satisfactions has been
attained.

But having distinguished the question of 'satiation of demand'
from the questions relevant to the conception of the 'margin',
we saw that a further distinction must be drawn, namely the
distinction between the marginal unit of equilibrium and the
marginal unit of utility (desiredness). When we are valuing, or
weighing one alternative against another, what we are evaluating
are 'contents' of demand, not 'objects' of demand. We are
weighing against each other two or more possible future states of
affairs (a little more satisfaction of 'this' demand as against a little
more satisfaction of 'that' demand) only one of which can in fact
be secured. It is to these contents of demand that we assign degrees of desiredness; so that the marginal units of utility will
always be contents of demand, not objects of demand. When,
on the other hand, we speak of the state of 'equilibrium', we are
referring to the proportions in which, after the completion of a
series or system of choices, we have allocated resources to competing demands. The marginal units of equilibrium are thus
'objects', not 'contents', of demand; the marginal unit of equilibrium of A, for instance, will not be 'the conception of the nth
unit of A to be purchased'; it will be 'the nth unit of A purchased'.
To define the marginal unit of utility we must first define the
marginal unit of equilibrium. The marginal units of equilibrium
are the units 'last' or 'finally' chosen, in the sense that no unit of A
will now be given in exchange for a further unit of B, and no
unit of B will now be given in exchange for a further unit of A.
We call these the marginal units of equilibrium, not because we
know independently that purchases in such a proportion are indeed the proportionate satisfaction of the total competing demands
within the limits allowed by the scarce resources at our disposal,
but because we assume or postulate that rational choice moves as
closely as possible to the proportionate satisfaction of demands,
and hence assume that proportionate satisfaction is achieved with
the nth A and mth B as the 'final' units *because* these (rather than

others) are the units which the person concerned has in fact chosen as his 'final' units. The units of equilibrium are therefore defined as 'the last chosen units . . . in the allocation of scarce resources'. The marginal units of utility are then defined so as to make it clear that we are really speaking of marginal utility, or the utility of marginal units, and not of utility or desiredness in general. To speak of the desiredness attaching to a marginal unit implies that we know what we mean by a marginal unit; and the primary meaning of marginal unit is bound up with the notion of equilibrium, or the 'last unit chosen'. The marginal units with respect to desiredness (marginal units of utility), therefore, must refer to the marginal units of equilibrium (which are 'objects' of demand), but must themselves be, nevertheless, 'contents' of demand. Both of these points are met by the recognition that the marginal units of utility must include, as one of the alternatives presented for choice, that particular 'content' of demand which, when chosen, will be a secured 'object' of demand constituting a marginal unit of equilibrium. The marginal units of utility are therefore those alternative contents of demand when the alternative actually chosen constitutes one of the marginal units of equilibrium.

The next contention in our argument up to this point was that the doctrine of margins is concerned with *relative* increases and diminutions in allocations to satisfy competing demands. The conception of marginal utility is not concerned with initial provision allocated to a hitherto absolutely unsatisfied demand, nor is it concerned with such allocations as would absolutely satisfy. Marginal utility—so our argument contends—is concerned with the realm of 'the more and less', with the relative utilities of additional units on the assumption that all the demands in question are already satisfied to some extent, although the resources available will never permit of complete satisfaction of all demands; and the general assumption appears to be that, in such a situation, choice will never result in the complete satisfaction of any one of the competing demands, inasmuch as such a choice would be contrary to the principle of equilibrium.

Lastly, we considered the question whether, in the light of our analysis of the conception of marginal utility and all it implies, it is possible to restate the orthodox formulation of the 'law of diminishing utility' so as to arrive at a true and significant law of valuation. We answered this question in the negative. The 'law' governing valuation must be stated in terms of the search for equilibrium, not in terms of increasing or decreasing utility.

(2) Equilibrium and Common Demand

We come now to the final step in the argument. We have to show that the law of equilibrium necessarily implies the conception of common demand. The notion of equilibrium, in this connexion, is that of the proportionate satisfaction of competing demands. It may be called an *a priori* rather than an *a posteriori* concept in the sense that we do not, on the basis of a series of empirical observations, see that, as a plain matter of fact, persons try to reach equilibrium or proportionateness in the satisfaction of their demands. We could only discover by empirical methods whether men aim at equilibrium if we could know antecedently the full extent of their competing demands, and then compare the full demands with the amounts of satisfaction accorded to each demand in conditions of scarce resources. But in point of fact we have not this direct, immediate knowledge of the full strength of demands. We can only infer it, as a general rule, and perhaps always, by observing the extent to which persons are prepared to put out effort, and forego other things, in order to satisfy given demands to a greater extent than they are actually satisfied. And even this observation of the effort and privation individuals are prepared to endure, in order to attain greater satisfaction, does not allow us to infer the 'absolute' extent of the demands whose satisfaction is sought. It only allows us to infer the strength of these demands *relatively* to the strength of other demands whose satisfaction is, for the time being, relegated to a subordinate place.

It is therefore impossible to regard the conception of equilibrium or proportionate satisfaction of demand as merely an *a posteriori* generalisation based on observation of human behaviour. It is no more *a posteriori* than is the concept of 'causality'. That *A* is in fact the 'cause' of *B* is a conclusion derived *a posteriori* from

K

empirical experience; but that 'every event has a cause' is an *a priori* category of all scientific reasoning. Similarly, the proposition that 'the *n*th *A* and the *m*th *B* are the marginal units of equilibrium for the individual *X* in the circumstances *e, f, g*' is a conclusion derived *a posteriori* from observation of *X*'s system of choices; but we only call these units the marginal units of equilibrium because we see that *X* actually adopts them as his 'last units chosen'. We are therefore assuming the general principle, 'every person, in evaluating alternatives in conditions of scarce resources, attempts to reach a position of equilibrium or proportionateness in the satisfaction of his competing demands'. This is an *a priori* conception in precisely the same way as is the conception of 'every event as conditioned by a cause'. It is a fundamental category of economic analysis in precisely the same way as the concept of causality is a fundamental category of scientific judgement. In particular, it is a category of thought without which the concept of marginal utility would be utterly devoid of significance.

Now to say that the concept of marginal utility postulates that, in all our valuation, we are aiming at equilibrium or proportionateness in the satisfaction of our demands is precisely the same as to say that the competing demands whose satisfactions we are weighing against each other are but different expressions of a more comprehensive common demand. The two statements amount to the same thing because the conception of equilibrium as between competing demands implies some more general demand of which the competing demands are expressions.

This can, I think, be shown quite briefly. Demand is not an aimless desiring of 'we know not what'. It always has an objective which, if achieved, implies that the demand is to that extent satisfied. The demand may not then cease to exist. In some cases this may be so; but, when it is so, the demand is likely to have been of trifling significance in the person's life. The objectives of all our most fundamental demands may well be the attainment of certain levels of existence, states of equilibrium the maintenance of which calls for continuous effort. This is a question which falls to be treated more fully in connexion with our theory of the attribution of 'goodness' in Part II. The only point of importance at the moment is that demand always has some objective, whether this be a continuous state of equilibrium or something which, once attained, implies the complete disappearance of the demand. That all demand has some objective is not affected by the fact that, with the limited resources allotted to us in this earthly life, we can never hope to attain all our demands in full. Scarcity of resources does not preclude an objective, but merely forces us to make choices between alternatives in order to approximate as closely as possible to the objective. But even though the demands cannot be satisfied in full, the fact that they have more or less definite objectives means that it is not a matter of indifference to us whether such satisfaction as we may be able to achieve should assume a relatively balanced rather than an unbalanced form. It is, indeed, the effort after balance of satisfaction which underlies our distribution of scarce resources so as to 'equalise, so far as possible, marginal uses'. That is why, if we are very hungry and not very thirsty, we shall spend relatively more on food than on drink, or, if we are both hungry and thirsty, we shall try to expend our available resources so as to get the most out of them in the right proportions of food and drink.

This, I think, is the real point which is intended in attempts to formulate a 'law of diminishing utility'—a law of the relative strength of competing demands, relative strength being determined by the proportions in which they are already satisfied. Thus, if it is true that the more one has of X the less will one demand an additional X rather than an additional Y, it is equally true that the more one has of Y the less will one demand an additional Y rather than an additional X. The 'law' is a law of *relative* diminishing (and increasing) utility or demandedness.

But this necessarily implies that X and Y are demanded in some sort of proportion, a proportion determined by the nature of the objective. We say 'the objective' and not 'the objectives', because, if we demand two qualitatively different things in some definite proportion, then we have not two quite separate and unrelated demands but a comprehensive demand for 'nX-plus-mY'. Thus —to take a quite arbitrary set of figures—suppose I say that I value a 46th X less than a 20th Y; then, according to the 'law of diminishing utility', there must be some additional Y which I shall say that I value less than an additional X. Assume that I value a 59th Y less than a 70th X. Now this is to say that, for the perfect satisfaction of the X-plus-Y demand, X must be present in some proportion *less* than 46 X : 19 Y and *greater* than 69 X : 59 Y. That is to say, the perfect satisfaction requires X and Y in a proportion somewhere between 2.43 X : 1 Y and 1.16 X : 1 Y. So far as my resources are limited, I cannot attain to perfect satisfaction; but this is the proportion—or rather these are the upper and lower limits of the proportion—which will determine my marginal valuations of X and Y.

Here, then, we have a unitary subject, having as an objective the proportionate satisfaction of demands. But a proportionate satisfaction of demands really means the satisfaction of a comprehensive demand which has different qualitative expressions. They must be qualitatively different expressions of the same comprehensive or common demand, because neither of the two competing demands is complete in itself. What is demanded is not 'nX rather than n-plus-1X' and also, quite separately, 'mY rather than m-minus-1Y'. What is demanded is 'nX-plus-mY', rather than 'n-plus-1X-plus-m-minus-1Y' or 'n-minus-1X-plus-m-plus-1Y'. In other words, it is strictly incorrect to say—as we have, up to now, tended to say—that we evaluate 'one more X' against 'one more Y'. What we evaluate is, strictly, one combination of XY against a different combination of XY, these being regarded as the 'better' and the 'worse' alternative ways of satisfying—as much as is possible with the resources at our command—the common demand for XY. Valuation always implies a complex demand. It must be complex because it must have different expressions sufficiently distinct, qualitatively, to enable us to refer to them as different 'competing' demands. But their difference must nevertheless be merely a differentiation within a common demand; for otherwise there could be no meaning in speaking of their 'proportionate' satisfaction, and hence no meaning in saying that our choices are governed by the 'law of diminishing utility', or—more correctly—the 'law of equilibrium'.

Chapter Four

VALUATION AND COMMON DEMAND
(Continued)

THE argument of the preceding chapter has been developed largely through criticism of doctrines sometimes advanced by economists. But behind all the criticism is the contention that our postulate of the 'common demand' is implied in the main doctrines of economics itself. And so, at the risk of seeming to waste the reader's time over an issue which may be regarded as already established, I propose in this chapter to continue the main theme of the previous one, taking the fundamental demand and supply concepts in order to see whether their main presuppositions square with the proposition being defended. To deal with these concepts at all entails a certain amount of elementary exposition of their meaning. Such an exposition will no doubt appear very elementary and possibly wearisome to the economist; but one cannot assume that all philosophers are familiar with the terms to be used; and, in any case, it is necessary that I should say what (rightly or wrongly) I myself understand the terms to mean.

Economists seem to be generally agreed that there are five concepts which, taken together, give an exhaustive classification of the main ways in which the demand for and supply of one thing can affect the demand for and supply of others. These are Composite Supply, Joint Supply, Composite Demand, Joint Demand and Derived Demand. What we have to consider is whether, individually or together, their implications for the theory of demand and valuation can be made intelligible on any hypothesis other than that asserted in our proposition that all valuation postulates the conception of common demand.

1. COMPOSITE SUPPLY

The heading of this section would be misleading to an economist without some explanation. He would naturally suppose that the main discussion will be about composite supply itself. It will, in fact, be mainly concerned with the nature of demand; for what I want to do is to ask whether the direct or indirect implications of the concept of 'composite supply' are consistent with the theory of demand and valuation developed in the preceding chapter. It would probably be true to say that I am really concerned, not with the nature of composite supply, but with 'complementary expressions of demand'; but perhaps the heading as given will be considered not inappropriate inasmuch as we are to deal with the implications of demand and valuation arising from the concept of composite supply.

The concept itself can, for our purposes, be stated very briefly. Things are said to be in 'composite supply' if the one can be a 'substitute' for the other in satisfying the same demand. Now here, quite patently, the question whether a common demand is involved admits of but one answer. Things in composite supply, by definition, refer to the same demand.

It may be thought, then, that we can pass without further discussion to our next concept. But this is far from being the case; for the concept of composite supply brings out an extremely interesting point, namely that the common demand in question may be of a complex nature, and that, with reference to it, the things in composite supply may sometimes be better described as 'complementaries' rather than as 'substitutes' for its satisfaction. The difficulty—at an elementary level of economic exposition— of drawing a sharp line of demarcation between things which are substitutes and things which are complementaries may be illustrated by the following case. Land, labour and capital will normally be described as 'complementary' factors of production; but for certain purposes it may be appropriate to speak of them as to some extent 'substitutes' for each other. Thus: 'Great changes take place from time to time in the scarcity of one factor of production in relation to the others, and corresponding changes take place in the use made of that factor relatively to the other. In some ages and countries labour is abundant and capital is scarce; methods of production, therefore, are such as to economise capital and use plenty of labour. In other ages and countries it is capital which is abundant and labour which has to be economised. The same services are rendered by combining the factors of production in very different proportions. . . . When we say that the factors of production can be combined in different proportions we are really saying that they are substitutes for one another. We can produce the same quantity of product by using more capital and less labour (substituting capital for labour) or by using less capital and more labour (substituting labour for capital)'.[1]

It is not suggested here that economists are using the same term to cover the two entirely different conceptions of 'substitute' and 'complement'. One understands, indeed, that in the more advanced exposition of supply and demand theory a technical terminology is employed appropriate to the complexity of the issues arising. The point is simply that in any general, elementary explanation of the concept of 'composite supply' which stresses the notion of things as 'substitutes' for satisfaction of the same demand, we find ourselves passing insensibly to the notion of these things as, in some sense, 'complementaries' when we recognise any element of complexity in the common demand to which they are relative.

Probably the best way to make this point clear is to leave aside examples which (like that of land, labour and capital) are concerned directly with questions of production rather than with questions of demand, and to consider some simple cases of composite supply in direct relation to demand.

An example of composite supply commonly given is that of tea, coffee, beer, milk and water as all in composite supply with respect to the demand for 'drink'. They are in composite supply because, with reference to this demand for drink, it can be met by beer if there is no tea, coffee if there is neither tea nor beer, and so forth. They are all substitutes for each other in the satisfaction of the same demand.

But we can describe them as substitutes only in so far as it is possible to regard the demand they each satisfy as absolutely the same demand; and there are facts of experience which show that

[1] Cairncross, p. 191.

this is not strictly true. What we call the demand for drink is not absolutely homogeneous in character. While the differences between the various substitutes—water, coffee, etc.—would be regarded as trifling and irrelevant by a man who had been deprived of the means of quenching his thirst for some days, they are not regarded as irrelevant by persons in normal circumstances. We can usually have tea or coffee or beer, or all three, for breakfast and afternoon tea if we care; and in such circumstances we do not even need to evaluate them against each other; but most of us have a relatively fixed behaviour pattern in our drinking, selecting, say, coffee for breakfast, tea in the afternoon, and so forth. If offered a mixture of tea and coffee we should probably decline the tea ingredient at breakfast and the coffee ingredient in the afternoon. Any such behaviour pattern in our drinking is quite inexplicable on the supposition that tea, coffee, beer, etc., are absolute substitutes for a demand which is absolutely homogeneous in character. The common demand must be complex in nature, and our behaviour pattern in selecting what we drink must be in the nature of a selection of 'complementaries' in some rough proportion to the complexities of the demand.

The point we have been making is that things, which at first sight seem best described as substitutes for satisfaction of the same simple demand, may on a closer view turn out to be also complements for the satisfaction of a complex demand. Similarly if we begin with the notion of 'complements', we often find that these turn out to be in some sense 'substitutes'. Thus bread, fruit and milk may be regarded as complementary in a balanced diet, each of them satisfying a different demand; but, as we saw,[1] they can also be substituted for each other in satisfying the general demand for sustenance.

The significance of the foregoing discussion, and particularly the stress laid on the manner in which things pass insensibly from the category of 'substitute' to that of 'complement' and *vice versa*, may not be obvious to the reader; but there is a point of great importance for our general argument. The point is that the economist's concept of 'composite supply' necessarily implies the

[1] Pp. 76-9.

notion of 'common demand' as this has been discussed and explained in our last chapter. Composite supply implies common
demand in the sense of a complex demand with various particular
expressions; for without this element of complexity in the 'same
demand' with respect to which things in composite supply are
'substitutes', the concept of composite supply would itself have no
significance; it could not be concerned with 'different' things
meeting the 'same' demand.

To show that this is so, let us consider three suppositions in turn.

Suppose, *firstly*, that two things are substitutes for satisfying the
same demand, and that these two things are absolutely homogeneous in character, being the same in every respect apart from
their numerical difference, e.g. two slices of bread cut from the
same loaf by the same machine. Now if they are substitutes for
each other in the satisfaction of demand, the fact that they are
exactly the same, except for their numerical difference, would be
compatible with the view that the demand they satisfy is itself a
simple, homogeneous demand. But in this case we are not
talking of composite supply as defined by the economist. Things
in composite supply are, by definition, of different kinds, although
they are substitutes for satisfying the same demand. Since, therefore, its satisfaction can be met by qualitatively different things, it
itself cannot be regarded as of an absolutely simple undifferen-
tiated nature.

Suppose, *secondly*, that we are really concerned with composite
supply in the proper sense—with things which are different in
kind. As we have just seen, we must in this case suppose that the
demand they both satisfy is not simple in nature. If then we assert
that they are substitutes for each other in its satisfaction, we can
only mean that their qualitative differences are not 'relevant' or
'important' with respect to the 'satisfaction in general' or the
'main character' of this demand. Thus, to a very hungry man,
the difference between a half-pound of white bread and a half-
pound of brown bread will probably be considered irrelevant to
the capacity of either to assuage his hunger. The two half-pounds
are different in kind, and the man will not suppose that they are
the same. Indeed his senses may be so sharpened by hunger that

he may even be more keenly aware of the flavour of the bread he is eating than he would normally be. If he is given brown bread, he may be perfectly aware of the fact that he is eating what he would normally reject in place of white bread, aware of a difference which would be relevant to demand in other circumstances. But all such considerations are, for the moment, 'irrelevant'. The qualitative differences are 'insignificant'; and what counts is the capacity of either brown or white bread to meet the demand for food.

Here, the irrelevance of the difference between brown and white, the irrelevance which enables us to say that the one is a substitute for the other, does not imply that we are dealing with an absolutely homogeneous demand, the 'demand for bread pure and simple'. It means only that, when demand is intense, satisfaction is sought initially on a quantitative plane with respect to the general character of the demand. A famished man is not fussy. He becomes finicky only when quantity is reasonably well assured and he can attend to the refinements of qualitative balance. That is to say, when different things satisfy the same demand, they can do so only to a limited extent. They cannot be absolute substitutes for each other; and they will only be considered substitutes up to that point at which quantitative considerations prevail over qualitative. When this point is passed, qualitative considerations bring the notion of complements more into the foreground. And when we actually do evaluate things against each other, the point at which quantity and quality begin to be balanced against each other may become quite evident in the character of our choices.

Suppose, *thirdly*, that the stage has been reached in which qualitative differences do become relevant to the ways in which we attempt to satisfy demand. Here, obviously, we have passed beyond the concept of composite supply; for composite supply is concerned with different kinds of thing in so far as they are regarded as substitutes; and when the differences between two kinds of things begin to be weighed against each other we are clearly concerned with different demands, not with 'the same demand'. It can I think be shown that, if we are forced to evaluate the contents of these different demands against each other, we are always liable to be forced back to the conception of them as to some extent substitutes for each other (and we are so forced when scarcity of resources brings the question of quantity of satisfaction into consideration); but it would not be appropriate to discuss this point in the present context. The principles on which the contents of different demands are evaluated against each other have been fully dealt with in the preceding chapter. Here we are concerned only with the strict implications of the concept of composite supply. These implications may be set forth in the following way:

Since things in composite supply are, by definition, *different* things which are substitutes for each other in satisfaction of the *same* demand, they must be qualitatively different (not merely numerically different), and yet their different qualities must be irrelevant in so far forth as they are considered as substitutes. Inasmuch as they are qualitatively different they cannot be absolutely and in every respect substitutes for each other; for if either of them exactly and perfectly met the demand in question the other could not possibly do so. If one of them perfectly meets the demand, none of its qualities will be irrelevant; for if any of its qualities were irrelevant to this demand then its satisfaction would entail the acceptance of and adjustment to something not in fact desired. But if one of them with all its qualities does in fact perfectly satisfy the demand, then the other which has some different qualities cannot possibly do so. So far, therefore, as we speak of different kinds of things as substitutes, the demand with respect to which they are substitutes must be a complex and not a simple demand, and the satisfaction of this complex demand which each of them provides must be the satisfaction only of some aspect (not the whole) of this complex demand, an aspect which, for the time being at least, is accepted as its 'main' or 'dominant' characteristic. Hence the concept of composite supply implies not only the notion of common demand (for this notion is contained in the very definition of the concept itself), but also the notion of this common demand as a complex demand, or complex conative disposition, the subordinate expressions of which are liable to give rise to valuation of the qualities in which the things in composite supply differ from each other, such comparative valuation arising at that stage at which crudely quantitative considerations of satisfaction become entangled with qualitative considerations of the complete satisfaction of the demand as a whole.

2. JOINT SUPPLY

Things are said to be in 'joint supply' when the one cannot be supplied or produced without the other. Thus, if we wish to produce meat, we have to accept also wool or cowhide or feathers. If we demand orange-juice, we must also accept pulp and rind. Mutton and wool, beef and cowhide, chicken-breast and feathers, orange-juice and rind are all instances of joint supply. When we speak of 'joint supply' we are thinking of something which, being composed of distinct parts, is a 'collection' of objects of separate actual or potential demands, objects which may be separately possessed and utilised once the 'collection' has come into existence, but which cannot come into existence except as items in that specific collection. If we attend to any one of these separate demands by itself, the concept of joint supply means that the object of that demand cannot be secured without our taking, at the same time, something which is completely irrelevant to the content of the demand.

Now, as a plain matter of fact, it is true that every object of demand is an item in joint supply. If you want meat, you get wool, hide or feathers as well. If you want tropical warmth, you get malarial mosquitoes as well. If you want the warmth of an overcoat, you have also to carry its weight. If you want to cultivate wheat, you must also cultivate straw. If you want an honest man to keep your accounts and handle your money, you must also accept a man who will assist the income-tax authorities to carry off some of your hard-earned profits. If you want gas, you also get coke and smell. If you want rapid transport by air you get political crises with oil producing countries. If you want a country walk, you will also get muddy boots.

From the examples just given, it will be apparent that the specific items which form the 'collection' in joint supply need not be eternally produced together. It is not inconceivable that chickens should be bred without feathers, country walks secured without getting muddy boots, oil produced without political crises. But if you don't get feathers with chicken-breast you will get something else. If you don't get political crises with oil fuel you will get some system of international agreement for control of the production and marketing of oil. While the items in the collection may be variable, the point is that nothing can be produced except as an item in some collection. With respect to any given demand, some at least of the items in this collection will be completely irrelevant; but this does not avoid the necessity of accepting them if the item in the collection which is the object of the demand is to be secured at all. It is true that, of all the parts or characteristics which a thing possesses (of all the items in the 'collection'), we attend at any given time to a selection only, and ignore the rest; but this does not justify us in supposing that the rest are not there.

However, this very wide conception of joint supply is not, I think, of any great interest to the economist. He is primarily interested in those cases of joint supply where the separate parts of the thing (the items of the collection) are in fact objects of different actual demands. He is thinking, for instance, of the case of mutton and wool which are both objects of actual demand, and which may be separated when the joint supply has matured, but which cannot come into existence separately. They can be produced only together by the rearing of sheep.

Taking joint supply in this limited, though perfectly legitimate sense, we have to state the concept rather more precisely than it is normally stated. The text-books are clear that, in an instance of joint supply, the different items can be produced only together and not separately; and they are also clear that the proportions in which the items are produced may be variable within limits; but they are not at all clear, so far as I can make out, whether the variability is included in or excluded from the concept of joint supply in the strict sense. It is important that this point should be cleared up. The view I shall press is that we are not here dealing with a situation analogous to that which we found with regard to the inclusion of the notions of 'substitute' and 'complement' within the concept of 'composite supply'. I shall argue that the concept of 'joint supply' becomes meaningless as a technical term unless we rigidly exclude from it the notion of variability in the proportions in which the items in joint supply can be supplied. I am, of course, talking of what is necessary if the concept is to have meaning in the theory of valuation. I do not pretend to say whether the same exactness is necessary or even useful from the point of view of general economic theory. But exactness is necessary in dealing with theory of valuation where we are concerned with the objective conditions which enforce a choice. We must think of a situation over which the individual has, at the moment of making his valuation, no control, and which therefore enforces upon him an act of choice. The fact that he may in turn react on those circumstances and alter the situation is not relevant to our study. Hence the conscious and deliberate manipulation of joint supply in the general sense, so as to vary the proportions in which the items occur, is beside the point if we are concerned to understand how valuation is affected by the fact of joint supply. Now the really important point about the concept is that, in joint supply, the object of demand cannot be secured unless the demander also accepts something else with it; and to grasp what this means we have to concentrate upon the fact that, at the moment of valuation, the proportions in which the items are supplied are fixed and not variable by the demander. If we allow the notion of variability to be included, then we are dealing not with joint supply but—to the extent that the proportions are regarded as variable—with the notion of independent supply.

A concrete example will, I think, make this clear. A wheat crop is an instance of joint supply. If you want any wheat-ear you must accept some straw. If you want any straw you must accept some ear. Let us suppose that a man is producing wheat in the proportion of 75% of its bulk as straw and 25% of its bulk as ear, but that he could if he wished vary the proportions. Let us say that, at the one extreme, he could produce 95% straw and 5% ear, and, at the other extreme, 30% straw and 70% ear.

This means that, if he wants any straw at all, he must accept something which contains at least 5% ear; and, if he wants any ear at all, he must accept something which contains at least 30% straw. In the production of wheat, then, there is 35% of the total product of 100% in which there is a strictly invariable proportion of 30% straw and 5% ear.

But what of the remaining 65% of the total? This 65% can be all straw or all ear, or partly straw and partly ear, exactly as he pleases. That is to say, of all his resources in land, labour and capital devoted to the production of wheat, he can regard 65% of what he is to produce as completely independent products. He can regard this 65% as though wheat-ear and wheat-straw had no more relation to each other than have wheat, sheep, potatoes, houses and tennis-courts. Just as he can devote his land to sheep or potatoes or housing schemes or tennis-courts, so (for this 65%) he can devote his land to wheat-ear or to wheat-straw. Obviously nothing is to be gained by including this variable 65% of the crop as 'ear and straw in joint supply', since it may actually contain not one grain of wheat or not one wisp of straw. The joint supply in any important sense of the term can mean only the 35% of the crop which comes in the invariable proportions of 5% ear and 30% straw. The concept of joint supply as relevant to our valuations, has a precise meaning only when we are talking of items which go together in invariable proportion.

The position, then, is this: We know very well that items in joint supply, in the broad practical sense in which the economist uses this term, can be varied in their proportions; and it would be foolish to suggest that for general purposes the term should be defined as though this were not so. But, when we use the term strictly, its significance must be limited to those objects of demand which are produced together in a proportion which is not variable; for our concern with them is the character which they present to a demander at the moment when he is confronted by the necessity of making a choice. If he wants one of the items, he has to accept both as they stand.

Having thus clarified the concept of joint supply, let us now return to our main question which is this: To what extent does the concept of joint supply support or run counter to the proposition that 'every valuational order postulates a common demand with reference to which the opportunity costs of the things in that order are estimated'?

It is possible to make out a strong case for the view that the concept of joint supply brings to light a factor in the process of valuation which renders our proposition completely untenable. I shall state this view as fairly as I can.

As we have seen, things in joint supply—mutton and wool, or straw and ear—may be regarded as a 'collection' of items which are necessarily produced together, but each of which is the object of a different demand. Mutton is an object of demand for food, wool for clothing; ear is an object of demand for food, straw for thatch and stable-bedding.

The items comprising a given 'collection' will therefore normally (perhaps always) belong to different valuational orders within the same individual mind. Thus we do not evaluate wool as against mutton in a single or common valuational order. We evaluate wool as against skins or grass or prepared bark with respect to the common demand for clothing. We evaluate mutton as against wheat-ear, fish, limpets, fowl, etc., in the 'food' valuational order. We evaluate straw as against rushes, common grass, palm leaves, etc., in the 'thatch and bedding' valuational order.

Thus, while the items in an instance of joint supply belong to different valuational orders, any particular item in the one joint supply will belong to the same valuational order as a particular item in another joint supply. Mutton, which belongs to the 'sheep' instance of joint supply, belongs to the 'food' valuational order, as does also wheat-ear which belongs to the 'wheat' instance of joint supply.

Let us, then, consider the process of evaluating mutton as against wheat-ear in the food valuational order. What is evaluated is the content of demand, the securing of mutton or the production and securing of wheat-ear. But the valuation is a process of assessing the relative opportunity costs. Now, since you cannot produce mutton without producing wool, or produce ear without producing straw, the costs of choosing mutton rather than wheat-ear are the costs of producing sheep rather than wheat crop; and the costs of choosing wheat-ear rather than mutton are the costs of producing wheat rather than sheep. Hence what you have to consider as the opportunity costs of choosing mutton are not merely the amount of food demand denied by the decision not to produce wheat, but also the demands for thatch and bedding which will also be left unsatisfied by the choice of mutton. Similarly, the costs of choosing wheat-ear are not merely the amount of food demand denied, but also the amount of clothing demand denied by the decision to produce wheat rather than rear sheep.

Now suppose that, with respect to the common demand for food, you would place mutton higher than wheat-ear; suppose also that you place wool very much below light and easily worked grasses in the clothing valuational order; suppose finally that you place wheat-straw very high in the thatch and bedding valuational order; then your strong preferences with regard to clothing, thatch and bedding may result in your choosing to produce wheat rather than sheep for food, despite the fact that, in the food order, you place mutton higher than wheat-ear. The opportunity cost of the mutton would be the denial of the demand for wheat-ear, plus the denial of the demand for straw thatch and bedding; and you regard this as a higher cost than the denial of the demand for mutton, plus the denial of the demand for woollen clothing. Therefore you choose the wheat crop.

The point upon which this kind of valuation throws serious doubt is not the contention that values are measured in terms of opportunity costs. The validity of that point is taken for granted. What is seriously in question is the contention that opportunity costs are necessarily measured in terms of a common demand. It is admitted that if you take any single valuational order by itself and estimate opportunity costs only in terms of the common demand to which that order is relevant, a very good case can be made out for our proposition. But to isolate valuational orders in this way is to omit one of the most obvious facts about valuation, namely the way in which valuations in one order can affect valuations in another. The example of the valuation of mutton as against wheat-ear makes this clear. Here we have a very

L

obvious case in which the final placing of two things, mutton and wheat-ear, within the food valuational order is not determined by reference to the common demand for food, but by factors outside the food order altogether, namely the places which two members of the food order (sheep and wheat-crop) occupy in quite different valuational orders, the order of clothing and the order of thatch and bedding.

What really does determine the final place of mutton and wheat-ear in the food order of value? It is (one may allege) the purely accidental fact (accidental from the point of view of the common demand for food) that two of the individual members of the food order also happen to belong at the same time to other valuational orders. That is to say, the sheep, by belonging to two orders at the same time, and the wheat crop, by belonging to two orders at the same time, form links between the three valuational orders of food, clothing and thatch-bedding. They are bridges across which influences from the one order can pass to another, affecting, and perhaps finally determining, the respective places of members in the latter order independently of the common demand implied in that order. If this be the case, then the concept of joint supply, when we follow out its full implications, renders our proposition invalid as a statement universally applicable to the activity of valuation.

I have stated this case for the prosecution as fairly as I can. We may now consider it from the point of view of counsel for the defence. It seems to me that the whole argument rests on the assumption that a thing which includes commodities in joint supply can be, at one and the same time, a member of two distinct valuational orders. I do not propose to challenge the view that valuational orders can somehow influence each other. Indeed in connexion with a later proposition,[1] I shall argue that they do. The question I shall now raise is not whether different orders influence each other, but whether the view of their mode of influence just suggested is tenable. The view we are now considering asserts that they influence each other through some particular object of demand which happens to be a member of two

[1] Proposition VIII, pp. 174-81.

or more orders at one and the same time. Suppose, then, that a thing cannot possibly be a member of two different independent orders at one and the same time. If it cannot, then it cannot constitute a link between them; and if it cannot be a link, it cannot constitute a 'bridge' by which influences can pass from one to the other. What I shall attempt is to destroy the foundations of the foregoing argument by showing that nothing can be a member of more than one valuational order at one and the same time.

This can be shown by consideration of the way in which we evaluate the sheep-as-mutton and the sheep-as-wool. Let us suppose that a sheep will produce 10 units of mutton and 8 units of wool, and that this will be an instance of joint supply in the strict sense, these proportions being invariable. Suppose also that a man's full annual demands are for 100 units of mutton and 96 of wool. Let us agree that the 'food' and the 'clothing' valuational orders are distinct. Let us further agree that it is the breeding of sheep (and not the 'acquiring of mutton' or the 'acquiring of wool') which has to be evaluated. That is to say, in the 'food' order the object of demand will be the sheep-as-mutton, and in the 'clothing' order the object of demand will be the sheep-as-wool. I set out the case in this way so as to allow every advantage to those who would maintain that the same thing can be in two valuational orders at the same time, since my object is to show that it cannot.

If the demand for mutton is for 100 units, this is equivalent to a demand for 10 sheep-as-mutton; and if the demand for wool is for 96 units, this is equivalent to a demand for 12 sheep-as-wool. In such circumstances, only the demand for sheep-as-wool will enter into a valuational order; the demand for sheep-as-mutton will not be, for it will not need to be, evaluated. The question will be whether it is worth breeding 12 sheep to satisfy the demand for clothing (or more strictly, perhaps, whether it is worth breeding 2 sheep (12 rather than 10) to satisfy in full the demand for clothing), or whether some substitute for 2 sheep's wool should be accepted instead. The question may even be raised whether the demand for clothing should not be so cut as to obviate the need to breed the 2 sheep or find any substitute. But whatever possibilities the person considers as alternatives to the 2 additional sheep-as-wool, so long as the contemplated number of sheep-as-wool does not fall below the number demanded for mutton, the sheep will not be placed in a 'food' valuational order at all. There will not be the slightest sense in evaluating them as food. Mutton will be a by-product of the sheep-as-wool, a free gift of nature. No choice between mutton and something else will be enforced; and, since no choice will be enforced, there will be no valuation.

Even if it were decided that the demand for sheep-as-wool could and should be cut to 80 units, the whole of the demand for mutton would still be supplied (exactly) as a by-product of satisfying the demand for clothing. The whole year's mutton would be a free gift to the man who bought his suits at Messrs Sheep & Co. The mutton is there for the taking. If the person happens to grow tired of it, that does not make any difference to the amount available. Mutton will then become to that extent a useless by-product or 'waste material'. Thus, on the assumption that sheep-as-wool is being seriously evaluated and balanced against other possibilities for clothing, the sheep-as-mutton will not be evaluated at all, even though it will be quite definitely an object of demand.

But suppose that for some reason, such as the discovery of another clothing material, the demand for sheep-as-wool falls below 80 units. Let us say that it falls to 72, while the demand for sheep-as-mutton remains at 100 units. Then, automatically, the sheep-as-mutton does enter a food valuational order. The question will be whether it is worth breeding 10 sheep (or 1 sheep beyond the 9 required for wool), rather than a smaller number of sheep and finding some substitute to satisfy the residue of the food demand. But as soon as the sheep-as-mutton enters the food valuational order, the sheep-as-wool falls out of the clothing valuational order. Wool can now be regarded as a by-product of the production of food. The man's suits are a free gift which comes to him because he buys his food at Messrs Sheep & Co. There is no need to evaluate the wool, for no choice is enforced requiring him to choose between wool and something else. The wool is there for the taking, and will be there whether he wants it or not. It will be there freely supplied as long as he does not decide to reduce his consumption of mutton below the equivalent of 9 sheep per annum.

The point of all this is that, while the sheep may leap back and forth from the one valuational order to the other, at any given time it is in one order only and never in both. In no sense can it be the cause of one valuational order's influence on the other. If it cannot be a link between them (and it cannot be a link if it is now in one and again in the other, but never in both), then it cannot be a 'bridge' by which influences can be transmitted from one to the other.

I must emphasise that I am not at all concerned to deny that valuational orders can somehow influence each other. I think, on the contrary, that there is such influence. There must be, because it seems plain that, if we set a low value on wool as clothing material, and a high value on straw as thatch and bedding (or *vice versa*), this may have a great influence on the decision as to whether we eat mutton or bread. It is not the fact of the influence which is in question but the nature of the influence and the manner in which it operates. The view I reject is that the influence comes through something being a member of two quite separate valuational orders at one and the same time.

This last point is what I wanted to establish in connexion with the concept of joint supply. It was suggested that the proposition with which we are concerned in this chapter can have only a very limited applicability, and cannot be true of valuation universally, because in joint supply we have evidence that the place of a thing in its own valuational order can be determined, not by reference to the common demand postulated in that order, but by reference to outside factors which affect the order through some member or members which are at the same time members of more than one. If my argument that nothing can be in more than one order at the same time be accepted, then no such conclusion as has been suggested can be derived from consideration of the concept of joint supply.

What conclusions can we draw from this discussion of joint supply? At first sight the conclusions seem to be entirely negative.

(1) There is no positive support for the contention that every valuational order postulates a common demand with reference to which the costs of the things in that order are estimated. But it is not in the least strange that there should be no positive support; for the concept of joint supply is exclusively concerned with the consideration of different demands when the objects of those different demands yet form a 'collection' which can be produced only together and not separately.

(2) There is no evidence against the proposition; what looked like contrary evidence is found to be nothing of the kind.

But while these principal results are negative in the sense of neither weakening nor supporting the argument for the proposition, we can draw some conclusions of a more positive nature.

(3) It seems quite clear, from the considerations arising in connexion with the concept of joint supply, that there must be many different valuational orders which can all exist within the one individual consciousness.

(4) It seems clear that, though there are these different orders, they do not necessarily exist in complete isolation from each other. They appear to be able to exert some kind of mutual influence; and there must be some method by which this influence is exercised.

(5) We can wholly exclude any suggestion that this influence is exercised through some particular member belonging at the same time to the different valuational orders which are influencing each other.

3. COMPOSITE DEMAND

The two concepts which we have been discussing up to now are both 'supply' concepts. The argument in favour of 'common demand' as implied in every valuational order would not be weakened if neither of our 'supply' concepts gave it positive support; for 'common demand' is, of course, a demand and not a supply concept. The argument would be weakened only if (and this we have seen, is not the case) any 'supply' concept not only failed to give positive support but also suggested a contrary view.

The position, however, is different when we turn to the main 'demand' concepts. If any of these occurs in a valuational context and can yet be made intelligible without postulating, either directly or indirectly, the conception of 'common demand' this will very seriously weaken the argument. If, in the case of 'supply' concepts, it may be said, 'those not against us are with us', in the case of 'demand' concepts it may—much more truly—be said, 'those not with us are against us'.

The following discussion of 'demand' concepts will, I think, show that, of the two fundamental ones (Composite and Joint Demand), composite necessarily implies joint, and Joint Demand, in the individual as distinguished from the social sense, necessarily implies Common Demand.

A thing is said to be in composite demand when quantities of it, as a whole, are demanded for different purposes. Since it is a quantity of the thing as a whole which is demanded for each of the purposes, these purposes are competitive. Thus gas may be used for cooking or lighting; and the quantity used for one purpose is denied to the other. Electricity may be used for cooking, heating, lighting, driving trolley-buses, operating industrial plant, or executing criminals; and the quantity used for one purpose is denied to the others. Intellectual ability may be used for organising crime or suppressing crime, for designing houses or devising methods of blowing them up; and the amount used for one purpose is denied to the others. All these—gas, electricity, intellectual ability—are objects of composite demand.

But the concept has to be somewhat further clarified, because it is frequently asserted that there is a close relationship between composite demand and joint supply. It is said, for instance, that, since a sheep produces wool and mutton, these can be regarded as in Joint supply; but, in so far as the proportions of wool and mutton are variable, we can also say that there is composite demand for sheep as producers of either wool or mutton.

There is presumably a point here of great importance in general economics; but it is difficult to see why the point should be put by asserting a special relationship between the concepts of joint supply and composite demand. In any exact sense of the term, joint supply must mean that things are produced together even though they are objects of different demands. Composite demand signifies that there are competing demands for the same object. The point which joint supply and composite demand have in common is that, in both cases, there are different demands concerned with what is in a sense the same thing. But it makes all the difference that, in the case of joint supply, the different demands are each for a different and separable part of the thing (separable, that is, once the thing has been produced, though not capable of separate production), and are therefore not competing. The more the one demand is satisfied, the more will there be to satisfy the others. But, in the case of composite demand, the demands are competitive, each being a demand the satisfaction of which consumes a quantity of the thing as a whole; and the more the one demand is satisfied, the less will there be to satisfy the others.

Since, then, I am concerned with the various concepts in their strict senses, I shall not assume that composite demand and joint supply are directly related.

On the other hand, the principal aim of this section is to show that the concepts of 'composite demand' and 'joint *demand*' are necessarily related. The meaning of joint demand will be discussed in our next section, and it is sufficient to say now that by joint demand is meant a set of demands which are so closely related that they rise and fall together. The importance of establishing the relation between composite demand and joint demand is this: The argument of the next section will seek to establish that joint demand in the valuational activities of the individual mind always implies 'common demand' such as is envisaged in the Proposition with which this chapter is concerned; and if we can show that composite demand has a necessary relation to joint demand, then composite demand will necessarily imply common demand in so far as joint demand does so.

In this and the following section on joint demand it is particularly important to bear in mind the distinction between the 'public order of value' and the 'valuational order in the individual mind'; otherwise the limited aims of the argument will be missed.

In the present section I shall make considerable use of illustrations from the public order of value. This seems expedient if we are to show that we are really dealing with the same general concept as the economist has in mind when he speaks of composite demand. Further, so far as the argument is concerned with the relation of composite to joint demand, it would seem to show that these two concepts are necessarily related both with regard to the public order and with regard to the valuational activities in the individual mind. But the really vital part of the argument is not to establish a relation between composite and joint demand; it is to establish a relation of composite to joint demand in order to show that composite demand implies 'common demand' to the extent that joint demand implies common demand. Now it does not seem to me to be true that joint demand in the public order of value always and necessarily implies common demand. Sometimes it does; sometimes it does not. The argument of our next section will be restricted to showing that joint demand in the individual mind necessarily implies common demand. The argument of the present section therefore is rather more broadly based than is strictly necessary for the conclusions in which we are primarily interested. We shall be dealing here indiscriminately with the public and the individual orders of value; but it must be clearly realised that what we are at present trying to show is not that composite or joint demand imply common demand, but simply and solely that composite demand has a necessary relation to joint demand.

When analysing the nature of composite demand, we have to abstract to some extent from the total situation in which it will normally operate. If, for instance, we take the composite demand for electricity—the items of demand being the demands for cooking, for road transport and for working industrial plant—in actual life there will also be composite supply, in the sense that the housewife will have the alternatives of oil, gas, coal and wood for her fire; it will be possible for road transport to adopt the alternatives of the motor-bus or horse-drawn vehicles; and industrial plant may be operated by steam. But to take composite supply into consideration would lead to such an elaboration of the argument that the main points would be in danger of being lost, and the elaborations would not in any event affect the principal issue. We shall assume, therefore, that composite supply is not present. That is to say, we shall consider composite demand on the assumption that the different demands for the same thing have no alternative methods of satisfaction, and that, so far as they do not secure an adequate share of the thing in composite demand, they will to that extent remain unsatisfied.

Let us set out our problem, first of all, in a very broad way, taking a case of composite demand in the social order. This will not give us a perfect picture of the situation for the individual, but it will at least show us the main issues to be dealt with. Consider the composite demand, in a community, for electricity. It is demanded for the domestic purposes of lighting, cooking and heating; it is demanded for the operation of public transport; it is demanded for offices and factories for lighting, heating and the operation of plant. So far as it is utilised for one purpose it will be denied to the others; and, in extreme cases, the policy of 'power cuts' will have to be adopted.

Is there any sense in saying that this example of composite demand is also an instance of joint demand? When things are in joint demand, an increase in the demand for one of the items necessarily carries with it an increase in the demand for all the other items. If, for instance, we say that the demand for electricity for domestic and for transport and for industrial purposes is both a case of composite demand (as it is), and also a case of joint demand, we must mean that any increase in the demand for electricity for domestic purposes will necessarily carry with it an increase in the demand for electricity for transport and industrial purposes as well. Can we really say that the competing demands for electricity are such that they will vary directly with each other, that an increase in one will carry an increase in the others?

If we care to divide the working day of the community into separate periods, we can draw a conclusion exactly the reverse. We can show that the increase in one of the demands necessarily carries with it a decrease in the others. If people are at home cooking and eating their breakfasts on a winter morning, the domestic demand will be heavy, the transport demand light, and the factory demand negligible. In the period when they are going to their occupations, the transport demand will be heavy while the domestic and industrial demands will be correspondingly light. When the day's work is in full swing, the industrial demand will be heavy and the others correspondingly light. This is, of course, a highly simplified statement of the situation, but the simple statement brings out the issue. In this case of composite demand there seems to be the exact reverse of what we mean by joint demand.

But we reach this conclusion only by considering the different parts of the working day in sheer isolation from each other; and it is important to notice that, when so isolated, they lose most of their significance. Their full significance can be grasped only when they are considered as the complementary parts of the total working day. We could not really explain the intense activity of the home in the morning without taking into account that, at a later period, the breadwinners (and the providers of the money to pay for electricity) have to be in their offices and factories. The demand for electricity in offices and factories cannot be understood apart from the demands which the members of the community are making for all sorts of things in their homes and out-of-work hours. The consumption of electricity in transport cannot be made intelligible without postulating that people have to move about for various purposes, one of which is to get from home to business, and back. That is to say, the demands on electricity for domestic, transport and industrial purposes do not exist except in relation to each other. They are diverse expressions of demand arising in the whole life of the community, and can be interpreted only in the light of the life of the whole. When we take them in their relations to each other, and not as artificially isolated, it becomes plain that, in some cases at least, they do react on each other in precisely the way that items of joint demand react on each other. The more power demanded for industry (the greater the demand for industrial products) the greater will be the demand for domestic power (the greater will be the number of people and homes required to operate the industries), and the greater also will be the demand for transport power (for trams and trolley-buses to take people to and from work). In this case, at least, what is an instance of composite demand is also an instance of joint demand.

Nor should it be supposed that the instance is exceptional. Land is in composite demand for purposes of agriculture, stock-raising, housing, tennis-courts, roads. The more it is used for growing wheat and potatoes, the less will there be for houses, stock-raising, and so on. And yet the more it is demanded for growing wheat and potatoes, the more will it also be demanded for all these other purposes, since the increase of demand for wheat and potatoes will come from an increasing human and animal population. Similarly the greater the demand for houses and tennis-courts, the greater the demand for wheat, potatoes and meat.

Our illustrations, so far, have been taken from the 'public economy'. Having seen broadly what the issue is, we should now deal more directly with the valuations of the individual and see whether, in this case also, composite demand implies joint demand.

Let us consider composite demand of the individual for gas. We have a poor author writing his great book in his garret. He needs gas, partly for light to see, and partly for the gas-fire; for, if he is too cold, he cannot concentrate on his job. (We are again supposing that the fact of composite supply does not operate; we are supposing that he has no substitute for gas either for lighting or for heating, although, in point of fact, he will be a very odd person if he can think of no substitutes.) If he has few coins to spare for the gas-meter, he will have to ration both his lighting and his heating, and the two demands will compete for the available supply of gas. There is here composite demand.

But there is also joint demand. The longer he requires the light, the longer will he also require the heating, and *vice versa*. He may, of course, be able to 'stagger' the consumption, as the social consumption of electricity for domestic, transport and in-dustrial purposes is staggered over the day. He may be more sensitive to the cold when he is doing the hard work of thinking out the contents of his book, than he is when actually committing his results to paper; and so, when doing his thinking, he may be able to turn out the light and slightly turn up the fire. But even if he thus staggers his consumption, the concept of joint demand will still apply. For the more periods of writing he requires, the greater number of periods for thought will he also require; and the more time required for working out his ideas, the more time will he require to set them out fully on paper. The composite demand for gas for heating and lighting will also be a case of joint demand for gas for heating and lighting.

These examples predispose us strongly to the view that composite demand implies joint demand. But, by working from examples we can, at the best, reach some sort of empirical generalisation; and our proposition is far too important to be left at the mercy of possible contrary instances. If any weight is to be placed upon it we must see whether we cannot give it a firmer base than a merely empirical generalisation. I think that its universal validity can be demonstrated in the following way:

We know that 'demand' is a conative disposition the content or end of which is the creation, maintenance or destruction of some state of affairs.[1] It is a subjective attitude which is a response to a perceived objective situation; and the response is what the demander himself feels to be the 'appropriate' response to that concrete situation. Thus, the housewife's 'demand' for tea on a given day is what she feels to be the appropriate response to the household conditions which she expects to obtain throughout that day. Any change in the conditions, actual or anticipated, will stimulate a new response, a change of demand, to restore the relation of appropriateness. If the family is unexpectedly invited to spend the day away from home, the demand for tea will automatically drop. If a son and four friends unexpectedly arrive, the demand will automatically rise. Alterations of demand are the responses appropriate to alterations in objective conditions.

Now, when we have composite demand—different demands for the same thing—the demands which constitute the items of

[1] See pp. 46-9.

composite demand may be either (1) opposed in themselves, or (2) complementary to each other.

(1) When the items are opposed (as, for instance, when criminals demand intelligence for employment in the organisation of crime, and police demand intelligence for employment in the breaking of criminal organisations), any increase in the one demand threatens to alter the objective conditions to which the other demand had been adjusted, and therefore causes an alteration in the character of the latter demand. Thus, if the demand for intelligence by criminal organisations increases, the demand for intelligence in police work, which had previously been adjusted to a less arduous form of detection, will automatically increase also. Hence, when the demands within composite demand are in their nature opposed, any increase in one will necessarily carry an increase in the other, owing to the fundamental nature of demand itself as an 'appropriate response' to a set of objective conditions. That is to say, composite demand will, in this case, always be an instance of joint demand also.

(2) When the items are complementary to each other (as, for instance, when the author demands both light and heat for the creation of his book), again, any increase in the one demand threatens to alter the objective conditions to which the other was adjusted. The more light demanded for the completion of the book (perhaps because the period within which it was expected to be completed has been underestimated), the more will this require readjustment of the demand for heat, if the latter is to be appropriate to the new conditions.

Hence, whether the items of demand in composite demand be opposed or complementary, an increase in the one will necessarily stimulate an increase in the other, and a decrease in the one will result in a decrease in the other.

In conclusion, we ought to remind ourselves of the main reason for this somewhat lengthy discussion of the relation between composite demand and joint demand. The main issue in this chapter is whether every valuational order presupposes a common demand; but we have not been trying to show that common demand is implied in the concept of composite demand. We have merely tried to establish that composite demand is always also joint demand. But, in our next section, we shall try to show that, so far as individual valuation is concerned, joint demand always implies a common demand in the sense required; and as it has already been established that there is a necessary relation between composite and joint demand, we shall, in making out our case for joint demand, also be making out a case with respect to composite demand.

4. JOINT DEMAND

When we speak of joint demand we are referring to a number of demands which together constitute a 'set' such that, if one arises, the others in the set will also arise. If one increases or decreases, the others will correspondingly increase or decrease. It is not assumed that the sets are eternally fixed in composition. The items in sets may vary from individual to individual, and for the same individual from time to time. Thus if we take the illustrations of joint demand given in the text-books—tea-sugar, bacon-egg, collar-tie, pen-ink, cooking-lighting-heating, and so forth—there is no necessity about these combinations. Some people like tea without sugar, some like bacon but not egg, the fashion of the moment may be against the wearing of ties, and the Chinese (one understands) will demand a brush and not a pen with his ink. But these considerations do not invalidate the concept of joint demand. If, in any given case, various demands are so related that they rise and fall together as a set, this is what we mean by saying that we have an instance of joint demand.

But while the variability of the items in the set which constitutes joint demand does not invalidate the concept, it does give rise to an important question: If there is this variability, what determines the constituents of a set at any given time? What determines how, on any given occasion, a set will be made up?

The answer is that, in some cases at least, namely in all cases of joint demand by the same person, joint demand postulates the existence of a 'common demand', and it is the specific nature of this common demand which determines the items which will, and those which will not, be included in a set. The common demand expresses itself in these various ways because only through its satisfaction in all of them will it achieve satisfaction as a whole. It is a complex demand, the various expressions of which may be simultaneous or successive, or partly simultaneous and partly successive, but will in any case together express a whole or common demand, and not a mere series of discrete demands.

If this were not the case, it would be impossible to understand why sets of joint demand should have the constituent items which they do in fact have. We could not understand why the sets arise, alter their constituents, and sometimes dissolve altogether. But these changes can be made intelligible if we assume that there is some common demand expressing itself throughout the set, and that this common demand is a general response to an objective situation which is itself subject to change. Thus the author in his bleak garret demands gas for light and heat, and these demands are related to each other as typical items in joint demand, an increase in the one carrying an increase in the other. But why do these demands exist and have this relation to each other? They and their relationship become intelligible only in the light of the general reason for his being in his room at all under these circumstances and at this particular time. The reason is his demand for the production of a book. The set of demands assumes this particular pattern because the objects of these particular demands— the lighted jet and the lighted gas-fire—together contribute to the satisfaction of the common demand. We need not spend time elaborating this argument from the point of view of the author's demands for light and heat; for the truth of the contention that the composition of this set of demands is due to the operation of the 'common demand' for the production of a book must be very plain.

The truth of the contention is plain here because we have selected as our example a case in which the items of demand are clearly 'complementary'. But we must now face a question which presents a formidable difficulty. In showing that composite demand is always also joint demand, we distinguished[1] between composite demands which are 'opposed' and those which are 'com-

[1] See p. 158.

plementary'. As an example of the former, we instanced the demands of criminals and police respectively for intelligence. It was established that we have here all the characteristic features of joint demand. But do we have here also a relation to some 'common demand' such as is now asserted to be implied in joint demand? To what common demand do criminal and police activities contribute? The answer we naturally give is 'none'—unless we are prepared to leap straight into the metaphysical empyrean and, with true Hegelian courage, personify the state, and ring the changes on thesis, antithesis and synthesis. For such a leap we are not yet ready; nor shall we venture to take it in any part of this book. That is not because we assume metaphysical doctrines of this sort to be untenable—we make no assumptions either way—but because we have a long way to go in the analysis of valuational problems before we can see what metaphysical issues are or are not raised.

Let us, then, accept what is apparently the commonsense answer to the question whether any common demand is implied in the opposed demands of criminals and police for intelligence. The commonsense answer would appear to be 'none'. Accepting this as probably true, we may suggest that, when the items in joint demand are in themselves opposed, then no common demand is implied, but that when they are complementary a common demand is implied; and further that in the individual activity of demanding there cannot be any composite or joint demand of which the items are in themselves opposed; they must always be complementary.

Before assessing the merits of this suggestion, we may try to see a little more clearly what it means. In illustrating composite demand and showing that it is always also joint demand, we selected some of our illustrations from the public order. For instance, there is the composite demand for electricity for domestic, transport and industrial purposes; and there is the demand for intelligence on the part of criminals and police. These two examples have one point in common, and also one respect in which they show an important difference. They are similar in that they refer to the public order, rather than to the individual mind. They

M

are unlike, in that the demands in the one case are complementary and in the other opposed. It is quite clear, therefore, that, in the public order, we can have both the complementary and the opposed type. What we are now suggesting is that this is not true of the individual mind; and that, in the individual mind, the constituent items in composite or joint demand are always complementary, and never opposed in themselves. They may compete for the same thing, but cannot be in their nature opposed. That is one part of our suggestion. The other part of the suggestion is that, if the items of demand constituting composite or joint demand in the individual mind are complementary, they must also necessarily imply the operation of a common demand. It may be that, when the demands are complementary even in the public order, something in the nature of common demand, such as we mean when we talk of 'the common good', is implied. But this raises issues which would take us beyond the theory of valuation in the proper sense. All we need discuss is whether, in the individual mind, if the items of demand are complementary, they imply a common demand. The suggestion as a whole, then, will amount to this: The operation of composite or joint demand in the mind of an individual demander is always the operation of items of demand which are complementary to each other, and when demands are complementary they imply the existence of a common demand.

It seems to me that the truth of this suggestion can be sufficiently demonstrated. The argument is as follows:

We have seen that a demand is what the subject feels to be the appropriate response to the objective conditions confronting him. Hence, when we say that in joint demand 'an increase in one of the items of demand stimulates a corresponding increase in the other items', this is a normally permissible but strictly inaccurate account of what happens; for in speaking of one demand as stimulating another, we are suggesting that demand is a response to demand, and not to an objective state of affairs. What is really happening is that two apparently distinct demands are responding to an objective situation. But the demands cannot, for the following reasons, be other than different expressions of one more general demand. If item *A* of the joint demand were a self-complete response or subjective adjustment to the objective situation, then there would be no other subjective response relevant to 'this' situation; that is to say, no conative response, whatever cognitive responses there might be. Demand *A* would be 'the' response. But the same would be true of demand *B*, and of all the other items in the joint demand. Now since the one (as we say) 'stimulates' the others, so that they increase and decrease with each other, none of them can be a self-complete subjective adjustment. It must be all the items taken together which constitute 'the adjustment'. Of none of them can we say that its specific content constitutes a 'whole' demand; for, if it did, there would be no parallel rise and fall in the others of the set. What happens is that, in contemplating the objective situation and the anticipated satisfaction of demand *A* in the set, our attention is also directed to that part of the situation which *A* does not cover—to which it is not the appropriate response. The 'uncovered' part of the situation evokes demands *B* and *C* and *D*, and so on, until the set constituting the joint demand is complete. The complete set may be regarded as a set of complementary demands, or as a whole or common demand with its varied expressions appropriate to the varied aspects of the complex objective situation to which the joint demand is the complex subjective response. Thus, when a person becomes aware of an opportunity to share in a deceased relative's fortune by replying to an advertisement requesting communications from kindred, the 'satisfaction' of the brusque demand, 'Get me a pen', will produce, not a sense of satisfaction, but only a sense of irritation and frustration if that demand is just literally satisfied, and there is neither ink nor paper in the house. The demand which gives significance to the demand for a pen, and the demand for ink, and the demand for paper, is the common demand of which these are merely particular expressions, namely the demand for the transmission of a letter with a view to sharing in the fortune.

5. DERIVED DEMAND

The concept of derived demand is an extremely interesting one, and many questions could be raised in connexion with it; but, so far as the main subject of this chapter is concerned, we can dispose of it without much discussion. Examples of derived demand come readily to mind. The demand for crude steel is 'derived' from the demand for steel products. The demand for timber is 'derived' from the demands for bookcases, tables, boats, etc. From any derived demand others may in their turn be derived. Thus from the demand for timber, there are 'derived' the demands for trained foresters, timber merchants and carpenters' tools; but these secondary derived demands refer us back ultimately to what may be called the original 'principal' as distinguished from the primary 'derived' demands; for if tables, bookcases and boats were to be made from steel and not from wood, there would be no demand for timber, and therefore no demand for foresters and carpenters' tools.

When we consider carefully the nature of derived demand, we see that derived demand is not essentially different from an item in joint demand. We talk as though it were derived from some other (principal) demand. But although this is a perfectly legitimate way of expressing ourselves in the ordinary course, we have to remember, as was pointed out in the discussion on joint demand, that no demand is a direct response to some other demand. Demand is always a response to our awareness of an objective situation, and derived demand will possess the essential nature of all demand. Derived demand must therefore be a response to an objective situation; but it is so obviously related to a principal demand that, in the last analysis, there can be no distinction between the relation of a derived to a principal demand and the relation of an item in joint demand to the common demand of which it and the other members of the 'set' are the varied expressions.

So far as it is important to distinguish between derived and joint demand, therefore (and I do not for a moment suggest that the distinction is superfluous), the importance is almost certainly due to the exigencies of general economics rather than to the requirements of pure theory of valuation. In any case, whether we regard derived demand as substantially the same as an item in joint demand or not, the fact that things in derived demand are evaluated primarily (though not wholly) in respect of their 'efficiency' in securing the satisfaction of the principal demand shows that, so far as the subject of this chapter is concerned, the concept of derived demand will support our main proposition. Things in derived demand are evaluated against each other by reference to a common demand.

6. CONCLUSIONS

We have now discussed in some detail the five concepts which, as I understand the position, economists generally accept as giving the main ways in which demand and supply affect each other. Our interest in the concepts has, of course, been to discover how demand reveals itself in detail, and especially to discover what implications they have in connexion with the assertion that every valuational order in the individual mind postulates a common demand with reference to which the opportunity costs of the things placed in that order are estimated.

Our conclusions are that the concepts of Composite Supply, Joint Demand and Derived Demand all give positive and un-qualified support to the proposition. The concept of Composite Demand likewise gives positive support in that, as the argument has shown, all Composite Demand is also Joint Demand. The only one of the five concepts which does not offer support is that of Joint Supply. But it does not, on the other hand, provide any argument on the opposite side; and this is because the concept of Joint Supply is concerned, not with the nature of a valuational order, but with an objective situation which, when studied in connexion with the nature of demand in general, reveals the exis-tence of more than one valuational order in the individual mind.

Now the proposition with which this and the previous chapter have been concerned—the proposition that every valuational order postulates a common demand—stated the *first* of two con-ditions which must obtain if the preceding proposition—that the order of value is the inverse of the order of opportunity costs—is to be accepted as universally valid. It may fairly be claimed that our argument shows this condition to be firmly established.

Chapter Five

ASSESSMENT OF OPPORTUNITY COSTS

In Proposition V it was affirmed that the order of value is the inverse of the order of opportunity costs; but while we saw that there was an initial plausibility about this view, we did find also that it implied two things: firstly, the postulate of 'common demand', and, secondly, that we can intelligibly speak of degrees of satisfaction of this common demand, i.e. that a quantitative conception of satisfaction can be applied sufficiently to enable us to speak of 'more and less' satisfaction. Having now completed our discussion of the first of these questions, we turn to the second.

PROPOSITION VII

The satisfaction of the common demand postulated in any valuational order may be measured in quantitative terms.

Up to the present we have been insisting on the complex nature of the 'common demand'. Only in so far as a demand is complex can we understand how it can have different 'items' or 'expressions' in relation to the different aspects of the objective situation to which it is a response. Even a demand so 'simple' as the demand for bread must be regarded as 'complex' if it is a common demand expressed as demand for bread today and demand for bread tomorrow. Indeed every demand will, on careful inspection, turn out to be a complex demand; for, no matter how simple and homogeneous it may seem to be when considered in relation to other demands, when we consider its nature in relative isolation as a response to a given situation, it will be possible to detect various aspects within it, corresponding to the complexity of the situation to which it is the response.

Nevertheless, while every demand may be regarded as complex, its satisfaction cannot be measured in quantitative terms unless it can also be regarded, from some point of view, as a simple or homogeneous demand. If we say, then, that the common demand postulated in a valuational order must be both complex and also measurable with respect to its satisfaction in quantitative terms, it follows that 'simplicity' and 'complexity' are themselves relative terms. So far as demand, at least, is concerned, there are no absolute and eternal 'simples' and 'complexes' as those who hold the objectivist theory of 'goodness' or 'value' are apt to assume. A 'complex demand' is not made up of a 'collection' of 'absolutely simple demands', any more than an extended line is made up of a collection of points possessing no magnitude. A complex demand is made up of complex demands. The 'simple' demands into which a demand may be divided are parts of a simple demand. There is here no mystery-mongering. We are not indulging in metaphysical subtleties which transcend the jurisdiction of the logical law of contradiction. We are merely pointing out that the terms 'complexity' and 'simplicity' are intelligible only in relation to each other, and that whether a thing is to be regarded as simple or complex depends on the universe of discourse. When we are considering the 'common demand' as that which is implied in its qualitatively different competing expressions we naturally stress its complexity; but when we are considering the degree to which it can be satisfied by one combination of things rather than another combination of those things, we naturally stress its unity or simplicity. We think, in the one case in qualitative terms, and, in the other case, in quantitative terms.

Since the point now to be established is that the common demand implied in a valuational order must be sufficiently 'simple' to have its satisfaction measured in quantitative terms, it will be proper to select for consideration a demand which, qualitatively, is indisputably 'complex'.

Let us suppose that a university proposes to extend its accommodation to provide for an additional 400 students distributed over Arts, Pure Science, and certain professional schools. A sum of money and an area of land are handed over to the university for this purpose. The university will not, in this case, be concerned with the 'social opportunity costs' of the project, in the sense of considering whether the land and money should be applied to university extension rather than to some other end. Presumably this question has been decided. The problem for the university will relate to costs within the four corners of the project itself. It will have to ensure that money and land are not wasted on hostel accommodation at the expense of teaching and recreational demands, or wasted on these at the expense of adequate hostel buildings. The money and land placed at its disposal will have to be distributed so as to satisfy the whole demand (the 400 extension project) in as full and balanced a way as is possible.

What will be the procedure in evaluating the methods by which this demand is to be satisfied? It seems to me that there are three distinct steps involved.

(1) The first step is to clarify the demand itself which is taken for granted. In the example selected, the demand is obviously of a highly complex nature: 400 students are to be given an education over varying periods of years, and the character of the education will vary according to the career ultimately envisaged. During the years of training they have to be provided with living quarters with appropriate amenities, recreation, and the necessary teaching, laboratory and library facilities. The clarification of the demand (the demand for the education of the 400) is the detailed working out of the specific demands in all these different directions. When the scheme has been roughed out in this way, we have an approximately correct picture of the demand as a whole.

Now this first stage is preliminary to any valuation which will take place. It is not itself an act of valuation. It is merely the clarification of the common demand which is taken for granted. The content of this demand, if it is ever to be evaluated as a whole, will be evaluated, not by the university as such, but by those who are responsible for deciding the comparative value of university extension as against other social purposes. It is presumed that the project has already been evaluated and chosen, and that resources have been assigned for the purpose, the function of applying these resources to the satisfaction of the demand being then handed over to the university. The demand is in this sense taken for granted; but it has required clarification.

(2) The second step is to undertake the 'administrative' or 'technical' calculation as to the amount of resources which will be necessary to satisfy each aspect or item of demand in the whole complex demand. Here again we are not evaluating but are merely engaged on a process preliminary to valuation. We are apprehending the objective situation. The social planners may have greatly over-estimated the amount of resources necessary for the project (in which case no valuation of the different items of demand within the project as a whole will ever be necessary). More probably they will have under-estimated. But whether they have over- or under-estimated (whether the items of the project will have to be evaluated against each other or not), this will not affect the need to undertake the administrative or technical calculations as to the amount of resources necessary for each item in the project. If the resources allocated are far more than sufficient, it will still be necessary to decide how much of them should be used to provide an adequate addition to the library, to the lecture-rooms, etc. etc.; just as it is necessary, when planning a salt-water swimming-pool on the Californian coast, to decide how much of the resources of the Pacific Ocean should be enclosed to make the pool adequate to requirements. Since the resources allocated to the university will not be scarce—any more than the waters of the Pacific are scarce—there will be no need to evaluate their use; but this will not mean that we can avoid the technical calculation as to the resources required for the project.[1]

If, on the other hand, resources are scarce, the problem of evaluating their allocation will arise; but it will still only arise after the technical calculations have been made. Indeed the valuation can arise only after this technical calculation has been done in some approximate way; for only then will it be seen whether the objective situation forces a choice in the utilisation of resources. The initial technical problem is not how to fit available resources to demand, but to see what resources the demand, as initially clarified, will require, irrespective of their availability.

[1] The reader may recall the distinction already emphasised (pp. 12-14 and 54-7), between the value judgement and the efficiency judgement.

(3) The third step—the stage of valuation in the proper sense —comes if, as is most probable, the demand as initially clarified is found, on the technical calculation, to be somewhat in excess of the supply. We may find that to build the hostels as contemplated will cut severely the plans for the library and laboratories. Some adjustment will have to be made. Now is the time for valuation of the hostel, library, etc., demands against each other. The question is: How do we reckon the costs of such qualitatively different demands against each other, and reckon these costs in terms of the 'greater' and 'less' satisfaction of a common demand so complex as the 'education of 400 students'?

Suppose that the scarcity which compels us to perform the act of valuation is scarcity of available land, and that the question confronting us is whether 5 acres should be cut off from the residential site and allocated to laboratory development; how do we decide whether the cost of denying this ground to hostels is greater or less than the cost of denying it to laboratories? We can compare the costs only by asking which of them more seriously affects the total project, which of them represents the greater frustration of the principal demand for the education of 400 students at a standard and of the quality envisaged. We ask ourselves: Does the absence of the amenities subtracted from the hostels, along with the retention of the more commodious laboratories, adversely affect the quality of education as a whole more or less than this would be affected by retaining those amenities and cutting down laboratory space?

If this is how we put the question, then it means that opportunity costs are measured, not simply in terms of the deprivation of satisfaction of one or other of the competing items of demand (competing expressions of the common demand), but in terms of deprivation of satisfaction of this demand *as* an expression of the principal demand itself. We cannot, in point of fact, measure the extent to which the hostels or the laboratories, taken in absolute isolation, could contribute to the total project. If we were to build hostels for 400, and nothing else, then we should have made no contribution to education of the standard and quality contemplated. On the contrary, we should have done a disservice to the community by offering maintenance at the public expense to a large collection of young bloods with nothing to do but devise mischief to relieve their boredom. If we were to build the laboratories and nothing else, we should have contributed nothing; for the prospective students would all have died of hunger or exposure before the laboratories had been open many days.[1] If, however, there is some residential, laboratory, library, etc., accommodation envisaged, we can intelligibly ask whether more of this and less of that would better realise the project as a whole. Opportunity costs are measured by the extent to which the common demand is frustrated more or less by alternative arrangements of the proportions in which the subsidiary demands are met under given conditions.

This means that we never can evaluate the items in a valuational order over against each other, unless the principal demand giving significance to that order can intelligibly be described as 'more' or 'less' well satisfied by alternative distributions of our resources amongst the various subsidiary demands constituting its particular expressions. However complex the demand may be—and we have purposely selected a highly complex one for discussion—it must be capable of being regarded as sufficiently simple or homogeneous in nature to render possible the distinction between 'amounts' of satisfaction. We must, in this sense, be able to measure its satisfaction quantitatively.

To reinforce the point we may take an example concerned with the valuations of the individual mind. A man is devoted to the ideal of art for art's sake, and not particularly inclined to paint or carve for the vulgar rabble which stupidly supposes that a cow's eyes should be in its head rather than on its hindquarters, and its hooves at the ends of its legs rather than sprouting from its ears. If our high-souled artist is wealthy, he can probably devote himself to the pursuit of pure art and posthumous fame. But if he is poor, he cannot ignore the fact that one of the subsidiary demands expressive of his principal demand for a dedicated

[1] Of course this would not be true if the university were non-residential with no responsibility for living conditions; but in that case the 'common demand' would not include hostels. The point at issue would then be illustrated by reference, say, to the competing demands for laboratory and library space.

life is the demand for life itself. He will have to clarify this principal demand sufficiently to get its various aspects or items into perspective. What standard of physical well-being does it include? Membership of suitable clubs, or merely enough bread and water to keep body and soul together? To what extent does pursuit of the ideal require that everything he does should bear its stamp? Do pot-boilers, as an evil but necessary side-line, enter into the scheme; or is it permissible to devote time to earning a living by stock-broking, street-sweeping, or route-marching through the division lobbies of the House of Commons? When the main pattern of the principal demand has been roughed out, the technical calculations as to resources will have to be faced; and then will come the valuation of this as against that, a little more of one thing as against another, in order to reach the best adjustment for the life envisaged as a whole. The valuation will be in terms of the realisation of this life as a whole. The question will be whether the quality of life demanded (lived over an anticipated period of years) will be, on the whole, richer if some pot-boiling productions or some extraneous money-making activities be admitted; or whether, on the contrary, the sense of having been false to the highest will have permanently detrimental effects such as no deprivation of creature comforts could produce. Whatever the outcome of this process of valuation may be, the nature of the process itself admits of little question. It will be the assessing of the opportunity costs of satisfying the various subsidiary demands by the extent to which the satisfaction of them in alternative proportions detracts from the satisfaction of the principal demand, the demand for a certain quality of life extending over a contemplated tract of time.

Now it may be questioned whether it is proper to say that this calculation of more and less of satisfaction of the common demand implies that we regard the common demand as, from this point of view, simple or homogeneous. As has already been explained, I hold that the terms 'simple' and 'complex' are intelligible only in relation to each other, and that there is no demand, however apparently simple, which cannot also be regarded as complex. My reason for insisting on the simplicity or homogeneity, from one point of view, of even the most complex demand, is merely complementary to the point that even the most simple demand is complex. The simplicity is stressed in the present context because it is plain that costs are measured in terms of the satisfaction of the common demand, and that the satisfaction is assessed as more and less; hence, in so far as quantitative measurement implies simplicity or homogeneity in the nature of the demand whose satisfaction is measured, to that extent the common demand must be regarded as simple.

Our general conclusion, then, is that Propositions VI and VII, taken together, justify us in attributing universal validity to Proposition V. That is to say, it is true, with respect to every valuational order without exception, that 'the order of value is the inverse of the order of anticipated opportunity costs'.

There is one question which may have occurred to the reader who has followed the argument thus far. It is this: Why should we adopt the cumbrous method of evaluating in terms of opportunity costs, when such costs themselves can only be estimated by reference to the extent of contribution to the satisfaction of a common demand? That is to say: If A costs more than B, this means that A leaves more demand unsatisfied; but this is merely a negative way of putting the positive statement that B contributes more to satisfaction of the common demand. To define value in terms of opportunity costs, then, is to adopt the curious procedure of (a) assessing 'contribution', (b) reversing this to get 'cost', and (c) reversing this again to get 'value'. Would it not be more sensible to say, not that the order of value is the inverse of the order of opportunity costs, but that the order of value is determined by the 'amount of contribution towards satisfaction of common demand'?

Superficially this is a sensible proposal. But is this really what we mean by the value of a thing? If a bottle of water from a mighty river will completely or 'absolutely' satisfy my demand for drink, does this water necessarily have a high degree of value or 'absolute value'? If we attempt to state value directly in terms of contribution, we confuse the question of 'administrative' or 'technical' calculation with the question of 'valuation'. If we do, in any given case, know the full extent of demand, it is possible to make the technical calculations as to what will contribute to the complete satisfaction of demand (and, if resources are adequate, proceed to act on the calculation) without ever raising the question of value at all. Valuation only arises when resources are inadequate, and we are forced to choose between 'amounts of dissatisfaction' with respect to the various ways in which the common demand expresses itself. The question which gives rise to the valuation of a thing is therefore not: 'How much does this contribute to the satisfaction of the common demand?' but, 'How much does this distribution of resources leave more demand unsatisfied than would be unsatisfied by an alternative distribution?' We indulge in the apparently needless somersault of defining costs by reference to contribution, and then value by reference to costs, because the conception of value is unintelligible if we attempt to relate it direct to contribution. The question of value will not arise unless and until the technical calculations with regard to contributions show that there will be a problem of choice, a problem of opportunity costs.

PROPOSITION VIII

When two or more valuational orders exist within a single consciousness, they are potentially subject to a more comprehensive valuational order, and hence to a more comprehensive common demand.

We are now in a position to deal with a problem noted but not pursued at the beginning of Chapter III. In saying that every valuational order postulates a common demand with reference to which the costs of the things placed in that order are estimated, we made it clear[1] that this does not exclude the possibility of our attributing values to two different things without relating these to any common demand. It was considered possible that there might be different valuational orders in the one individual mind; and if x is valued in one such order and y in another, each will be relative to the common demand of its own order, but there need not necessarily be a common demand to which x and y are

[1] Pp. 80-1.

both relative. In Chapter IV, when dealing with the concept of joint supply,[1] we saw that there must be these different valuational orders within the one consciousness. There are orders which are at least relatively independent, although they are not so permanently isolated that they cannot under any circumstances affect each other. In point of fact, they do at times influence each other.

We have now to consider the process by which, when they do influence each other, this comes about. The proposition indicates the manner of this influence. The orders affect each other by entering into a more comprehensive valuational order, and thus become relative to a more comprehensive common demand. The proposition asserts that all valuational orders are 'potentially' related to each other in this way. What converts the 'potentiality' into 'actuality'? The answer is that they become actually related in this way when anything becomes an object of composite demand with respect to two or more valuational orders in the same consciousness.

Before illustrating this point with reference to the individual, it may be helpful to see the principle operating in the wider social system. One of the first points impressed upon us in the textbooks of economics is the extraordinary way in which the economic order may develop without any kind of central planning. Any given member or section of the community counts on being fed, clothed, entertained and carried about the country, through the assistance of millions of his fellow mortals at home and abroad, most of whom know nothing of his existence and would not, in any case, greatly worry whether he lived or died. There are many different demands which exist in society. The food demand has its particular expressions directed to meat, fish, fowl, cereals, etc., and a great deal of man-power, machinery and other resources are utilised in providing for its satisfaction, as valuations within the relevant order direct. There are demands for clothing, buildings of many kinds, roads, products of the heavy industries, education, health services, holidays and recreation.

In a free or 'competitive' economy, these demands seem to be relatively external to each other, relatively independent in the

[1] See esp. pp. 149-50.

sense that the intricate system which they form is not a result of conscious and comprehensive planning.

Contrast this with the economy of a modern society in time of war or under an intensely 'socialist' régime. All the principal demands listed above, and countless others, become evaluated against each other in some more comprehensive order, and have their places fixed, within broad limits, in the light of some comprehensive 'end'. If the end is very precisely envisaged, such as winning a war, the valuation of the demands is fairly precise. The kinds of food available are restricted and the quantities rationed; building projects are 'screened' and operations to a great extent directed; the development and maintenance of transport facilities, the emphasis in types of university and technical education, the policy with regard to public health, the operation of heavy industries, the facilities for holiday and recreation, all become caught up in the effort at central planning. Where the end is less precise, such as an ideal of welfare in the socialist state, the central control will be correspondingly less tight, but the principle at work will be the same. All those various demands which, in a competitive economy, seem to achieve some sort of intricate system without forming part of a comprehensive valuational order, are, in a planned economy, brought within such a comprehensive order.

What forces all the common demands of these various valuational orders to be evaluated against each other? It is the extent and urgency of composite demand for resources, such as manpower, coal, steel, machinery, fuel oil and spirit, and many others. The competition for these things enforces an assessment of the relative values of the contents of the demands to which they minister. The question is whether it is better that a given object should be utilised in this rather than in that way. But the relative valuation of the competing demands could never be undertaken except in the light of some more comprehensive demand of which they are regarded as the particular expressions. They are assessed as items in a general project, to win a war or to maximise the wellbeing of the society as a whole.

Looking at the question from the point of view of the individual consciousness, we have no difficulty in suggesting illustrations of the same principle. Robinson Crusoe will have a variety of demands which are all capable of being regarded as relatively independent in their nature. There will be the food, clothing and housing demands, and he may be a keen naturalist. Taking a purely abstract view of these demands, we see no reason why his preferences—his order of choices or values—in relation to any of these demands should interfere with the order of values in relation to any other. If his first choice in food is for cereals, his passion in clothing for woollen garments, his inclination for a house of seasoned timber, and if he has a longing to spend hours in his boat studying marine biology, the demands in themselves are not obviously competitive in a way such as to enforce choice. Nevertheless choice may be enforced. Thus, if the land available makes it possible to grow wheat or raise sheep, but not both, he cannot have both cereal food and woollen clothing. If the seasoned timber available makes it possible to have a timber house or a boat, but not both, he will have to do without his elegant house or severely limit his range in biological study. The fact that land and timber are in urgent composite demand forces him to evaluate the principal demands of the various valuational orders against each other. And, as we saw in Chapter IV,[1] composite demand implies joint demand, and joint demand implies a common demand.

Hence—to repeat the substance of our proposition—the different valuational orders which may exist in the one mind are only relatively independent inasmuch as they are liable, through the fact of composite demand when such exists, to have their respective principal demands brought within a more comprehensive order, and thus to have their opportunity costs assessed in relation to a more comprehensive end.[2]

[1] Pp. 157-8; 162-3.
[2] Perhaps the foregoing discussion will throw some light on a difficulty noted on p. 152. Economists frequently say that there is a close relationship between joint supply and composite demand, and I have ventured to suggest that this is a mistake, if the concept of joint supply is to be understood in any strict sense. Elaborating that suggestion, I should distinguish between three, not two, supply concepts. There is 'composite supply', there is 'joint supply' and there is a third concept which I may call that of 'complex supply'; and when economists say that

N

So far I have stressed the *liability* of relatively independent valuational orders to be comprehended within a larger one. I want now to stress the *contingent* nature of this tendency towards 'wholeness' in our valuational life. It is for this reason that the word 'potentially' figures in the proposition. It is not contended that all valuational orders are actually synthesised into a whole. It is merely contended that, under certain conditions, this integration will take place. So far as I can see, the necessary condition of the potentiality being translated into actuality is that there should be composite demand for some 'scarce' object or objects as between the different orders. Hence the question how far the movement towards wholeness in our valuational life will go, can only be answered by discussing the question how far-reaching composite demand for scarce commodities is likely to be.

To what extent, then, do things tend to be in composite demand?

There are two things and possibly others which appear to be universally in composite demand, namely time and energy (including both physical and mental); for it is impossible to attempt to satisfy any demand without utilising these, and what time and

there is a close relation between 'composite demand' and 'joint supply', there seems to be a confusion between the concepts of 'joint' and 'complex'. It is complex and not joint supply which is bound up with the notion of composite demand.

The difference between 'joint' and 'complex' is this: When we say that things are in joint supply, we are referring to such things as wool and mutton, or wheat-ear and straw. A sheep is not in joint supply; wheat is not in joint supply. But wool and mutton are in joint supply, and are provided in joint supply by a sheep; ear and straw are in joint supply, provided by the wheat plant. Things are in joint supply only if they satisfy two conditions: (*a*) they can never be produced except together, and (*b*) when produced, they can be separately utilised for the satisfaction of different demands. If they do not satisfy condition (*a*), then they are in independent supply. If they satisfy condition (*a*) but not condition (*b*), then they are in complex (not joint) supply. That is to say, when things are in complex supply, not only must they be produced together, but the one cannot be utilised without using up a quantity of the whole product. Thus timber, because it has properties which adapt it for use either in house- or in boat-building is an object in complex supply; for we have to use a quantity of the whole of the timber, and not merely some of its properties, if we are to build a boat, and similarly if we are to build a house. Land is in complex and not in joint supply in that we have to use an area as a whole, and not merely some of its properties, if we propose to grow cereals, and the same applies if we propose to use it to breed sheep. Now, clearly, it is an object which is in complex supply, not one which is the 'collection' of things in joint supply, that is intimately related to composite demand.

energy are expended for one purpose will not be available for others.

Most resources, however, are not in composite demand in this comprehensive way, and the extent to which they are in such demand seems to depend mainly on our knowledge of their nature and specific properties. Time and energy can be in composite demand although we may be hard put to it to say what their natures are. But with respect to most things, this is not the case. However rational a being may be, he may be very ignorant of the universe around him; and, so far as he is ignorant of things and their properties, to that extent he will not be able to think of them as 'causes' productive of 'effects' which he may actually desire. We are probably safe in saying that the composite demand with respect to any given thing will be the more extensive, the deeper our knowledge of that thing and its potential relations to other things. Hence, while the potential movement towards wholeness in our valuational life is grounded in the nature of man as a unitary self-conscious 'demander', the extent to which this movement is actually realised will depend upon his intellectual progress as a 'knower'.

Thus, it is highly probable that the initial demands of primitive man for coal were demands for missiles to heave at enemies and wild animals; and later there would be a demand for coal to build, say, defensive ramparts. Here would be composite demand; and the competition might become quite acute when an enemy pressed the attack and forced the besieged to choose between scarcity of ammunition and employing parts of their ramparts for that purpose. Composite demand would become still more extensive when some busy housewife accidentally set fire to the ammunition dump or the defensive wall in cooking the Sunday joint. Anyone with the necessary interest and imagination can follow through the process, compare the primitive with the twentieth century composite demands for coal, and judge how far this extension of composite demand has forced us to include valuational orders, which initially were relatively independent, under a more comprehensive one.

There is one other factor besides that of increasing knowledge which affects the extent to which things will be in composite demand, and hence the extent to which our different valuational orders will tend to influence each other. This factor is the degree of complexity of the social organisation within which we live. The complexity of the social order does, it is true, depend largely upon expanding knowledge, but still it deserves particular mention on its own account.

When life is lived at a relatively primitive level without intensive specialisation of function between the members, no individual can secure the resources for satisfying many of his demands without himself doing many different things. If, to take an extreme case, Robinson Crusoe wants food, he has to hunt for it, or grow it or breed it. If he wants it cooked he has to expend still more energy and use other implements. The satisfaction of each demand or group of demands requires its own mode of approach, and to a great extent the use of different materials. So far as the materials to be consumed in satisfying different demands are different, to that extent there will be no composite demand for them. But the position is very different for a member of a society such as ours. Robinson Crusoe can talk as much as he likes but this will not bring him food. More likely it will scare food away. But by simply talking longer on a rostrum, or gesticulating and declaiming for more nights on a stage, the academic teacher or the actor can secure the means to satisfy more and more of his demands. For doing such things he will receive money, and thus be able to command the services of countless numbers of people who will not only provide him with cooked food, but also bring him all the necessaries and many of the luxuries of life. Hence, in a highly complex society, money becomes almost as universally an object of composite demand as are time and energy.

At the same time, social specialisation and a monetary economy will cause an individual to integrate his values more systematically than he otherwise would or could. Money is in general composite demand because it secures such a variety of services. But this means that all the services which it can purchase are liable to be evaluated against each other. A man may not show great wisdom in these valuations, but that is hardly relevant to the main point.

It is because of this specialisation within society that it is possible for parents to think beforehand of 'careers' for their children, and for young men and women to undergo prolonged training with a reasonable expectation of being able to devote themselves to some specially interesting activity and have all their main needs satisfied as a consequence of doing so. If one has an intense demand to tear through space operating levers and switches, to be the lord of the footplate on the 'Barchester Express', to exhibit oneself in the latest fashions, to talk for hours about the universe, or to punch holes in tramway tickets; and if other people are prepared to support one for doing so; it is very easy, when reflecting about the way in which one's values can be integrated as an indirect result of this specialisation, to fall into the habit of thinking that there must be some specific thing or state which can, in the abstract, be described as the 'supreme good' or the *summum bonum* to which all else is relative and subordinate. This is to forget that such highly integrated valuational systems are not at all characteristic of human nature, as such, in its pursuit of what is good, but are due to the fact that the individual's valuational activity is being carried on in a complex society, organised towards specialisation of function, and presupposing a vast store of inherited knowledge. The extent to which the valuational activity itself is responsible for such integration can best be assessed by trying to imagine how much the individual's composite demands would be reduced (and therefore how 'compartmentalised' could be his 'common demands') if he were dependent on his own efforts to satisfy his demands, and knew nothing but what he had himself discovered by original investigation.

To sum up: The potentiality of a greater and greater synthesis in the valuational life of the individual, given a certain amount of knowledge and social organisation, depends upon the unity of self-consciousness and the principles of valuation which have been explained in this and the preceding chapters. The extent to which this potentiality actualises itself depends upon increase of knowledge and other strictly non-valuational factors which give rise to the conditions in which composite demand is stimulated.

Chapter Six

THE ULTIMATE GROUND OF VALUATION

1. PROVISIONAL STATEMENT OF CONCLUSIONS

WHILE our analysis of the nature of valuation is not yet complete, we may attempt to make a provisional summary of the conclusions so far reached.

Value is always relative or comparative and never absolute; for 'value' means degree of goodness which one thing has in comparison with others.

Our valuations are never of 'existing' things; for valuation is undertaken only when choice is enforced upon us, and choice always has a future reference. We find ourselves demanding this, that and the other; the contents of our demands are provisional 'ends'; and it is these provisional ends or contents of demand which we compare with each other and place in a valuational order, the one which stands highest being the one which will become an actual end to us.

The order in which we place our contents of demand is determined by the amount of their opportunity costs, i.e. by the sacrifices entailed respecting the contents of other demands; and the order of value will be the inverse of the order of opportunity costs.

For such an order of costs to be possible, we must be able: (*a*) to assess the opportunity costs of all the things valued against each other in relation to a demand common to them all, and an examination of the 'law of diminishing utility', as well as an analysis of the main concepts of 'supply' and 'demand' employed in economic theory, shows that such a common demand is in fact an essential postulate in economics; and we must be able (*b*) to attach real significance to the notion of 'more' and 'less' satisfaction of this common demand, a notion which becomes fully intelligible once we realise that, when we are apparently weighing one distinct content of demand against another, what we are really doing is weighing one combination of both against a different combination of both, and evaluating the different combinations as satisfying more and less the common demand of which the particular demands for the different items in the combination are but diverse expressions. It is this fact (that we weigh combinations) which gives significance to the conception of 'marginal' analysis in economic theory.

While each valuational order postulates a common demand, a number of relatively independent valuational orders may exist in the one unitary consciousness. This independence is, however, only relative or conditional; for we know that these different orders can at times influence each other in such a way that a tentative assessment of opportunity costs in one order will not finally determine our choice within that order. This is because anything which is in 'composite demand' as between the common demands of two orders, will force us to weigh the common demands of the two orders against each other in terms of some still more comprehensive common demand. In this way, and in accordance with our degree of knowledge and our particular circumstances, we tend to develop highly complex systems of values, approaching (to a less or greater degree) the conception of 'complete happiness' or 'the realisation of the self as a whole'—to use expressions which have in the past played an important part in the theory of value.

To complete our analysis of the nature of valuation we shall have to consider whether there is any single principle (e.g. the concept of the *summum bonum*) which is the ultimate ground of all our comparative value judgements. But before we can prudently attempt to carry the analysis further it will be necessary to consider a possible criticism of the argument up to this point. The argument, it may be said, can have but a very restricted application even within the field with which it professes to deal. Granting that it does not profess to answer the question as to what we mean by 'goodness', as such, but is concerned solely with the question how—assuming that we take several things to be good —we range these good things in an order of degree of goodness; still, even within the field of the merely comparative value judgement, the theory cannot pretend (it may be said) to cover the ground, for it works exclusively with concepts derived from economics. But are there not also aesthetic and moral values? How can we suppose that these are governed by the concept of marginal utility, or that the values of the aesthetic or moral order are ranged in orders of preference according to their 'opportunity costs'? Is there not something slightly humorous in the very idea?

2. THE CONCEPTION OF 'MORAL VALUES'

While the foregoing questions can be raised about both aesthetic and moral 'values', it is probable that most people will be interested in the latter, and I shall confine myself to a discussion of the bearing of the foregoing theory on the conception of 'moral values'. We shall find, as we proceed, that the greatest difficulty is not in answering objections to our theory of the comparative value judgement, but in getting any clear idea of what the objections are, and what is meant by the 'moral values' for the protection of which the objections are raised.

In the summary form in which the objections have been stated above they are quite impossible to assess. Objections cannot be answered unless they are put with a reasonable degree of precision. If it will help the critic to put them more precisely, I may say that I should have the same difficulty in understanding what was meant if someone were to say that the theory as developed above did—or did not—apply to 'economic values'. I do not think that I have been talking about a class of things or ends called 'economic values' or 'economic goods'. I think that there is a particular kind of relation—called the 'economic' relation—which men may assume towards each other. What this relation is has been explained in Chapter I,[1] and I should at once agree that it is different from the 'moral' or 'juridical' relation in which persons may also stand to each other. I think, further, that it is the economic relation which is the special field of study of economics, and that the economist, in building up his theory of its complex development, makes certain assumptions about the per-

[1] Pp. 38-40.

sons entering into the economic relation. He assumes that their minds operate in a certain way when they make the choices and preferences on the foundations of which the complex of economic relations is erected; and he is forced to proceed a considerable way in giving these assumptions a systematic, explicit expression in the form of a theory of valuation. The economist carries the theory of valuation as far as he thinks necessary for his special purposes—which are to explain the phenomena of production for, and the process of, exchange. But since the economist is here providing a much more systematic and solidly based theory of the comparative value judgement than moral philosophers generally attempt, it seemed to me worth considering whether, despite the fact that the theory originated in an attempt to explain the order of economic relations, it could serve as a theory of the comparative value judgement in general. My conclusions are that, with certain corrections and some amplification, the theory is a sound theory of the comparative value judgement in general, and that, whenever we make comparisons of degrees of goodness, or express choices between alternatives open to us, our minds operate in accordance with the general principles set out in this theory. In other words, I regard it not as a theory of the comparative value judgement in so far as 'economic things' or 'economic values' are concerned, but as a theory of the comparative value judgement in general which was originally developed by economists.

Now if it be objected that this theory does not cover 'moral values' (whatever these may be), the criticism will, I think, have to take one or other of two lines: (a) It may be said that we do make comparative value judgements in matters of 'moral goodness' or 'moral values'; and the principles governing such judgements are not those about which we have been speaking in the foregoing chapters; or (b) It may be said that we do assert moral values or judge ends or actions to be morally good; but since these are absolute and unconditional values, the comparative value judgement can have no relevance to them.

Before we can deal with either of these two possible objections it is necessary to clarify as far as possible the conception of 'moral value' or 'moral goodness' itself. When we attribute 'moral goodness' to something, does 'morally good' mean something like 'virtuous', 'right' or 'dutifully motivated'? That is to say, are we simply *asserting* that the end or action has a 'moral quality' (of a certain sort)? Or, alternatively, are we (*assuming* that the end or action has in fact a certain 'moral quality') *placing a value* on the quality or on the action-as-embodying this quality? These are two quite different things.

In case the distinction is not clear to the reader, we may perhaps illustrate it sufficiently by reference to the famous proposition with which Kant opens the *Groundwork of the Metaphysic of Morals*: 'It is impossible to conceive anything at all in the world, or even out of it, which can be taken as good without qualification, except a good will.'[1] Talents of the mind (he goes on), qualities of temperament, or gifts of fortune may be good and desirable in many respects; but they are not good without qualification.

In the proposition quoted Kant uses the word 'good' twice ('... für *gut* könnte gehalten werden, als allein ein *guter* Wille'). Nothing, he says, is (*a*) 'good' without qualification except (*b*) a 'good' will: but apparently the word 'good' means something quite different in the second use from what it means in the first. In sense (*a*) 'good' seems to mean 'desirable', since 'good without qualification' is contrasted with 'good and desirable in many respects but not without qualification', the one being applied to a certain type of will (the 'good will'), and the other to gifts of fortune, etc. What does he mean by 'good' in sense (*b*)? We know, from the subsequent development of his argument, that by the 'good will' he means 'the law-reverencing will'. The proposition could therefore be stated in the form: 'It is impossible to conceive anything ... which can be regarded as unqualifiedly (*a*) *desirable* except a (*b*) *law-reverencing* will.' Hence, in sense (*a*) the term 'good' is being used in what I should call a genuinely valuational sense, while in sense (*b*) the term 'good' is being used descriptively, 'good' meaning 'law-reverencing'.

Now if 'moral goodness' or 'moral value' be understood in sense (*b*)—if it be the quality of the will indicated when Kant, for

[1] Paton's translation, p. 61.

instance, speaks of the 'good will'—then it would be perfectly
true to say that the foregoing theory of the comparative value
judgement has nothing to do with moral value or moral goodness.
This is indeed a point on which I have insisted from the outset.[1]
Any theory which dealt with moral goodness in this sense would
be a theory of the 'moral' judgement, not a theory of the 'value'
judgement as I understand it. A theory of the 'good will' which
attempted to explain the nature of 'goodness' in this sense would
be a theory of the nature of virtue, or moral obligation, or (perhaps more strictly) of that quality of will which is expressed when
a person does what he thinks he 'ought' to do. Valuation, as I
have used the term, has nothing to do with the conception of
'ought' or 'obligation'; and my own personal view (which, however, is quite irrelevant here) is that Kant's theory of the ultimate
ground of obligation—of the 'good will'—is the most far-seeing
and sound analysis of the moral judgement which has ever been
made in the history of ethics.

But it is an entirely different matter if 'good' is to be understood
in sense (a) as equivalent to 'desirable'. If we use it in this sense,
and say that 'the good will is good, and even unconditionally
good', we are not asserting that the law-reverencing will is unconditionally law-reverencing, while talents of the mind or gifts
of fortune are merely 'conditionally', or 'with qualification', or
'only relatively', law-reverencing. We are asserting that the
law-reverencing will is desirable; and, as Kant would have it, it is
even unqualifiedly or unconditionally desirable; while talents of
the mind and gifts of fortune are only qualifiedly or conditionally
desirable. This is a truly valuational sense of the term 'good'.
Kant is passing a value judgement on the law-reverencing will;
and he is apparently passing a comparative value judgement on it,
in so far as he calls it unqualifiedly good in contrast to other things
which are only relatively good. So far as he is making a comparative value judgement on the law-reverencing will, then, the
theory developed in the foregoing chapters does profess to express
the principles governing his judgement (in so far as this
value judgement is one to which he would adhere after thinking

carefully about the meaning of the terms he has employed).

We are now in a position to return to the two possible lines of criticism which, it was suggested, might be made against our theory. It might be argued (a) that we do make comparative value judgements on the 'good will' which do not follow the principles explained in our theory of the comparative value judgement; or it might be argued (b) that we do not make comparative value judgements about the 'good will' in the sense that we never for a moment contemplate weighing its value against that of anything else.

(a) Let us consider the first of these possible criticisms. To avoid ambiguity, we should not speak of the 'good' will when we are thinking of Kant's sense of the 'good will'. But we cannot assume general agreement that this means the 'law reverencing' will. Let us therefore call it the 'virtuous will'; or, better still, let us assume that what we are speaking about is 'virtue'. The objection we have to answer, then, is that we do not, in our comparative value judgements where virtue is concerned, value in accordance with the principles of the foregoing theory.

Perhaps one of the clearest statements of a view on which such an objection would be based is found in Ross's chapter on 'Degrees of Goodness' in *The Right and The Good*. He has argued that there are three intrinsically good things, virtue, knowledge and pleasure; and he proceeds to a discussion of the question whether these are either comparable or commensurable in value. His conclusion is that they are all comparable but not all commensurable. We can say that pleasure or knowledge is less valuable than virtue, and we can say (unless the amount of pleasure is very large and the item of knowledge very small) that knowledge is more valuable than pleasure; but we cannot measure the value of virtue against that of knowledge or pleasure to the extent of saying that a given amount of pleasure or knowledge would have more value than a given amount of virtue.

Faced by the question, '*What* amount of pleasure is precisely equal in value to a given amount of virtue?' ... I see no possibility of an answer or of an approach to one. With regard to pleasure and virtue, it seems to me much more likely to be the truth that *no* amount of pleasure is equal to any amount of virtue, that in fact virtue belongs to a higher order of value, beginning at a point higher on the scale of value than that which pleasure ever reaches; in other words, that while pleasure is comparable in value with virtue (i.e. can be said to be less valuable than virtue) it is not commensurable with it, as a finite duration is not commensurable with infinite (p. 150).

When we turn to consider the relative value of moral goodness and knowledge as ends, here again I am inclined to think that moral goodness is infinitely better than knowledge. Here too the question seems to become clearer when one considers these two goods not in the abstract but as objects to be striven after for ourselves as individuals. When I ask myself whether any increase of knowledge, however great, is worth having at the cost of a wilful failure to do my duty or of a deterioration of character, I can only answer in the negative. The infinite superiority of moral goodness to anything else is clearest in the case of the highest form of moral goodness, the desire to do one's duty. But even of the lesser virtues the same appears to be true. And if virtue is always the thing best worth aiming at for oneself, it is the thing best worth trying to promote in others (pp. 152-3).

A view of this kind is quite clearly a rejection of any suggestion that a comparative value judgement involving virtue and knowledge, and still more virtue and pleasure, as alternatives would be in terms of marginal utilities in accordance with the 'law of equilibrium'. And yet it is difficult to see how Ross can be so confident about the point when it is considered that, in countless cases, what we do is precisely to evaluate virtue in accordance with that law. Valuation is the making of a choice or preference in a given situation when we have to choose between alternatives, both of which we want. If, say, knowledge and virtue are both regarded as good, this does not mean that we shall necessarily evaluate them against each other. We may not need to do so. We may be in the fortunate position—as are, presumably, the angels in Heaven—that to have the greatest possible amount of one is perfectly compatible with having the greatest possible amount of the other. But if, in any given case, they are alternatives between which we must choose, then we evaluate them against each other. It follows from this that there can be no sense in asking whether we think virtue in the abstract better than knowledge in the abstract; for, in the abstract, if it were impossible to have both, this would be a logical, not a factual, impossibility. It would be as impossible for the angels or God as for us. But we do not suppose that to seek both virtue and knowledge is to seek a self-contradiction. We suppose that they can both be achieved to some extent; and that, in so far as they are alternatives in a choice situation, this is because of the particular objective situation itself. So far, then, what applies to securing bags of corn, cups of tea, pounds of potatoes or helpings of jam-roll applies also to acquiring virtue or knowledge. In so far as we are driven to evaluate them against each other, this is because the particular situation presents the hard alternatives: either this particular expression of virtue or this particular acquisition of knowledge must be renounced. We evaluate, not in universals, but only in particulars in given situations.

If we consider a particular case involving the valuing of virtue, it is difficult to avoid the conclusion that our valuations conform to the law of equilibrium, as in all other cases, whether we are evaluating talents of the mind, food and clothing or gangster bodyguards. Thus, an employer complains that much waste goes on in his factory because some of the operatives are seriously defective in a sense of duty towards the enterprise. His friend may suggest a remedy. He may say: 'I know A, B, C and D who are extremely conscientious fellows, and they happen to be out of work. It is true that they are not so intelligent or technically skilled as the men you normally employ, but you will find them absolutely first rate so far as honesty and conscientiousness are concerned. Or—if they do not appeal to you as suitable—I know E, F, G and H who have got all the technical ability and intelligence you normally demand, and they are, in addition, completely reliable. Indeed they are now, because of this reliability, in positions of some responsibility; so that you will have to pay them a rate considerably higher than you are offering if you want to secure their services.' The answer of the employer may well be: 'I fear that neither of your solutions is helpful. A, B, C and D will, no doubt, exhibit all the virtues I require to a satisfactory degree; but, as you say, they will be defective on the technical side. E, F, G and H will have to be paid more; and that will produce a demand for an all-round increase of wages for men in my factory engaged on that kind of job. I simply could not stand the cost, in view of what my goods fetch on the market. I am better, on the whole, to put up with the position as it is.' What the employer is, in effect, saying is that he does not evaluate virtue as such; he evaluates, in a certain context, a particular virtue of a certain degree, and the value he sets upon it is relative to the function it performs in some enterprise as a whole. For this enterprise he requires not only virtuous disposition but also certain skills, machines, materials, premises, etc.; and the resources at his command have to be distributed over these requirements. There comes a point when an 'additional amount of virtue' is less valuable than a 'certain amount of knowledge'. The marginal utility (demandedness) of virtue, knowledge, machines, premises, etc. shifts with any shift in composition of the complementary demands or amount of resources, in accordance with the law of equilibrium. Perfect skill and complete lack of virtue would be worthless. Perfect virtue and complete lack of skill would be worthless. There must be some of both; but an additional degree of virtue at a certain point will be of less value than the amount of skill (or of something else) which would have to be sacrificed to secure it.

It may be suggested that this illustration has nothing to do with the position adopted by Ross. The illustration is concerned with an employer's valuation of virtue as a mere means to an end, while Ross is talking about the comparison of the 'intrinsic goodness' of virtue with that of other things such as knowledge and pleasure. It is, I think, extremely doubtful whether we are using words with any intelligible meaning when we say both that things are 'intrinsically good' and also that one has a goodness 'superior' to that of another; but I shall let this pass. Suppose that we can speak of evaluating against each other things which are 'intrinsically good', *as* intrinsically good and not as contributing to some end, how are we to discover how people do actually evaluate them? Here again, it must be remembered that valuation is a choice between alternatives, either, but not both, of which the person concerned can have in a given situation. We cannot evaluate 'intrinsic goods' any more than we can evaluate 'instrumental goods' in the abstract; for 'alternatives' in the abstract would be logical alternatives. We always evaluate in concrete situations where the objective order, on this particular occasion, enforces a choice.

To see how we evaluate virtue, knowledge and pleasure in concrete situations, then, we must look at the ways in which a person will utilise his resources when the distribution affects the extent to which virtue, knowledge and pleasure, respectively, are likely to be produced. Now societies for the rehabilitation of habitual criminals help in the production of virtue; the possession of books helps in the production of knowledge; the possession of wine helps in the production of pleasure. And according to the view we are considering (that no amount of knowledge or pleasure, however great, can equal in value any amount of virtue, however small), if we are to choose according to our valuations (and choice *is* the outward expression of valuation), then we shall never choose to spend a farthing on books or wine unless we are satisfied that, irrespective of their effects on the production of knowledge or pleasure, these expenditures also promote virtue to a greater extent than would have been possible on any other method (e.g. a subscription to 'The Criminal's Friends, Ltd.') known to us. Is that, indeed, how we make up our minds in deciding whether we should buy a bottle of wine, a coveted first edition or a ticket for *The Mikado*?

It may, of course, be suggested than an argument of this sort is merely slick; and that the life devoid of knowledge and pleasure can exhibit but a distorted and unlovely 'pussyfootish' sort of virtue. To give all our spare ten shilling notes to 'The Criminal's Friends, Ltd.', or to decide that it is better to spend some of them on wine and Gilbert and Sullivan *because* indulging in these pleasures will increase our virtue more than the money would have promoted the reform of criminals, and *not* because the wine or song will give pleasure, would be the mark of the insufferable prig, to say nothing of its being the unpardonable insult to any self-respecting wine merchant or Savoyard. A robust healthy virtue (the argument may continue) develops only in those who, within reasonable limits, pursue knowledge and take their pleasures as intrinsically good, and not as merely instrumental goods; for, taking the long-term view, virtue will be more truly developed if people are not always thinking about being virtuous and supporting deserving causes from a sense of duty, but are sometimes concerned with the pursuit of knowledge and pleasure, as ends, for themselves and others, without any thought of their ulterior implications for virtue.

Now this sort of reasoning may be sound wisdom and common-sense; but for a defender of Ross's view to indulge in it is to jump with both feet on to a very slippery slope. It means that, when confronted by a situation where there is a definite choice between increasing virtue (by subscribing to the rehabilitation society) and indulging in pleasure (by spending the money on wine or the theatre), it is *sometimes* the pursuit of pleasure which has the higher value. It will not do to say, 'Oh, but this is because virtue is, in the long run, best produced by selecting pleasure in this instance'. It will not do to say this, because, on the argument, anyone who says so writes himself down as an insufferable prig. He must choose the pleasure as his real objective, as an intrinsically good thing; and therefore he must not be influenced in his choice by the conception of pleasure as a means to the production of virtue. That is to say, he is, in this particular case, on this particular occasion, giving the production of a certain amount of pleasure a higher value than the production of a certain amount of virtue; and probably most of us would say, 'Stout lad! Good luck to him!' At any rate, what we are here describing is a person who, in his general habits of life and his valuations over a long period, is evaluating 'intrinsic' goods as the factory employer is evaluating 'instrumental' goods; he is valuing virtue, knowledge and pleasure (and everything else) in accordance with the law of equilibrium.

(*b*) The second possible objection to the claim for the universal applicability of our theory of the comparative value judgement was that we do not, in fact, make comparative value judgements about 'moral goodness' or virtue, in the sense of weighing its value against that of anything else. As Kant puts it, we regard the good will as good without qualification, although we regard all other things as merely relatively good.

o

Now if this were really true, then of course our theory of the comparative value judgement could not possibly apply to our value judgements on virtue, for our theory is a theory of the comparative (not of the simply positive) value judgement.

Is it true? The foregoing discussion under (a) should make us extremely sceptical of any such contention. The view has, however, been held. It was held—or at least asserted (which is not quite the same thing)—by Kant; and curiously enough Ross comes to hold something like this view in *The Foundations of Ethics*. We have already remarked on the point.[1] While in the earlier work Ross considered that pleasure and virtue are comparable but not commensurable, he came to the conclusion, on further reflection, that if they are even comparable, we have to admit that, theoretically at least, there is a point at which a certain amount of pleasure will have a higher value than a certain amount of virtue. As he is not prepared to accept the conclusion that virtue can ever be less valuable, he feels bound to deny comparability.[2]

But if two things are not comparable in value, this means that they can never be alternatives for a rational being. To compare values is to assign degrees of goodness; and this comparison is inseparably bound up with the activity of choice itself. The reader may be wearied by insistence on the point, but we must repeat that choice is neither more nor less than the expression of valuation, and valuation is the comparative value judgement. If, then, we deny that virtue and pleasure are comparable in value, we are at the same time denying the possibility of a choice situation with 'virtue' and 'pleasure' as the alternatives. To deny this possibility may mean one of two things. It may mean, *firstly*, that the universe is never so harsh a taskmaster as to present us with such alternatives, that we never compare the values of virtue and pleasure because the securing of the one never does and never can interfere with the securing of the other; the 'choice situation' never does in fact arise, so far as these two things are concerned. On this view, it would be very difficult to understand why the two are so often supposed to be harsh alternatives; and we should,

---

[1] See footnote to p. 82 above.   [2] *F. of E.*, p. 275.

I think, have to reconsider some of the stock criticisms of hedonism.

To deny that virtue and pleasure can be alternatives for rational choice may mean, *secondly*, that, though the universe does on occasion present virtue and pleasure as alternatives, we are in fact incapable of making any rational choice in such a situation. This would be a strange view to take. If I see, or believe, a certain line of conduct to be my duty, and a contrary line of conduct to be conducive to much more pleasure than would be afforded by taking the former line, is it really impossible for me to make a rational choice, to evaluate, to prefer to take the one line rather than the other, knowing what I shall gain and lose in each case? I do not know what the defender of this later view of Ross would answer to such a question; and it is not very profitable to speculate. It may be that the assertion of incomparability was made without realising all the implications, particularly the implications with regard to the psychology of choice.

One final observation. It would not, I think, be proper to say that we have 'proved' that 'moral value' or 'moral goodness' or 'virtue' is assessed in value in the same way as other things, namely in accordance with the concept of marginal utility and the conception of common demand. We have not been concerned to 'prove' this, but merely to answer the objection that our theory of the comparative value judgement is defective as a theory of the comparative value judgement in general—that it is inadequate to cover the case of 'moral values'. No one can prudently claim for any theory that it is so true and perfect that it will never stand in need of modification; and the imperfections which are discovered in theories are either logical defects or failures to cover facts which the theories profess to cover. But every theory is at least an attempt to cover a certain inter-related group of phenomena; and the contention is that the theory here developed is, broadly speaking, adequate to explain our comparative value judgements generally. It can at least be said that such objections as we have considered—objections designed to remove 'moral values' from the field which the theory might truly be said to cover—have not been found particularly plausible

3. The 'Summum Bonum' and the 'Principle of Economy'

We shall now attempt to complete the analysis of the nature of valuation. Valuation is the choice between combinations of the contents of different expressions of demand, and therefore postulates a common demand in every valuational order. Further, there is no theoretical limit which can be set to the extent to which different valuational orders may be synthesised under increasingly comprehensive common demands. Whenever, and so far as, choice is required and made, to that extent a common demand is implied.

What, then, is the ultimate ground of the comparative value judgement? It may be thought that this is a premature question in view of the fact that we have not yet discussed the nature of the simply positive value judgement—the attribution of goodness itself. The conception of something as good is more fundamental than the conception of it as having a particular degree of goodness. Hence it may be considered that the ultimate ground of the conception of degree of goodness (and hence the ultimate ground of the comparative value judgement) must lie in the notion of goodness itself.

But this would be a mistaken line of argument. It seems to assume—or at least might lead us to assume—that the comparative value judgement is based on the notion of an 'end', the 'chief good' or *summum bonum*; and that, as we shall presently see, is precisely the point at issue. I think that the real nature of the question we are now concerned with may best be put in the following way:

To attribute comparative value to anything is to attribute, by implication, goodness. But to attribute goodness is not necessarily to attribute value (a comparative degree of goodness). We only evaluate things against each other when we have, hypothetically or really, to make a choice between them. The conception of goodness, therefore, while *a* necessary ground of the comparative value judgement, is not a sufficient ground. It does not explain why one good thing should be considered better or worse than another; and what we are now trying to understand is just the ultimate ground, not of the notion of the goodness of things, but of the 'better-ness' and 'worse-ness' of good things. Assuming the simply positive value judgement of goodness on both X and Y, on what ground, ultimately, do we base the comparative value judgement upon them?

In seeking an answer to this question we may cast our eyes hopefully in one or other of two directions. We may suppose that the ground must be some sort of 'end'; or we may think that it must be some sort of 'principle'. To illustrate the significance of this distinction it may be helpful to refer to the analogous problem in connexion with the moral judgement. The Greek moralists, or at any rate Plato and Aristotle, thought that the ultimate ground of the notion of virtue is the idea of the 'good' or the 'chief good'; and, following this line of thought, some of the best known modern schools, notably Utilitarianism and Idealism, have accepted the 'idea of the good' as the ultimate ground of the notion of duty. The fundamental concept is that of the *summum bonum*. On the other hand, while Kant reflects this view to a considerable extent, what seems to me to be his main contribution to ethics is that line of thought in which he conceives the ultimate ground, not as an 'end' in the proper sense of 'end', but as a regulative 'principle' operative in our minds. It is the principle of respect for the pure form of juridical law—in other words, respect for personality universally—which regulates our pursuit of ends when we act from a sense of duty. On this view, the ultimate ground of the moral judgement is the principle of the 'autonomous self-legislative will' rather than the idea of an 'absolute end' or *summum bonum*.

As the present work is concerned with the value judgement and not with the moral judgement, the foregoing remarks are offered, of course, not to recommend a particular theory of the moral judgement, but merely to show how an 'end' theory may differ from a 'principle' theory.

Now, superficially, it would seem that, with regard to the comparative value judgement, the ultimate ground must be the notion of the *summum bonum*. We cannot measure degrees of goodness without postulating some common demand, the content of which must, of course, be an 'end' to us. Further, the more we synthesise our valuational orders, the more comprehensively must we envisage the common demand. We can set no theoretical limit to the extent of this synthesising process. Is it not plain, then, it may be urged, that the whole inspiration of the synthesising process is the *a priori* concept of the *summum bonum*?

There are, however, serious difficulties in this view. If there is any concept operating *a priori* in valuation, then its influence must be discernible, on reflection, in *every* valuation. To say that this *a priori* concept is the *summum bonum* is to say that the ground is the conception of an 'end'. But an 'end' has always a content, something which can be envisaged as an 'objective' to strive after; and the real difficulty is to discover any such 'objective' which is presupposed *a priori* in *every* valuation.

To illustrate the point, let us consider the Aristotelian—and indeed the popular—view that the 'chief good' or supreme end is 'happiness'. If this is an 'end' in any proper sense of the term, the content of the end must be capable of being stated as we can state the content of a demand, for it will in fact be an *a priori* content of demand. The statement, 'This book should be completed in ten weeks from now', is the statement of the content of a (hypothetical) demand, or an end. But is 'happiness' an end which can be stated in such a way? Aristotle realised that, if happiness is an end, we must be able to describe it in some more or less intelligible way as an objective towards the realisation of which we can direct our action. He comes to the conclusion that, for man, 'happiness' consists in the 'development and exercise of his rational nature'. Assuredly, this could be *an* end. It could be the end for which a person might (wisely or mistakenly) undertake the study of logic. But it is plainly not the *summum bonum* in the sense required—in the sense of an end postulated *a priori* in every comparative value judgement. 'This kind of lipstick is better than that' could be (though it is not necessarily) a comparative value statement. The same is true of 'Nothing like Bloggs boots for happy hikers!' Is there any necessary reference in either of these to the development of rational nature?

There is, indeed, no way of giving real content to the notion of 'happiness' such as will make it a significant 'objective', and, at the same time, preserve its universal character as that which is presupposed in all comparative value judgements. We have no difficulty in agreeing that 'all men seek happiness', so long as we do not take this expression strictly and try to translate the concept of happiness into an 'end'. This suggests that, while 'happiness' is a significant concept, it is not an end, but simply an idea of the maximum realisation of all such ends as form the contents of our demands in the course of our lives. The point is well made by Kant.[1]

Unfortunately the concept of happiness is so indeterminate a concept that although every man wants to attain happiness, he can never say definitely and in unison with himself what it really is that he wants and wills. The reason for this is that all the elements which belong to the concept of happiness are without exception empirical—that is, they must be borrowed from experience; but that none the less there is required for the Idea of happiness an absolute whole, a maximum of well-being in my present, and in every future, state. . . . Happiness is an Ideal, not of reason, but of imagination—an Ideal resting merely on empirical grounds, of which it is vain to expect that they should determine an action by which we could attain the totality of a series of consequences which is in fact infinite.

The same observations apply if, for 'happiness', we substitute 'self-realisation'.

The case against the theory of an 'absolute end' or the *summum bonum* as the ultimate ground of the comparative value judgement may be put—conclusively, I think—in this way:

The ultimate ground of comparative value judgement must be *a priori* in the sense in which Kant held that certain principles or categories of the understanding, such as 'substance', 'causality', and so forth, are *a priori* grounds of all theoretical judgement. These principles, he holds, are operative in our minds whenever we make a theoretical judgement claiming to be true (whether it is in fact true or false is immaterial). Similarly, an *a priori* ground of valuation must be one which can be shown to be operative in every comparative value judgement (however much the judge-

---

[1] *Groundwork*, Paton's translation, pp. 85-6.

ment may be disputed). Now we can say with confidence that
every comparative value judgement presupposes a common demand or common 'end'; but to say that it postulates an absolute
end or *summum bonum* is to go beyond what the situation requires.
It is to go beyond the requirements of the situation because the
difference between the notion of 'common demand' and the
notion of the *summum bonum* is this: the former refers to the
postulate made when alternative ends are actually evaluated
against each other, but not necessarily made when there are different ends pursued but not evaluated against each other; while
the latter refers to something which is supposed to be implied in
our having different particular ends at all, whether they are evaluated against each other or not. It is quite patent, therefore, that
to postulate the *summum bonum* as the ultimate ground of the
comparative value judgement is to go beyond what the comparative value judgement actually requires. There is a necessity about
the conception of the 'common demand', and there is no necessity
whatsoever about the conception of the *summum bonum* so far as
the act of valuation is concerned.

Thus, to evaluate *A, B* and *C* against each other postulates the
common demand *X*; and to evaluate *D, E* and *F* against each other
postulates the common demand *Y*. But we cannot infer from
this that *X* and *Y* are themselves expressions of a still more comprehensive common demand, the demand for the *summum bonum*.
X and *Y* may not in fact be evaluated against each other, and
therefore there is no evidence (from the valuation of *A, B* and *C*,
or the valuation of *C, D* and *E*, against each other) that *X* and *Y*
are expressions of a common demand. If we are forced to evaluate *X* and *Y* against each other, then we do at once postulate a
common demand *Z* of which they are the expressions. But this
postulation of *Z* arises from the purely contingent fact that *X*
and *Y* are actually being evaluated against each other. There is
no reason for supposing that they *must* be so evaluated (in fact
they may not be), and therefore no reason for supposing that
they *must* assume a common demand.

Hence the comparative value judgement does not presuppose
as its *a priori* ground the conception of the *summum bonum*.

It will probably be wise, at this point, to warn the reader against a possible misunderstanding of the foregoing argument. The argument is *not* offered as a proof that there is no such thing as the *summum bonum*. That is to say, we are *not* arguing that, if X and Y are not evaluated against each other, they *cannot* be the expression of a common demand Z. We are merely arguing that the *summum bonum* is not necessarily implied in every comparative value judgement; and are not arguing that the conception of the *summum bonum* is incompatible with a theory of the comparative value judgement as here expounded.

Thus, although X and Y are not evaluated against each other, they may nevertheless be expressions of a more comprehensive common demand Z. I may, for instance want to travel abroad (X) and I may also want to run a car (Y). I may evaluate against each other different schemes for my foreign travel (A, B, C); and I may evaluate against each other different makes of car (D, E, F). A, B and C are all expressions of the common demand X; and D, E and F are expressions of the common demand Y. These two different valuational orders do not, in themselves, postulate any relation between X and Y. X and Y may not be evaluated against each other; and therefore the valuations made with respect to X and to Y respectively do not postulate Z to which X and Y must be assumed to be relative. But while Z is not postulated for purposes of the valuations, it may nevertheless be true that X and Y are in fact expressions of a common demand Z. Z may be a project I have for writing a book about the eighteenth-century Jacobites; and the demands for X (the continental travel) and Y (the car) may be but expressions of the common demand for Z, the car being desired for travelling around the Highlands collecting material for my book. The fact that I am fabulously rich, and never have to give a thought to a possible choice situation involving the continental travel and the car as alternatives, and therefore do not need to evaluate X and Y against each other, does not detract from the fact that X and Y are in very truth expressions of Z.

In short, we are not discussing the question whether and to what extent all our ends are, without exception, expressions of some total common end (though any assertion that there is such an end has still to meet the difficulties pointed out by Kant and left unresolved by Aristotle); we are only discussing the question as to what is implied *a priori* in the comparative value judgement. Our argument is this: When we have distinguishable ends X and Y, either or both being common demands postulated in one or two valuational orders, this does not presuppose *a priori* that X and Y are expressions of a more common demand, Z. That they are such expressions may be shown in either of two ways: they must be if they do indeed become evaluated against each other; and it may be shown that they are in fact such expressions even though they never need to be evaluated against each other; but the proof that X and Y are expressions of Z will in both cases be based on empirical grounds; either on the empirical ground that a particular set of circumstances enforces a choice, or on the empirical ground which connects the two as parts of a single project. But the conception of the *summum bonum* is not supposed to be a mere generalisation from experience. It is supposed to be an *a priori* postulate respecting the relationship of all our possible ends; and such an *a priori* postulate is not implied in the comparative value judgement.

We must, then, abandon the search for the ultimate ground of valuation in terms of the conception of an 'end'. The alternative is to seek it in some kind of 'principle' native to and operative in the human mind in every valuation.

With this latter alternative in mind, let us look once more at the conception of 'happiness'. There is no difficulty, we have seen, in agreeing with the popular view that, in some sense, we all do as a matter of fact seek happiness or self-realisation, so long as 'happiness' or 'self-realisation' is not conceived of as an 'end' or 'objective' in the proper sense. But if happiness is not an end in the proper sense, what is meant by saying that we all do seek it?

It would seem that the notion of happiness as a pseudo-end really arises from the obscure awareness that all demands imply the demander—a unitary self-conscious subject aware of itself as unitary, and expressing its nature in all its diverse demands. That is to say, the unifying principle in demand is not to be found

objectively in the content of demand—in the notion of 'end'—
but subjectively in the nature of the demander. The conception
of 'happiness' or 'self-realisation' is a kind of pseudo-concept, an
'ideal of the imagination' which we project as a fictitious objective;
but we have the tendency inevitable to this imaginative way of
thinking because there is in fact a genuine awareness of ourselves
as unitary self-conscious agents, as single subjects-of-ends, expressing our nature in diverse ways through specific demands.

This unitary self-consciousness expresses itself in all our conative
life underlying valuation. When we try to give this awareness
an explicit formulation, to express it as a conative ideal, we speak
in terms of 'the most complete satisfaction' or 'happiness'. The
awareness of ourselves as unitary agents is present in all our demanding whether we are evaluating things or not. That is to say,
if we could suppose a blessed state in which there was no scarcity
of resources, we should still attempt, in 'technical' or 'efficiency'
and 'aesthetic' judgements, to co-ordinate our uses of resources in
the search for the perfect equilibrium of satisfactions. We should
not conceive of 'marginal units' of equilibrium or utility, because
marginal units only arise when resources are scarce. But we
should, freed from the conditions in which the 'law of diminishing
and increasing utility' operates, still make calculations on technical,
administrative and aesthetic grounds, at least, so as to select from
the richness of our inheritance the combinations of things suited
to the complete satisfaction of our demands; and we should do so
because our unitary self-conscious nature requires such a form of
rational activity.

Now it is this same principle which is operative under conditions of scarcity; but in conditions of scarcity it induces us to
evaluate alternatives in accordance with the law of equilibrium
and marginal utility; and, as so operative, we call it the 'principle
of Economy'. Hence the ultimate ground of the comparative
value judgement is the principle of Economy.

Having reached this conclusion, it will be evident that there is
one further point requiring explanation. A great deal of time and
argument have been devoted to establishing what was said to be
a fundamental point in the theory of the comparative value judge-

ment, namely the postulate of 'common demand' in every valuational order. But, it may be asked, has not this been something of a waste of time and labour since, in the final analysis, we reject the notion of 'end' in favour of that of the 'principle of Economy' as the ultimate ground of valuation?

I do not think that there has been any waste of time here.. It can, I think, be shown that our final conclusion makes more intelligible the notion of the common demand. What we were arguing, in support of the proposition with regard to common demand, was not that this is the ultimate ground of valuation, but simply that it is necessarily presupposed in all valuation. What we now see is that the ultimate ground is the principle of Economy. How have we to express the relation between the concept of common demand and that of the principle of Economy? The best way to express this relation is to say that, while the notion of common demand is necessarily implied in every valuation, common demand is itself dependent on the existence of the principle in ourselves as unitary agents which, in conditions of scarcity, is called the principle of Economy. Common demands are generated through the awareness of ourselves as unitary agents. They could be generated in circumstances where scarcity did not apply, as has been explained in the illustration given on page 201. But in conditions of scarcity they are bound to be generated through the operation of this awareness in the form of the principle of Economy. To explain this point:

It is probably natural, though in fact a mistake, to suppose that our theory of common demand postulates a pre-existing hierarchy of 'common demands' all lying ready to function as their services are required—as a hierarchy of courts may exist, all ready to function as appeals pass from the lower to the highest. But that is not the view here adopted. Common demand may indeed exist before it is called on to function for purposes of valuation; but it may not. There are many situations where it is the necessity to make a choice which compels us to formulate the common demand in order that the choice may be made. There are situations where we find ourselves with two or more demands which have no obvious relation to each other, but in circumstances which make it impossible to satisfy both. It is in such cases that the principle of Economy operates to generate common demand in the sense of making us formulate, as clearly as the situation requires, a conception of what, on the whole, we really want, so as to enable us to choose rationally between the alternatives (or some other possibility which, on reflection, reveals itself).

For example, suppose that a woman has embarked on a medical career to which she is much attached, and then receives a marriage proposal which is very attractive to her. She may not have to choose between her professional career and marriage; she may be able to have both. But the circumstances may be such that she has to choose the one at the cost of the other. We cannot assume that there was any original connexion between these two demands. Let us say that there was none. Nevertheless, it will be necessary to think out, on a broad basis, the quality of life she wants to lead, to consider what are the dominant tendencies demanding fulfilment, and how far one combination of activities will compare with another with respect to opportunities for living 'the fullest possible life'—a life which must in some form or other include some satisfaction for those aspects of her nature which attract her to her professional career, and also those aspects which give attraction to the prospect of marriage. She has got to formulate and make explicit to herself this 'overall demand'; and she must formulate it with a clarity sufficient to show how it bears on the alternatives open to her before she can exercise a rational choice between them. It may be said that she will not choose rationally at all; but that is a rash assumption; and, so far as it is true, we are not concerned with her case. We are concerned with the theory of rational valuation and choice; and the point of the illustration is that we have not here a pre-existing common demand ready to come into operation when required. We have, initially, two demands, between which there is no obvious connexion at all; the common demand, on the basis of which choice must be made between them, is generated because a choice situation has in fact arisen; and it is generated by the operation of the principle of Economy.

Hence, to repeat the final conclusion of this analysis of the comparative value judgement: Common demand is postulated in all valuation; but it is the principle of Economy which is the ultimate ground of the comparative value judgement, because it is this principle which drives us to evaluate, and because it is this principle which also operates to generate common demand, if such does not already exist, without which valuation cannot take place.[1]

[1] The argument of Part I has concentrated on the formal analysis of the principles of valuation, and illustrations of their practical application have been of the simplest kind. As to how these principles actually express themselves in the major realms of human experience, creating and sustaining individual ways of life and social institutions, the reader is referred to Professor Macbeath's recent Gifford Lectures, *Experiments in Living*.

Professor Macbeath does not accept the emphatic distinction I draw between the 'value' and the 'moral' judgement. Broadly speaking, he regards the moral judgement as the supreme form of the value judgement. He therefore introduces moral concepts into his theoretical analysis in contexts where I should not.

But this important difference affects my agreement with his main line of argument rather less than might be supposed. For this there are two reasons. Firstly, I think that our moral judgements, being assessments of what is objectively equitable or categorically imperative in a given situation, have the force of judgements of matter of fact as constituents in our 'apprehension' of the objective situation presenting us with choice alternatives, and have therefore a powerful influence on our effective value judgements (see below, pp. 310-18). Secondly Professor Macbeath is concerned not only to state the principles of valuation but also to exhibit them in action in important realms of experience. He is therefore taking the value judgement at a level on which I agree that moral judgement is exerting its influence. On this level, it is our substantial agreement on the nature of value judgement (see e.g. *Experiments*, pp. 57-65 and 404-21), rather than our disagreement on the relation of 'value' to 'moral' judgement, which is most in evidence. With Macbeath, I would say that the older Idealist theory, despite its defects, had a sounder approach to the problem of valuation (as distinguished from the problem of obligation) than its twentieth century critics; and I also agree that his restatement of the 'self-realisation' theory (as a theory of valuation) has removed its major defects and transformed it into a powerful instrument for the purposes to which he has applied it.

PART II
THE ATTRIBUTION OF GOODNESS

Chapter Seven

GOODNESS AND APPROVAL

The Problem of Goodness

In surveying our general problem,[1] a distinction was drawn between the conception of value and the conception of goodness.[2] By presupposing the validity of this distinction, we were able to take it for granted that valuation is essentially comparative. It appeared that we were doing no injustice to any school of thought in making this assumption, since the distinction was found to be inherent in the views of objectivists such as Moore and Ross who, of all contemporary philosophers, would naturally look with most suspicion upon relativist assumptions. Both of them distinguish between the questions (*a*) What things are good? and (*b*) What are the relative degrees of goodness (values) which different things possess? The second of these questions is concerned with comparison, and comparison is a matter of relativity.

It is true that we have been concerned with a question rather different from the one with which Moore and Ross were concerned. They were discussing the 'value or goodness which things are asserted to possess' and the question whether this is something intrinsic to the things of which it is predicated. We have been concerned with the question as to the nature of the subjective activity which we call the value judgement. But this transformation of the issue does not affect the importance of the distinction between the problem of goodness and the problem of degrees of goodness. It is just as necessary to distinguish the question (*a*) What is the nature of the attribution of goodness to a thing? from the question (*b*) What is the nature of the attribution of a degree of goodness (value) to a thing? as it is to observe this distinction when we profess to be talking about goodness as a quality of the thing concerned.

[1] See the Introduction.   [2] P. 20.

The validity of the distinction being taken as granted, then, we concentrated in the subsequent chapters on the nature of valuation. Our task now is to analyse the subjective activity which consists in the attribution of goodness to things. In attributing value, we are assigning to a thing a place in an order. In attributing goodness, we are characterising the thing as a member of that order. In this and the following chapters I shall adopt the plan used in the analysis of valuation. The main steps in the argument will be set out in a series of propositions, such explanation and commentary as are necessary being subjoined.

PROPOSITION IX

All things, and only those things, to which we attribute goodness can be members of a valuational order.

This first proposition, like our first proposition in the theory of valuation, is of the nature of an initial postulate which may, without prejudice, be accepted by all. It helps to make clear the fundamental meaning to be attached to 'goodness' in all the subsequent argument. We make no assumptions with regard to the subjectivist-objectivist controversy. We are merely indicating that 'goodness' is the term we propose to use in designating 'that in virtue of which a thing is potentially a member of a valuational order'. 'Goodness' only confers potential membership, because, as the theory of valuation has made plain, things are not evaluated unless they are alternatives in an enforced choice as well as being esteemed good. But this requirement of choice being taken for granted, we can best indicate the sense in which 'attribution of goodness' is to be used by saying that it signifies 'that which is the fundamental condition of membership of a valuational order.'

PROPOSITION X

The attribution of goodness or badness is the expression of approval or disapproval.

Here, it would at first sight appear, we plunge into the heart of the great controversy. But that is not the case. We are still on ground which is, one understands, common to all parties in the subjectivist-objectivist controversy. It may be taken for granted that the subjectivists will not dissent from our proposition; and it only remains to show that it is acceptable also to the objectivists. One need not argue that all objectivists without exception will agree. It will be sufficient to show that the proposition is not felt by all objectivists to be incompatible with the essentials of their position. For the purposes of our argument, therefore, we may consider how this proposition would be viewed by Ross.

Taking the relevant sections[1] of *The Right and The Good* and *The Foundations of Ethics* as expressing generally the same point of view, Ross's position may be summarised thus:

When we ask what there is 'common' to all things which we call good, we have to be content with the primary definition of 'good' given in the *Oxford English Dictionary*. 'Good' is 'the most general adjective of commendation, implying the existence . . . of characteristic qualities which are either admirable in themselves or useful for some purpose.' Goodness in a thing depends upon its having specific qualities of a certain sort; but the sort of quality which is relevant depends upon the nature of the thing. Thus the goodness of an action (Ross is here bringing in the 'moral' issue, but the point need not be discussed in the present context) depends upon the fact that the action has sprung from a certain kind of motive; the goodness of an intellectual activity depends upon the fact that it is an instance of knowledge; the goodness of an affective state depends upon the fact that it is pleasant.

But the question may be raised: Granted that goodness depends or arises consequently upon the presence of these various qualities, can we not say that, when they are present, we can also discern a characteristic common to each and all of the things called good, this common characteristic being the quality we denote by the term 'goodness'? The answer is 'Certainly not; there is no such common characteristic discernible to which the name "goodness" can be applied'.

Nevertheless, there is something which is common to every situation in which we call things good. The universal precondition—and apparently the only one—of our using the word 'good' is the existence of a favourable attitude, an attitude of commendation or approval, in us towards the things in question. The attribution of goodness is the expression of approval. We must, of course, be clear as to the distinction between 'expression' and 'meaning'; for what we express is not the same as what we mean. But, still, it is true that one thing we are doing when we call a thing good is expressing approval of it.

[1] See *R. and G.*, pp. 131-2; and *F. of E.*, pp. 254-5.

Now I am not at the moment concerned with all that is implied in this view of Ross. Some important questions will have to be raised in subsequent stages of our argument; but our sole concern at present is with the question whether our proposition, as it stands, is acceptable to both objectivists and subjectivists. The agreement of subjectivists can be taken for granted; and it appears very plain that Ross, an objectivist, is committing himself explicitly to precisely this proposition. 'What we *express* when we call an object good is our attitude towards it. . . . When we call an object good we are commending it'.[1]

That there should be this common ground is immensely helpful to us in taking our departure and setting the course for our voyage of discovery. Since we may take it that the attribution of goodness is at least the expression of approval, and since what we are specially interested in is the subjective activity constituting this attribution of goodness, we are able to concentrate on the analysis of the nature and presuppositions of approval itself.

PROPOSITION XI

Approval is primarily a conative, not a cognitive or an affective, attitude.

1. THE COGNITIVE THEORY

With this proposition we do embark on controversial issues of considerable importance; for it would, I think, be rejected both by the extreme objectivist and also by the extreme subjectivist who holds what has come to be known as the 'emotive' theory of goodness. The proposition is so fundamental to the main thesis of this book—as the conception of 'common demand' was fundamental to the theory of valuation—that its discussion will occupy us for some time.

Let us start with the question whether approval can be regarded as a cognitive attitude.

It will be convenient to adopt the old terminology which distinguished three aspects of mental life as cognitive (knowing, etc.) affective (feeling) and conative (willing and suchlike). The valid-

---

[1] *F. of E.*, p. 255.

ity of these distinctions will have to be discussed later; but, for the time being, it may be taken for granted. What, then, is the nature of our question? It is the question whether that special subjective activity which we call approval is cognitive or not. We might be led to the conclusion that the activity is essentially cognitive, but that it implies the existence of some prior or subsequent conative or affective activity. Now the latter part of this conclusion—if this were our conclusion—would, no doubt, be of very great interest; but it would be a conclusion with respect to the antecedents or consequents of the act of approval. It could not in any way detract from the first part of the conclusion, namely that the activity of approval in itself is cognitive, and not conative or affective. Precisely the same thing would hold if we came to a different conclusion—that approval is itself a conative (or affective) activity but presupposes the prior or consequent operation of some cognitive activity. The fact that cognition was a pre-condition of approval would not make approval itself a cognitive activity. It would be conative (or affective).

From the general line of argument adopted by objectivists, it is natural that they should lean to the view that the act of approval which constitutes the attribution of goodness is a cognitive activity. Let us therefore put the view that it is conative, and see how a philosopher such as Ross would be inclined to react. Approval, we may say, must be regarded as conative for the following reasons: When I commend or approve of something, I am expressing an active tendency in myself to bring it into existence or to maintain it in existence if it is already there. I am not suggesting the 'truth' that 'the thing is there'. I am expressing myself in such a way as to indicate that I 'want it to be true that the thing is there'; I want this thing with such and such qualities to exist. The 'wanting the thing to be' is something quite different from 'apprehending that it is'. The latter is an instance of cognitive activity; the former is not. If, then, following Ross, we regard the existence of this non-cognitive activity as the universal pre-condition of the ascription of goodness to anything, we must be regarding the ascription of goodness as a non-cognitive activity.

The argument just presented is not by any means logically impeccable. There is some confusion between an activity and its preconditions. But our chief interest at the moment is not in this somewhat crudely presented argument. It is in the sort of reply which an objectivist, such as Ross, would probably make. Ross does not, so far as I recollect, deal specifically with the question whether the attribution of goodness expresses a conative attitude. His main preoccupation is with the question whether it can be regarded as an assertion of a 'feeling' state in the subject judging; but how he would receive the suggestion that the attribution of goodness is essentially the expression of a conative attitude may perhaps be inferred from the line of argument he takes.[1]

The substance of his argument, so far as relevant to our present problem, may be given under two main headings, (1) the distinction between 'expression' and 'meaning' and (2) the relation between 'feeling' and 'judgement' in the attitude of approval.

(1) *'Expression' and 'meaning'*: Following Meinong, Ross holds that language performs a double function. It expresses our state of mind; it also means or refers to the object of that state of mind. Thus, what we express when we call a thing good is a state of mind called approval; but what we mean is something about the object itself and not about our attitude. To commend or approve of a thing is not to say that we are commending or approving of it. It is to say that the object has a certain character, a character which we think it would have whether we were commending it or not.

Now this insistence on the distinction between expression and meaning either (*a*) begs the whole question at issue, or (*b*) leaves us precisely where we were before the distinction was made.

(*a*) The first alternative is that it begs the question. Our question is whether approval is or is not a cognitive attitude. We can express cognitive and conative and affective attitudes; this I think will be admitted. But can conative and affective attitudes 'mean' something? If they cannot 'mean' anything, then we beg the question by bringing in the distinction as though it were relevant. If conative and affective states cannot 'mean' anything, to say that approval expresses a state of mind, but means or refers to the

[1] R. and G., pp. 131-2 and F. of E. pp. 254-5.

object, is to assume that approval must necessarily have a meaning
as well as an expression. But it will have no meaning at all if it is
not cognitive (on the supposition that conative and affective
activities have no meanings); and therefore to say that it means
such and such is to assume that it must be cognitive. This, however, is the very question at issue.

(b) The second alternative is that the distinction contributes
nothing to the solution of the question and leaves us precisely
where we were. For, suppose that conative and affective states
of mind do, like cognitive state, have meanings. Then the fact
that approval has a meaning as well as an expression does not
prove that the state of mind expressed is cognitive. It could perfectly well be conative or affective.

(2) *Relation between 'feeling' and 'judgement' in approval.* The
second consideration which would seem to be relevant is Ross's
contention that the attribution of goodness expresses either an act
of apprehension or an act of which the precondition is an act of
apprehension. That is to say, he seems to hold that approval is
either a cognitive act or presupposes a cognitive act. Thus, when
contrasting beauty and goodness,[1] he tells us that in predications
of beauty—in attributing beauty to things—we find it impossible
to make such a predication unless we have first derived aesthetic
enjoyment from the thing; the 'feeling' is the primary factor and
the 'judgement' is based upon it; but in our attitude to those
objects called good, the opinion or judgement that they are good
seems to be the primary factor, and the 'feeling' (of approval) to
be consequent upon this. If we ask ourselves what 'approval' is,
we find that 'the basic element in it is not feeling at all but the
judgement that an object is good'. Again, we are told in round
terms[2] that it is impossible to approve of anything without thinking it worthy of approval—without thinking that it has a goodness of its own which makes it fit to be approved.

Now the first comment on all this is, I think, a fairly obvious
one. Ross has not quite made up his mind which of two quite
distinct and incompatible statements he wishes to defend. He
can say (a) that approval is essentially a cognitive activity, that

[1] *R. and G.*, p. 131.   [2] *F. of E.*, p. 261.

the basic element in it is not feeling at all but the judgement that an object is good. Or he can say (b) that the approval is an affective (or conative) state, but that it only arises as a consequence of the opinion or judgement that the thing is good. He can say either of these things, but he cannot consistently say both; and the trouble is that he does try to say both.

(a) If he really wishes to defend the first statement—that approval is itself a cognitive state, that its basic element is a judgement and not a feeling—then this puts in rather a new light what one supposed to be the difference between Ross's view and that of the 'emotivists'. Both are saying that to assert goodness is to express approval; but Ross thinks that 'to express approval' is the same as 'to state a truth', while the emotivists think that expressing approval is different from stating truth. I shall not at present pursue the problems which confront anyone who takes the view which Ross seems here to be maintaining. They are very considerable as we shall see later[1]; but it would be unprofitable to go into them now, for the reason that Ross is at least as much inclined to another and quite incompatible view, namely that approval is not itself an opinion or judgement but is consequent upon an opinion or judgement.

(b) Turning then to this second view, the thesis would seem to be that approval is a state which supervenes upon a judgement that a thing is good or worthy of approval.

This is the sort of thesis which one might reasonably expect an objectivist to maintain. But it is one which Ross cannot maintain without retracting what he has said on other occasions. Two difficulties seem to present themselves.

(i) In trying to show that the basis of approval is a judgement that the object is good, he argues[2] that the judgement and not the feeling must be the significant factor, because 'we can give an account of what the goodness of good things depends upon without introducing any reference to the feelings they produce in a spectator'. Thus the goodness of an action depends upon its springing from one or other of certain motives; the goodness of an intellectual activity upon its being an instance

---

[1] See pp. 230-8.   [2] R. and G., p. 132.

of knowledge; the goodness of an affective state on its being pleasant. But surely there is a serious confusion here. What he is professing to show is that 'a judgement of goodness' is pre-supposed in approval. What he is actually showing is that we must be aware that actions have certain motives, intellectual and affective states certain qualities, before we can approve of them. Granted that we must judge these qualities (which are patently not what is meant by 'goodness') to belong to the things before we approve of them, this is an entirely different thing from saying that a 'judgement of goodness' is presupposed.

(ii) But perhaps the really conclusive reason, on Ross's own showing, for rejecting the view that approval presupposes a judgement of goodness is this: If it be true that 'the only universal precondition of our using the word ('good') is the existence of a favourable attitude (approval) in ourselves towards the object'; then it cannot also be true that the judgement that a thing is good is primary, and the approval consequent upon this judgement of goodness. My reason for paying attention to this present point is not that it runs counter to our proposition now under discussion —the proposition that approval is conative not cognitive—for it would be consistent to hold that approval is a conative activity and also to hold that approval supervenes upon the attribution of goodness in a theoretical judgement; but that it runs counter to our Proposition X which stated that the attribution of goodness or badness *is* the expression of approval or disapproval, a propo-sition which Ross supports in saying that the universal precon-dition of our using the word good is an attitude of approval in ourselves.

Where do we stand now with regard to the assertion that approval is a conative and not a cognitive or affective attitude? So far, we have advanced no positive argument in favour of the view that approval is conative. We have merely been engaged in negative criticism of arguments purporting to show that it is cognitive.

2. THE AFFECTIVE THEORY

In this next stage of our argument we shall continue this negative form of criticism, but shall direct it now against those who seem to hold that approval is an affective attitude; that when we attribute goodness to things we are expressing our feelings or emotions. There is a tendency nowadays to suppose that, if the attribution of goodness does not express a cognitive attitude, it must be the expression of an affective or feeling state. I speak of this merely as a tendency, for there are many philosophers who do not go from one extreme to the other; and it may well be that some of those who profess to adopt the emotive theory are not altogether clear in their own minds whether they wish to lay the stress on conation or on feeling.[1] It is important that we should not be misled into confused argument through failure to distinguish between conation and feeling. I propose, therefore, to consider in a very general way the plausibility of the view that, when we attribute goodness to anything, we are expressing not a cognitive, and not a conative, but merely an affective attitude.

In assessing the merits of such a view we must be guided mainly by what the psychologists have to tell us about feeling and its

[1] C. L. Stevenson's *Ethics and Language* contains perhaps the best-known statement of what is called the 'emotive' theory. His discussion of particular topics is often acute and stimulating; but he frequently uses the term 'emotive' when the nature of his argument suggests that 'conative' would be more appropriate. I agree that no state of mind can be exclusively cognitive, conative or affective (see below, pp. 223-8); but if we distinguish these three aspects at all, we must be clear as to which one we are emphasising in any given context. Stevenson does recognise that he is to a very great extent dealing with conative attitudes; but a general recognition of this sort, without a careful analysis of the value judgement so as to show the significance of the affective and the conative elements respectively, can lead only to confusions, giving a certain plausibility to an 'emotive' theory precisely because it is not, properly speaking, an emotive theory.

This criticism of Stevenson in particular, and of the 'emotive' school in general, is, I think, strongly supported by a consideration of the papers in the symposium on 'The Emotive Theory of Ethics' in the *Aristotelian Society* Sup. Vol. XXII. While my own positive views on the nature of the value judgement are, I think, different from those of Professor Paton, I find myself in substantial agreement with his two main charges against the 'emotive' theory. Firstly, I consider that any theory which proceeds on the assumption that one can lump together value judgements and moral judgements, under the general heading of 'ethical statements' or 'ethical attitudes', is bound to produce muddled arguments and un-illuminating conclusions. Secondly, even if the emotivists had made this necessary distinction between the 'value' and the 'moral' judgement, and had professed to be dealing only with the value judgement, I consider that their theory fails to appreciate the difference between an 'emotive' and a 'conative' theory of the value judgement.

relation to cognition and conation. I do not pretend to be well versed in contemporary psychological theory; but, for the limited purpose we have in view, we are presumably safe in taking any recent reputable text-book as a sufficient guide.[1]

Apparently the terms 'feeling' and 'emotion' are not synonymous. Feeling is the affective state considered in abstraction from cognition and conation. In this case, the conception of 'feeling' may be considered without any definite reference to motor activity directed towards the alteration or maintenance of a situation, for it is merely an internal condition and, by itself, produces no external results. There is, of course, the question whether feeling can ever exist without any tendency to action. But, so far as there can be 'mere feeling', to that extent there can be an internal state which does not issue in external action of any kind.

Feeling is, however, often demonstrably associated with a motor tendency; and this is the situation which is of interest to us in connexion with the theory of goodness, since, according to the 'emotive theory', in attributing goodness or badness, we are to some degree expressing a tendency towards changing or maintaining a state of affairs. It is significant that those who speak of the 'so-called value judgement' as an expression of our affective nature do not use the somewhat colourless term 'feeling'. They use the rather more explosive term 'emotion'.

Now, psychologists, I understand, regard emotion as the feeling-tone of a 'motor set' or a tendency towards activity. It is the 'moved' or 'stirred-up' feeling associated with such a tendency. Sometimes, indeed, emotion is the term used to describe the whole state which includes the motor set and its feeling tone. Thus the emotion of anger may be described as the set towards attack, fear as the set towards flight, and so forth. But, whether 'emotion' should signify the whole conative-affective state, or merely the stirred-up feeling characteristic of a motor set, this is a point to be settled by those concerned with the systematic exposition of psychological doctrine. Whatever be the decision on this point,

[1] E.g. *Psychology* (20th edition, 1949), by Woodworth and Marquis, Chapter XI, 'Feeling and Emotion'.

our main contention is not affected. We may take the James-Lange theory, or any other one; but I think that no contemporary psychologist maintains that 'mere emotions' as such can be described and distinguished from each other. We distinguish them either by reference to organic processes or by reference to an objective situation of which the subject is aware, and by the type of overt conative response which he has a tendency to make.

This general view of the nature of an emotion may be illustrated with reference to 'fear'.

Fear arises under the following main conditions: There is some 'end' towards which the subject is strongly disposed. A set of circumstances arises constituting an imminent threat to its attainment. The threat is so strong that the subject has no confidence that the resources at his command will be adequate to meet it.

The strength of the emotion will not depend upon the importance he attaches to the end alone (though this is a factor), nor upon the magnitude of the danger, nor upon the magnitude of the effort required to overcome it. It will depend upon the importance attached to the end plus the extent to which the subject lacks confidence in the adequacy of his power to meet the danger. Thus, if the end is relatively trivial—such as that of reading the morning paper before going out to work—any disturbance of expectation may cause annoyance, but will not cause fear. Again, if the threat is to personal freedom, or to life or limb, or to one's house by an approaching fire, or to some scheme into which one has thrown one's enthusiasm and resources, fear will not arise if one is confident that, however great the threat, one's power to meet it is greater still. If, however, there is a lively sense of the importance of the end and, at the same time, of defective power, fear tends to be aroused. If the threat comes with such suddenness and menace that the significance of its outcome grips the imagination, the subject may become so mentally adjusted to the idea of the consummation of the threat that this 'expectation adjustment' inhibits any effort to counter or even escape from it. He becomes 'stupid with fear', and does not even take obvious measures which an outside observer sees to be perfectly practicable. The response is of the 'all-out' type. But if, in this state of mind, some method of evasion occurs to him, there will again be an 'all-out' response, but a response of a different type—one of intense activity in the manner suggested by the avenue of escape, and this escape-response may take the form, not of flight, but of attack. Here fear does not make the subject 'stupid'. It 'lends superhuman strength to his arm and courage to his heart'. It is not courage in any proper sense of the term. It is recklessness which shows little evidence of the influence of reason; it may take the form of throwing all caution to the winds, or behaving with utter brutality, because the mind is intensely concentrated on this specific response to the inhibition of all other considerations. The concentration can become so complete that the end from which the fear initially drew its significance may be forgotten, and fear be replaced by a different emotion, the sense of exhilaration in carrying out the response itself.

If this is an approximately correct account of fear—or even if it is seriously wrong in many respects—it shows that the attempt to explain the nature of an 'emotion' has to be made by putting a 'feeling' into a cognitive and conative context. One has to postulate a strong prior conative tendency towards some end, and the cognitive awareness of a threatening situation. The rise, fall and transformation of the emotion of fear into a different kind of emotion are all described in terms of the interplay of the cognitive and conative aspects of the subject's psychical states. It may be quite significant to say, in general terms, that the emotion of fear indicates disapproval of that which constitutes the threat. But it would be very strange indeed to suppose that one is 'explaining' this disapproval by saying that it is 'the expression of an emotional and not a cognitive or conative state'; for you can offer no explanation of what an emotional state is without describing it in terms of the interplay of conative and cognitive activities. The most commonly accepted view in psychology, I understand, is that, while the cognitive aspect of the psychical state cannot be ignored, emotion is best regarded as the affective aspect of motor sets or activity tendencies. That is to say, it is most intimately associated with conation. Since it is not self-explanatory in the sense in which the terms cognition and conation appear to be, it is not a particularly useful conception for explaining the nature of the 'attribution of goodness'.

3. PRELIMINARY STATEMENT OF CONATIVE THEORY

So far, our arguments in support of the proposition have consisted of attacks on other views. No really positive evidence has been adduced in favour of the contention that approval is a conative attitude. Before developing the argument more positively, it may be helpful if I state, quite dogmatically and somewhat crudely, the position I shall try to establish; and it will be convenient to define my own view over against that of Ross, saying how far I agree and how far I disagree with him.

(1) I accept Ross's contention that there is no common quality which we apprehend in things when we call them all 'good'. His case on this point is, it seems to me, well made out.

(2) Consequently, I agree with him that, so far as the objective order of things is concerned, the attribution of goodness arises from the awareness of specific qualities in things, these qualities differing from thing to thing. For instance, there is presumably a difference between the kind of quality in an action which makes us attribute goodness to the action and the character we call knowledge which makes us attribute goodness to a cognitive state. I do not necessarily agree that virtuous action, psychical states of knowledge, and affective states which are pleasant, stand out from all other things to which we attribute goodness, because I am not prepared to accept his doctrine of intrinsic goodness. But that difference in our views is of minor importance so far as my present point is concerned. The point is that I agree that the objective grounds of the attribution of goodness are specific qualities in the things we call good, there being no common quality (goodness) which we apprehend in all those things.

(3) I accept his view that, on the subjective side, the assertion that a thing is good is an expression of approval of the thing.

(4) But, taking all these three points together, I come to a general conclusion rather different from that which commends itself to Ross. The position, as it appears to me, is this: We perceive certain actions done from certain motives, certain psychical

states to be instances of knowledge, certain affective states to be pleasant (I take Ross's examples for simplicity's sake), these states of affairs all being apprehended by us in cognitive activities. Immediately we become aware that those actions, and those cognitive and affective states are so qualitatively characterised, we respond with an attitude of approval (which is a non-cognitive activity), and express this approval by saying 'That action (or cognitive or affective state) is good'. The attitude of approval thus depends and is consequent upon a prior cognitive activity; but the cognition is not of any 'quality' called 'goodness'. It is the cognition of a thing with specific qualities (the action done with a certain motive, etc.); and it is the cognition of this which directly evokes the approval and its expression in an attribution of goodness. There is not, sandwiched in between the cognition of the thing with its specific qualities and the attitude of approval, something which may be called a further cognitive apprehension (the apprehension of 'goodness'). It is the approval itself, supervening directly upon the cognition of the thing with its specific qualities (none of which is a quality 'goodness'), which is expressed as the 'judgement' of goodness. This approval, since it is not an apprehension of what exists in the objective order, but a response to such an apprehension, is not a cognitive attitude. It is a conative attitude, a 'conative disposition' as distinguished from an overt conative activity.

This is admittedly a purely dogmatic statement of a view, and not an argument. The view is stated here simply to indicate the direction which the subsequent argument will take.

4. APPROVAL AS CONATIVE

(1) *Distinction between 'Cognitive', 'Conative' and 'Affective'*

The first point to consider is the basis of the distinction between the cognitive, conative and affective aspects of psychical life. How far are these distinctions themselves valid; and, if they are valid for certain purposes, have we any ground for supposing that they are ultimate?

There is one consideration which may perhaps throw some doubt upon the validity of the distinctions, and this is the information we derive from physiologists. The nature and functioning of the nervous system suggests that, if any parallel can be drawn between the activity of the nervous system and psychical activity, psychical activities must be all of the same kind.

The reason for this suggestion will be clear if we consider the nature of nervous activity, beginning first with reflex action. The whole course of a reflex action, such as blinking when a small object is suddenly thrust close to the eye, from the first application of the stimulus to the muscular movement of blinking, involves the activity of several neurons. A neuron is a nerve cell having branches connecting with other such cells; and the path traced through those neurons from the sense organ to the muscle is called the reflex arc. Now, leaving aside the question of 'feeling', we can, if we wish, distinguish the total activity in the reflex arc into the cognitive and the conative stages. The impulse passing through the neuron immediately connected with the sense organ would quite definitely be cognitive, and the impulse passing through the neuron immediately connected with the muscle would quite definitely be conative. But, taking account of all the neurons which compose the reflex arc, how far does the cognitive activity proceed before it becomes transformed into the conative; and does the nature of the activity in the nervous system change when it is transformed from cognitive to conative? It appears that any line drawn between cognitive and conative aspects of the reflex arc would be quite arbitrary, and would indicate, not different kinds of activity, but merely the fact that at the one end we have the reception of a stimulus, and at the other end an active response.

This will be clearer if we assume that a reflex arc could be made up of one neuron only, connecting at the one end with the sense organ and at the other end with the muscle (although I understand that the simplest reflex arc contains several neurons). The nature of the 'impulse' travelling through this neuron would be of precisely the same nature from beginning to end; and its 'cognitive and conative aspects' would be convenient distinctions drawn by us to indicate that the nerve cell has received a stimulus (cognition) and transmitted it to the muscle (conation). The reception and transmission would be the first and the last stages of a homogeneous process or activity.

The position is really no different if we take account of the fact that a reflex arc is composed of several neurons. The neuron connecting with the sense organ transmits what is apparently an electro-chemical 'wave' through the nerve fibre to the neuron next in line; and it is an impulse of precisely the same character which is transmitted from the second to the third, the third to the fourth, and so on, until it reaches the neuron directly connected with the muscle.

Apparently this applies not only to those neurons which operate in reflex action but also to all those, without exception, which make up the nervous system. The fundamental structure of all is the same; the nature of their activity is fundamentally the same. Every one of the millions of neurons constituting the nervous system is engaged in the activity of transmitting an impulse in the form of an electro-chemical wave to its next in line astern. This is true whether we are dealing with those which make up the simplest reflex arc or with those constituting the cerebrum with which conscious life is supposed to be most intimately connected. Apparently there is some localisation of function within the cerebrum—motor area in the frontal lobe, auditory area in the temporal lobe, etc.—but these are spatial areas, and there is no suggestion that the fundamental nature of the cells or of the activities varies from area to area.

Hence, if we were to attempt to draw any kind of inference from what is known of the nervous system, there would be nothing to suggest that, on the psychical plane, there are activities which are different in kind, such as we normally suppose cognition and conation to be.

But considerations of this sort may be completely irrelevant. However closely physiological and psychical activities may be related—even if they are actually the same activity from the points of view of two different universes of discourse—the factors most significant in physiology may not be those which are most signi-

Q

ficant in psychology. It may even be doubted whether our pro-
pensity to distinguish between cognition, feeling and conation,
has anything to do with our knowledge or ignorance of physiological processes. In our inner experience we can draw significant
distinctions between knowing and feeling and willing; and perhaps the terms cognitive, affective and conative are merely representative of the attempt to furnish a systematic account of the
human mind, starting with the 'facts revealed in inner experience'.

How far contemporary psychology is inclined to retain this
terminology I am not certain. The terms do not appear in some
discussions of psychological problems in which I should have expected them to occur; and it may be that the philosopher who
continues to use them is out of date. However that may be, the
problem with which I am now concerned presupposes that the
terms do have some significance. There would be no 'objectivist',
'subjectivist' or 'emotivist' theories of the value judgement if
these distinctions were not supposed to stand for real differences
in our psychical make-up.

Whatever may be in doubt, then, we may take it for granted
that the distinctions referred to are accepted by the various philosophical schools; and I think we may also take for granted the
assumption that there is no such thing as an exclusively cognitive
—or conative or affective—'mental state'. Every mental state has
all three aspects. Hence, when we disagree as to whether approval
is cognitive, affective or conative, the question is not whether
approval is a mental state consisting wholly of one of these. The
question is rather more complicated. In speaking of 'approval'
we may ordinarily have in mind a total mental state with special
emphasis on one of its three aspects; or we may, while agreeing
that every complete state has all three aspects, be attending exclusively to one of these aspects. It will, I imagine, be agreed that
traditional logic is interested, not in the total mental state with an
emphasis on the cognitive aspect, but exclusively in the cognitive
aspect. It also seems clear that modern psychologists (particularly
Freudians), even when specially concerned with the study of our
reasoning processes, are not interested exclusively in the cognitive
aspect but rather (when theorising about our inferential processes)

in the total mental state with an emphasis on the cognitive aspect.

Now it seems that our theoretical interest in approval is like the interest of the modern psychologist in 'reasoning', rather than like that of the traditional logician. If we were really exclusively interested in one aspect, it is extremely unlikely that we should find cognitive *and* conative *and* affective theories of approval widely canvassed. It would almost certainly be generally agreed (as, I take it, in logic) that considerations arising from two of these are irrelevant to the problems we are studying. The fact that all three types of theory of approval have their champions strongly suggests that we are really concerned with a total state of mind; and the difficulty is to be certain as to which aspect is being emphasised when we are said to 'approve', rather than 'know', 'will' or 'feel'. Almost certainly the main emphasis is being laid on one of the aspects, x, rather than y or z; and we have to find out which is x.

(2) *Level of Psychical Development Presupposed in Approval*

There is one further general question of the greatest importance. At what level of psychical life do we suppose approval, properly speaking, to emerge? While it is true that every mental state, at every psychical level, has cognitive, conative and affective aspects, the cognitive aspect at least shows great variations. There is, in man, the level of 'reflective cognition', or 'self-consciousness', or 'awareness of awareness of things'; but, even in man, cognition is present in lower forms, some of which, so far as we can make out, are shared by man and animals fairly low down in the biological scale. Do we think it proper to speak of 'approval' when discussing, for instance, the 'psychology of fish'? When a fish is attracted by bait, can we ever say that the fish 'approves' the presence of the morsel, and violently 'disapproves' the hook caught in its mouth? Many would warn us sternly against using terms such as 'think', 'desire', 'infer' and 'choose', in these connexions; and, so far as I can discover, they would also exclude the term 'approve' as illegitimate. They may be right or wrong in being so cautious, but that is not the important point. The important point is—as I understand—that, if they warn us against using con-

cepts appropriate to the higher form of psychical life, they seem
to deprecate the use of the term 'approve' or 'disapprove'. That
is to say, they appear to regard approval as appropriately used
only when we are dealing with the higher psychical levels, presumably the level of reflective cognition, there being no approval
in the proper sense unless we are aware of our awareness of that
which elicits our approval. To take this view does not imply that
a sharp line can be drawn between the reflective and the non-
reflective cognitive levels, or that a given experience can unhesitatingly be placed in one or other of the categories. It merely
implies that, in so far as we hesitate to place a mental state in the
reflective category, to that extent we hesitate to use the term
'approval' in connexion with its 'pro-attitude'.

Probably we are safest in taking this view. It would, indeed,
seem to be the only possible view when we are considering the
significance of approval in connexion with the 'value-judgement',
in the wide sense, as that which attributes goodness or some degree
of goodness to a thing. We must here, surely, be reflectively aware
of that to which the judgement refers.

(3) Approval 'Potentially Formative of', not 'Informative about' the Objective Order

Granted, then, that, when we speak of 'approval', we are thinking of a total mental state which, on the cognitive side, belongs
to the reflective level; the question is, which of the three aspects
—cognitive, conative or affective—is receiving the emphasis? For
reasons already given, I trust that I shall be excused from considering the 'emotive' theory, and for assuming that the really serious
issue is between the 'cognitive' and the 'conative' theories.

When we speak of cognition, we are thinking of those aspects
of psychical life, such as perceiving, reasoning and believing,
which are concerned with the apprehension of the nature of things
as they are, were, or will be; and when we speak of conation, we
are thinking of those aspects, such as willing, striving and desiring,
which operate as 'forces' determining what the nature of things
will be. Cognition is 'informative about' the objective order,
conation is actually or potentially 'formative of' the objective

order. Is approval 'informative about', or is it actually or potentially 'formative of', the objective order?

It must be clearly understood that we are here discussing the
nature of approval, and not the nature of its expression. There are
various problems concerning the 'expression of approval' which
will be dealt with in our next chapter.

Restricting our discussion, for the present, to the nature of
approval itself, it seems hardly intelligible to say that approval is
cognitive. I can cognise that the three internal angles of a triangle
equal two right angles; the cognition is 'informative about' this
aspect of the objective order. I can hardly imagine anyone asking
himself whether he approves or disapproves of this fact about
triangles. I can also cognise that my rich old uncle is alive and
well; and this cognition is also informative about that part of the
objective order. But, in this case, I can well imagine myself asking
whether I approve or disapprove of the fact cognised; and my
approval or disapproval will be 'potentially formative of' this
particular part of the objective order. If I approve of that which
I cognise or apprehend (that my uncle is alive and well), I shall
tend to take the steps in my power which I consider conducive
to his continuance in life and health. If I disapprove, I shall omit
to take such steps, and possibly take steps to bring about his death.
Now if my 'approval' of my uncle's condition were the same as
my 'apprehension' or 'cognition' of his condition, if it were informative about the objective order, then to approve of his being
in life and health would be the same as to perceive, know or
believe him to be in life and health, and to approve of his being
killed (i.e. of his not being in health or life) would be precisely the
same as to perceive, know or believe him to be dead.

We all know that this is not the way in which the terms
'approval' and 'disapproval' are used. Approval does not mean
'cognitive apprehension'. To say 'I apprehend (cognise) the fact
that A exists', and also, 'I do not apprehend the fact that A exists'
would be to contradict myself. But there is no such contradiction
if I say, 'I apprehend the fact that A exists', and also, 'I do not
approve the fact that A exists'. Or to say, 'I apprehend the fact
that A is x', and then add, 'I do not apprehend the fact that A is

x', would be a contradiction; but it would not be a contradiction if I had added, instead, 'I do not approve the fact that A is x'.

To elaborate on this point would be a waste of time. It is so clear that there seems no ground on which one could plausibly maintain that approval is cognitive or informative about the objective order. Or, putting the case more accurately, there seems no case for the view that, when we speak of approval, we are laying the emphasis on the cognitive aspect of the total mental state.

(4) Theory of Approval as Cognition of 'Non-natural' Quality

I imagine that those who hold the cognitive theory would readily agree with the essential point made above. But their contention, apparently, is that our conclusion follows only when we limit our attention to the relation of approval to 'natural' existence and 'natural' qualities. The whole point about approval, they would say, is that it is the cognition of a 'non-natural' quality, 'goodness'; and (they would continue) we do get a real contradiction between an 'apprehension' statement and a 'disapproval' statement if the quality for which x stands is not a natural quality such as colour, sound, and so forth, but the non-natural quality, goodness. To say, 'I apprehend that A is good', and also, 'I do not approve of A', would be just as much a contradiction as to say, 'I apprehend that A is good' and also 'I do not apprehend that A is good' or 'I apprehend that A is not good'. Approval must therefore be primarily cognitive; but it is the apprehension of the specific non-natural quality, goodness.

It will not be unfair, then, to say that the defenders of the cognitive theory of approval rest their case entirely on this allegation that, in approving, we are cognising a non-natural quality; and that if this ground is found to be indefensible the case for the cognitive theory goes. How difficult both the attack and the defence must be will be appreciated if we note the peculiarities of the situation. The cognitive theory based on such a ground can make no use of illustrations, analogies or parallels drawn from cognition in the ordinary sense (i.e. our cognition of 'natural' qualities); for its whole case is that arguments based on cognition of natural qualities are completely irrelevant. The case has to be expounded and defended entirely within the four corners of the conception of approval as a 'cognition of the non-natural quality, goodness'. The criticism, for those who do not accept this view, must be conducted wholly along the lines of a straightforward examination of the logic of the doctrine.

The doctrine that approval is cognition of the non-natural quality, goodness, may mean either of two things. It may mean either (a) that approval is a very special kind of cognition the object of which we call goodness, or (b) that approval is cognition of a very special kind of thing, goodness.

(a) Approval as Special Kind of Cognition

On this view the fundamental distinction between approval and other forms of cognition will be a subjective, not an objective, distinction. If we were permitted to argue from the analogies of 'cognition of natural properties' (which, on the non-naturalistic theory, we are not), we might say that just as there are various forms of 'sensing' distinguished as 'seeing', 'hearing', 'tasting', so (on the view) there will be different forms of 'cognising', 'approving' being one of these. And just as we can have different kinds of 'sensing' the same thing (seeing and hearing the same trumpet, for instance), so we can 'approve' and have other forms of cognition of the same thing.

Now we can distinguish between different forms of 'sensing' by indicating the organs of sensing. We talk of seeing when we sense through the eyes, hearing when we sense through the ears, and so forth. If we were permitted (as we are not) to ask what are the 'analogous' distinctions between the methods of 'cognising' in different ways, we might expect that anyone holding the view that 'approval' is a particular *kind* of cognising would indicate some 'mental organ' or 'faculty' of approval.

About the only thing we can say about this view (if indeed anyone does really hold it, which is a matter for doubt) is that it is suspiciously like a subjectivist, rather than an objectivist, theory of goodness. This is all we can say, in the absence of any champion to defend and explain it; for it is useless to undertake any elaborate discussion of what it *might* mean, in view of the fact that speculation as to what it might mean would inevitably be based on 'natural' analogies.

As a matter of fact, I do not think that anyone, nowadays, who holds the view that approval is a cognitive activity has suggested that approval is a special kind of cognition. The view seems to be that approval is the cognition of a special kind of thing, namely the non-natural quality, goodness.

(b) *Approval as Cognition-of-Goodness*

On this view, approval is not, in itself, different from any other form of cognition. We call it approval rather than cognition-in-general simply because it is the cognition of a special object, namely goodness; just as we speak of 'marginal utility' when referring to the utility attached to the 'marginal unit'.

The question to be considered is whether, on this view of the nature of approval, we can explain why it is thought that the statement 'I approve A' is equivalent to 'I apprehend A to be good', and that there would be a real contradiction in saying both that I approve A and also that I do not apprehend A to be good.

Throughout the whole of the following argument the reader should bear in mind that I am not at all challenging the view that 'I approve A' is equivalent to 'I apprehend A to be good'. In my view these statements are so substantially the same that I should regard it as a contradiction to express disapproval of what one professes to regard as good, or to express approval of what one professes not to regard as good. The sole question at issue is whether this substantial equivalence of 'approval' and 'regarding as good' can be made intelligible on the theory that approval is the cognition of the non-natural quality goodness.

Now if approval means cognition-of-goodness, we ought to be able to express not merely the term 'approve' in terms of cognition, but also the terms 'do not approve' and 'disapprove'. It may be that 'disapprove' means exactly the same as 'do not approve'; but we must not assume such equivalence at the outset. It will be necessary to examine whether any distinction can be drawn between the two when we try to translate into cognitive terms.

Prima facie, if we translate the language of approval into that of cognition (on the assumption that approval means cognition-of-goodness), we get the following equations:

'I approve A'   = 'I cognise goodness in A'
'I do not approve A'   = 'I do not cognise goodness in A'
'I disapprove A'   = 'I discognise goodness in A'

What are the meanings and implications of these 'translations'?

I cognise goodness in A. In order to follow the logic of the position more easily let us use x to stand for 'goodness'. 'I cognise goodness in A' will thus appear as 'I cognise x in A'. This is apparently a statement to the effect that I have a certain mental state, the cognitive content of which (if I have truly described it) necessarily implies that, in the objective order, A is x.

The statement 'I cognise x in A' could therefore be contradicted in either of two ways: firstly, and directly, by the statement 'You are not, in fact, cognising Ax'. This is not a denial that, in the objective order, A is x. A may well be x. What is being denied is that Ax is being cognised by the person in question. Secondly, the statement could be contradicted, by necessary implication, by the statement 'A is not, in fact, x'. Here what is being denied is the very possibility that the mental state could have the content alleged. It is being asserted that the necessary objective conditions for the state to have such a content do not exist.

I do not cognise goodness in A. This simply denies that I have a mental state with a certain content. Here there is only one way of contradicting the statement, namely by saying, 'You are, in fact, cognising goodness in A'. The contradicting statement must be a statement about the state of mind; and any assertion about the relevant objective order would not be a contradiction either directly or by implication. Thus, 'I do not cognise x in A' is not contradicted by 'A is, in fact, x'.

I discognise goodness in A. What can this mean? If it can have any significance at all it probably means the same as 'I do not cognise goodness in A'. We either do or do not cognise. There is no intermediate concept. We can cognise in a greater or less degree; but this is still cognising, and not something different.

It might, of course, be said that, since 'I approve A' means 'I apprehend or cognise goodness in A' and since 'I disapprove A' means 'I apprehend that A is bad', then 'I discognise A' means 'I cognise badness in A'. Now granting (as I do grant) that 'I disapprove A' means 'I regard A as bad', it appears that we can substantially equate these statements only if we take a view *other than* the view that 'approval' means 'cognition-of-goodness'. If we adopt the cognitive theory of approval we reach strange results in attempting to equate the statements. 'Goodness', on the theory under discussion, is a specific non-natural quality. 'Badness' is presumably a quite different specific non-natural quality. If, then, 'I discognise goodness in A' means 'I cognise badness in A', the statement has nothing whatsoever to do with goodness; it is a statement with respect to a quite different non-natural quality. It would indeed be strange if 'I *dis*-cognise *good*-ness in A' really meant 'I cognise *bad*-ness in A'; but this is certainly the result we reach if we attempt to explain the equivalence of 'I disapprove' and 'I regard as bad' on a cognitive theory of approval. And therefore on a cognitive theory of approval we must rule out the conception of 'discognition' ('disapproval') as relevant to the non-natural quality 'goodness'. It can be relevant only to the non-natural quality 'badness'.

We can therefore leave the term 'discognise' out of account in the sense that it must be either irrelevant or equivalent to 'do not cognise'.

What is most significant, then, about these 'translations' of the language of approval into the language of cognition? It is this: If these are genuine, *bona fide* translations into the language of cognition, then the language will be subject to the conditions governing the language of cognition. Now the most important point here, for purposes of the present discussion, is that, when we are making statements about a mental state with special reference to its cognitive aspect, there are certain ways in which such statements can and cannot be contradicted. If we make a *positive* statement in the form, 'I cognise goodness in A', this positive affirmation that my mental state has a certain content may be contradicted, *either* by a denial that the mental state has that content, *or* by an assertion about the objective order ('*A* is not, in fact, good'); but, when we simply *deny* that the mental state has a certain content—'I do not cognise (or discognise) goodness in *A*' —we can contradict this *only* by a statement about the mental state ('You are in fact cognising *Ax*'), and *not* by any statement about the objective order (such as '*A* is, in fact, *x*').

Let us now ask whether these 'translations' of approval into the language of cognition are plausible. What is the proper interpretation of the language of approval itself? We should probably be suspect if we took an interpretation of our own. Let us therefore try to see what one who regards 'goodness' as a 'non-natural' quality, and who (sometimes at least) takes approval to be cognitive, has to say on the point.

The *Oxford English Dictionary* very judiciously gives as its primary definition of 'good': 'the most general adjective of commendation, implying the existence in a high, or at least satisfactory, degree of characteristic qualities which are either admirable in themselves or useful for some purpose.' Probably no more definite account than this will cover the whole variety of the applications of the word. Probably the only universal precondition of our using the word is the existence of a favourable attitude in ourselves towards the object. And this may give rise in some minds to the thought that what we are asserting of the object is that it is the object of such a favourable attitude —which would at once imply that 'good' is a relational term, signifying that there is a certain relation between the object and him who judges it to be good. To correct this, it may be enough to refer to a point made by Meinong, and thus summarised by one of his expositors:

> 'Language serves a double function: it *expresses* our states of mind and it *means* or refers to the objects of those states of mind' (J. N. Findlay).
>
> ... In the same way what we *express* when we call an object good is our attitude towards it, but what we *mean* is something about the object itself and not about our attitude towards it. When we call an object good we are commending it, but to commend it is not to say that we are commending it, but to say that it has a certain character, which we think it would have whether we were commending it or not.[1]

Ross's main point here is that 'goodness' is not a relational quality; but the passage is quoted in the present context for what

[1] Ross, *Foundations of Ethics*, pp. 254-5.

it has to say about the language of approval or commendation. His view is that, when we express approval, we are certainly expressing a state of mind, but are not saying something about that state of mind; we are saying something about the objective order. For instance, to express approval of A is not to say 'I apprehend or cognise goodness in A'. This would be to say something about my state of mind. To express approval is to say 'A is good'. But I can also express approval by saying 'I approve of A'; and, according to Ross's view, this does not really mean that I am talking about a state of the 'I'. I am *expressing* that state; but what I *mean* is something about the object—'A is good'.

Is this a plausible account of the nature of the language of approval? I think that, substantially, it is. We are drawing attention to the object—not always, but probably in nine cases out of ten—when we express approval, whether we say 'That is good' or 'I approve of that'. This comes out more clearly if we take the negative form, 'I do not approve (or disapprove) of A'. We think that a man would be talking rubbish if he were to say both 'I disapprove of A' and also 'A is good'.

Both the view of Ross and also what one understands to be the popular view, then, are agreed that to say 'I approve of A' is the same as to say 'A is good'. But this is extremely interesting when we come to consider the implications of the language of approval as so understood. If I make the affirmative statement, 'I approve A', this would be contradicted *either* by the statement 'You do not, in fact, approve A' (a statement referring to my mental state) or by the statement 'A is not, in fact, good' (a statement referring to the objective order). But again, if I make the negative statement, 'I do not approve (or disapprove) A', this would be contradicted *either* by 'You do, in fact, approve A' (referring to my mental state) *or* by 'A is, in fact, good' (referring to the objective order).

The implications of the language of approval are therefore *quite different* from those of the language of cognition. A statement such as 'I cognise Ax' can be contradicted either by 'You do not cognise Ax' or 'A is not x'; but a statement such as 'I do not cognise Ax' can be contradicted only by 'You do cognise Ax'. It cannot be contradicted by 'A is x'. When, however, we turn to the language of approval, we find that what is apparently a statement about a state of mind ('I approve A') can be contradicted *both* in the affirmative *and* in the negative form by a statement about the objective order. 'I approve A' can be contradicted by 'You do not approve A' or by 'A is not good'; and 'I do not approve A' can be contradicted by 'You do approve A' or by 'A is good'.

Since the language of approval and the language of cognition thus follow quite different principles, the inevitable conclusion would seem to be that approval cannot be a cognitive attitude.

The defender of the cognitive theory may reply: 'Ah, but you forget that approval is a very special kind of cognition. The reason why the language of approval does not follow the principles of the language of ordinary cognition is that approval is the cognition of the "non-natural" quality "goodness".' But I fear that such a defence will collapse at the blast of the logicians' trumpet. It can be shown quite clearly that, *if* approval is a form of *cognition*, then, whatever else it may be, it cannot possibly be 'cognition of *goodness*'. The proof is as follows:

According to Ross, the expression of approval, while *expressing* a state of mind, is a statement *about* the objective order. Now the proposition '(1) A is good' is clearly not the same as the proposition '(2) I cognise goodness in A'; but proposition '(3) I approve A' is, by hypothesis, the same as (1) and not the same as (2). How, then, do (2) and (3) differ? Both are about the 'I' as cognising subject; and both are, by hypothesis, expressing a cognitive attitude. The difference must therefore lie in the respective contents of the two cognitive states. Since A is common to both cognitive states, the difference must be concerned with the only remaining element, namely 'goodness'. Proposition (2) asserts goodness to be part of the content; and so proposition (3) will necessarily assert the cognition of some (undisclosed) characteristic of A *other* than goodness. Hence, if approval is a form of cognition, it cannot be the cognition of 'goodness'.

It will be observed that this argument is directed against the view that 'approve' means 'cognise goodness in'. It is not directed against the view that 'I approve A' is the same as 'A is good'. The difficulties would all be removed if it were admitted that 'A is good' is not essentially the expression of a cognitive attitude. But so long as we assert that it is, and hence that 'I approve' is essentially the expression of a cognitive attitude, we are driven to the conclusion that approval cannot be the cognition of goodness. And yet the whole point of the theory that approval is cognitive is to support the view that it is the cognition of a non-natural quality, goodness.

To sum up: We saw that, *prima facie*, cognition or apprehension of the objective order is quite different from approval. Cognition is 'informative about', while approval is potentially 'formative of', the objective order. To any such conclusion it was objected that this is true only if we take cognition and approval as applying to the world of 'natural' existence and 'natural' qualities; and that approval is really the cognition of the 'non-natural' quality, goodness. In considering this view, we noted that it may mean either (*a*) that 'approval' is a very special *kind* of cognition, or (*b*) that 'approval' means 'cognition-of-the-non-natural-quality-goodness'; but we have found that no logically coherent presentation of the view can be made out on either interpretation. On all counts, therefore, we must reject the doctrine that approval is primarily a cognitive attitude.

(5) *The Conative Theory*

Since the 'emotive' theory of approval is ruled out on the ground that 'emotion' is not itself explicable except by reference to cognitive and conative attitudes, we are left with the remaining possibility—that approval is primarily a conative attitude; or rather that, when we speak of approval, we are referring to a total mental state or activity which is at once cognitive, affective and conative, but with the emphasis on the conative aspect.

Conation, as already explained, is that attitude or aspect of our psychical state which is practically activist; it is not 'informative about', but actually or potentially 'formative of', the objective order; and perhaps the main point requiring clarification on this view is the nature and significance of the cognitive element in a total mental state of approval. If by approval we mean, not exclusively the conative aspect of a given mental state, but the total mental state with the emphasis on the conative aspect, what, in any specific case, will be the cognitive aspect corresponding to a given conative attitude?

It might be suggested that this is precisely where we have to re-introduce the assumption of cognition of the non-natural quality goodness; but, apart from all the difficulties to which we have already referred in this connexion, it is well to bear in mind the general principle of theoretical analysis that assumptions and postulates should not be unnecessarily multiplied. If we can reach an intelligible theory without assuming the cognition of goodness, that assumption will be unjustified.

There is a further weighty consideration against assuming the cognition of goodness, if this can be avoided. We have every reason to suppose that the cognitive level of psychical life implied in approval is the reflective level—that level at which we are aware of our awareness. If, then, we are seeking the cognitive aspect of the total mental state of approval, we may reasonably expect that the content of our cognition will be something of which we are quite reflectively aware. It should be pretty clear to the 'owner' of the mental state what it is that he is cognising. It should be so clearly focussed that it can be definitely indicated even if it eludes 'definition'. The remarkable thing about the view that we have a cognitive apprehension of 'goodness' is that those most convinced that we have such cognition are most hesitant in saying, either by definition or by simple indication, just what it is that we are cognising. Their difficulty is that, if they try to go beyond the mere word itself and to attach any intelligible meaning to it, they find their words bearing a sinister 'naturalist' meaning. They have no difficulty at all in telling us what 'things' are 'good' (even though they do not all agree on this point). That is to say, they have no difficulty in pointing to the things and to the 'natural' qualities of the things to which they attribute goodness; nor have they any difficulty in indicating what they mean when, referring to some specific natural quality (e.g. 'That there is what I mean by yellow-ness'); but they seem quite unable to indicate the content of their cognition of 'good-ness'. This would be extremely strange if the cognitive aspect of the state of approval were cognition on the reflective level, and cognition of 'goodness'; but it is precisely what we should expect if the cognitive aspect of the state of approval were cognition on the reflective level but were not cognition of 'goodness' but of the thing and its natural properties or qualities.

Let us see how the conative theory of approval will work out on the assumption that the relevant cognitive aspect is the cognition of the thing approved and its natural qualities. There is, let us say, a radiator in my room, adjusted to work at half-capacity. Suppose that I approve, or think it good, that the power should be turned full on. On the conative theory of approval, to say that I approve the turning of the radiator full on means that I have a conative attitude towards turning it full on. What will be the cognitive aspect of this state of mind? It will be the conception or idea of the radiator as turned full on. The cognitive aspect of an approval attitude is thus nothing other than the idea of that which is approved; and it will be noted that what is approved is not a state of affairs which exists, but a future state of affairs. The cognitive content corresponds to what we call an 'end' or 'content of demand'. We are not asking here why I should have this conative attitude towards turning on the radiator. We are merely asking, granting that there is this attitude, what the cognitive aspect is.

Suppose that, instead of approving, I disapprove of turning the radiator full on, and approve its remaining exactly as it is. What will be the cognitive aspect of this disapproval? One might argue that the content of the cognitive aspect in disapproval is exactly the same as that which we find in the approval attitude. We have the idea of the radiator as turned on, but have an anti-attitude to this state of affairs. If this be the true account of the situation, it would seem to follow that, on the conative theory of approval, approval and disapproval mean exactly the same thing; for if we suppose that every mental state has cognitive, conative and affective aspects, and that the cognitive content in the dis-

approval of a specific state of affairs is exactly the same as the
cognitive content in the approval of it, the conative attitude of
approval must be the same as the conative attitude of disapproval
unless we bring in some other factor to explain the distinction
between approval and disapproval—say the cognition of 'goodness' in the one case, and the absence of this cognition in the other.
I am prepared to agree that, if the cognitive content is the same
in both cases, this will have serious implications for the conative
theory of approval; but I do not believe that the content is the
same. It seems to me that the cognitive content relevant to the
disapproval of turning up the radiator is not the idea of the radiator as turned up, but the idea of the maintenance of the radiator
in its present state of adjustment. Here we still have, as the cognitive content, not a present state of affairs, but the continued or
future maintenance of this state of affairs. To say 'I disapprove of
the radiator being turned up' is the same as to say 'I approve of
the radiator not being turned up (in this case, remaining at its
present adjustment)'. What we have to remember is that we are
here concerned with two conative attitudes with opposite tendencies; and conative attitudes are always positively activistic
even when we can, for convenience, describe two opposed conative attitudes by stating the one in positive and the other in
negative terms. Conation is never simply the 'refraining from'.
It can never be interpreted in terms of *laissez-faire*. That would
be the absence of conation. It is always actually or potentially
formative of the objective order, formative in the sense of positively altering or positively checking alteration (maintaining).
This is the real reason for the distinction we have already discovered between the language of cognition and the language of
approval. The simple denial that I cognise so-and-so does not
characterise the objective order; but a simple denial that I approve
is as much a characterisation (in the opposite sense) as the assertion
that I approve.

To say that the cognitive content in the approval of turning up
the radiator is the idea of its being turned up, and that the cognitive
content in the disapproval is the idea of its being maintained at
its present adjustment, does not mean that, when considering

R

whether we shall not turn it up, we do not think of both. We are, after all, beings with a unitary self-consciousness, and our cognitive life does not consist in a 'mere stream of ideas'; but neither does our conative life consist in a mere succession of un-related conative attitudes. If it did, we might possibly be able to regard specific things as good or bad (though I doubt even this), but we certainly could not evaluate them. The question is not whether the attribution of goodness or the act of approving takes place in a 'fragmented' consciousness, but—supposing that we can distinguish 'this' approval from 'that'—what is the cognitive aspect of 'this' attitude of approval, so far as it can be distinguished from other approvals within our total conative life; and the answer here given is that the cognitive aspect of a given attitude of approval, so far as thus distinguishable, is the idea of the future state of affairs which we call the 'end'; it is that which we de-scribed as the 'content of demand' in our theory of valuation. The cognitive content is not 'the goodness of turning up (or leaving as it is) the radiator'; it is the 'turning up (or leaving as it is) the radiator'.

Now it may be asked how, on this theory, we reconcile what has been said with the fact that we can think about turning up, or leaving alone, the radiator adjustment, without ever having, apparently, any conative attitude on the subject. It is, apparently, possible to think quite dispassionately about the way the apparatus works, to have the idea of turning up and turning down, without wanting to do anything about it in fact. But I think it entirely proper to reply that what is being called in question, here, is the whole psychological theory that cognition, conation and feeling are three aspects of every mental state. Does the questioner really want to raise that as an issue? If so, the centre of the discussion has been shifted right away from the theory of the value judgement to a fundamental question of general psychology; and there is no presumption that the conative theory of approval would suffer from a refutation of the generally accepted psychological theory about the relation of cognition, conation and feeling. Indeed, it might perhaps be more reasonably assumed that it is the cognitive theory which would suffer. Our argument here takes it for granted that the general psychological theory is accepted by the holders of the cognitive theory, as well as by the holders of the conative theory of approval. If both take this general psychological theory for granted, then they both take it for granted that, even when a person is engaged in the most dispassionate and 'purely theoretical' study of, say, the mechanism of a radiator, his mental processes will not be purely cognitive but will have their conative and affective aspects. It is not for the theory of value judgement to explore this sort of question. By hypothesis, the question posed in this 'objection' is about an attitude in which the cognitive aspect is the centre of attention. The theory of the value judgement, on the other hand, is concerned with the attitude of approval in which the emphasis is on the conative aspect; and all we can fairly be asked to do is to make intelligible the place of cognition as an aspect of the total mental state in which the conative aspect occupies the centre of attention.

The conative theory of approval, as so far developed, raises a number of issues which we shall have to consider under subsequent propositions; but perhaps enough has now been said to let the reader make up his mind on the merits of the view which we are here specifically recommending. The limited object of this present argument is to defend the proposition that 'approval is primarily a conative, not a cognitive or affective, attitude'. The view is that, when we contemplate the objective order, and become informed about its existing structure and behaviour, we may judge some of that structure or behaviour to be good or bad. The value judgement here made is the expression of approval or disapproval. The approval (disapproval) is a conative attitude arising in response to an apprehension of what this order is and what we believe it could be. It is the cognition of this objective order which directly evokes the conative attitude. In the total mental state of which the conative attitude is the aspect emphasised when we speak of approval, there is also a cognitive aspect, the idea of a future state of affairs which is 'the existing conditions as maintained' (if the attitude is approval) or 'the existing conditions as altered' (if the attitude is disapproval). The cognitive factors in the situation are therefore sufficiently described by saying that there is the cognition of the factual and potential nature of the objective order (what would be called the 'natural order' by those who speak of 'non-natural qualities' such as goodness), and that the cognitive content of the approving mental state is the idea of that (again 'natural' in the above sense) which is being approved. There is not, sandwiched in between the cognition of the objective 'natural' order and the approval or disapproval, something which may be called a cognition of goodness or badness. It is the approval itself, supervening directly upon the cognition of the 'natural' objective order, which is expressed in the value judgement.

PROPOSITION XII

Approval is a conative disposition to create or maintain a state of affairs.

The previous proposition sought to show that approval is essentially conative, not cognitive or affective. The emphasis in the present proposition is on the distinction between a conative disposition and a full conative activity. While the distinction between 'disposition' and 'full activity' can only be a matter of degree, the distinction is useful from many points of view; and so far as it is valid, the reasonable doctrine would seem to be that approval is a 'conative disposition' rather than a full 'conative activity'.

Some psychologists use different terms to mark this distinction. They speak of an 'activity set' or a 'motor set', corresponding to the term 'conative disposition' here adopted, and of an 'overt activity', corresponding to 'conative activity'. But whatever terms we use for these two notions, the states referred to may be readily understood from the following examples.

If two boys are engaged in a rat-hunt, one trying to drive the rat from its refuge and the other standing ready to deal with it at the point where it is likely to emerge, the attitude of the latter illustrates very well what is meant by an 'activity set' or 'conative disposition'. His body will be tensely poised, his eyes will be focussed directly on the exit, his stick will be raised; if one observes his hands and feet, it will be seen that his hands are constantly testing the 'feel' of his grip, and his feet testing the suitability of his stance. The whole attitude indicates that he is highly 'charged' with a force which will, at any time, issue in movement; his whole being is held in readiness to make that movement when the occasion arises. When the rat dashes for the exit and reaches just the appropriate position (appropriate from the boy's, not the rat's, point of view), this is the 'occasion' or the signal for the transformation of the 'activity set' or 'conative disposition' into 'overt activity' or 'conative activity'.

Similarly, when competitors are lined up for a race, their bodily poise constitutes an 'activity set'. The pistol-shot is the occasion for the transformation of the set into overt activity—for the transformation of a conative disposition into conative activity.

Now it may be asked whether it is proper to contrast in this way a 'disposition' with an 'activity'. Surely the disposition is itself an activity, and not a merely passive state. The objection is perfectly reasonable. The boy poised ready to deal with the rat is certainly not in a passive state. There is a great deal of internal activity, and without this activity the disposition could not be maintained. It would not be a disposition. One might even say that this internal activity—at times manifesting itself in small outward movements—is the maintenance of the disposition. Strictly speaking, then, a disposition is not different from, but is a kind of, activity. But, as is usual when one is dealing with psychical phenomena, we have to use terms which suggest absolute distinctions when the distinctions themselves are only relative. We speak, for instance, of a 'state' as distinguished from an 'activity', although no psychical state can be other than an activity. The fact of the matter is that every manifestation of mental life can be called either a state or an activity according to the context in which it is being discussed. Before an army is given the order to attack, the troops will be in a 'state of preparedness' for attack, as distinguished from being engaged in 'the activity' of attacking; although it is quite patent to anyone in the army that this state is itself one of great activity. But we call it a state or disposition rather than an activity, when contrasting it with that towards which it is the disposition, namely the overt activity of engaging in battle. Any conative disposition is, as an expression or manifestation of psychical life, a form of activity. But, by contrast with that activity into which it will become transformed on a given occasion or signal, it may legitimately be described as a 'disposition' rather than an 'activity' of a person.

Chapter Eight

THE EXPRESSION OF APPROVAL

UP to this point we have been concerned with the nature of approval itself rather than the nature of its expression. It is quite true that we can only discuss its nature by considering it as manifested in its expressions; but it will I think be agreed that the two problems are not identical.

As, however, our fundamental question is the nature of the value judgement which is the mode (or at least one mode) of expressing approval, it is obvious that the general nature of the expression of approval is a question of vital importance for us. That is the question which will engage our attention in this chapter. The principal issue will be the problem how, if approval is primarily a conative disposition, the expression of approval can be called true or false.

PROPOSITION XIII

Approval and disapproval imply the prior and continuing cognition of an objective order.

That approval and disapproval imply the prior or antecedent awareness of an objective order was argued[1] under Proposition XI. In the course of the argument it was shown that approval cannot be explained in affective or in cognitive terms. But to explain it in 'conative' terms we had to assume that conative attitudes arise as responses to the perception or awareness of objective situations. The whole case for the conative character of approval breaks down unless we assume that there is this prior awareness of the objective order.

That the cognition must be continuous throughout the approval however, is a point which requires some further explanation. The

[1] See pp. 238-44.

247

reader will find ample confirmation of this point if he tries to explain the nature of approval without expressing himself in such a way as to suggest that approval is a cognitive activity. Thus Ross tells us that 'the basic element in approval' is a 'judgement' that such and such a thing is good; and it is just as natural for us to say 'I *know* that *x* is good', as to say 'I approve of *x*'. While the cognitive theory of approval is wrong, the tendency to adopt it is very intelligible. This tendency is due to the fact that the cognitive aspect of the total mental state, of which 'approval' emphasises the conative aspect, is itself part of our total cognitive life—our view of what the universe is, has been and may become. Were this not so, then it would be difficult to see how approval could be a 'response' to awareness of an objective situation. Approval is an attitude which continues over a tract of time. It is not a momentary state, but a 'disposition' or 'activity set' which will express itself in some appropriate way when the 'occasion' occurs in the objective order. To sustain itself as a disposition, and to be capable of transformation into full conative activity when the occasion or signal occurs, the disposition must be a sustained or persistent response to a continuous cognition of the objective order.

PROPOSITION XIV

To attribute goodness to anything is to express the disposition to adopt its maintenance or creation as an end.

This proposition does, I think, follow inevitably from what has already been said. The cognitive content of the total psychical state of approval is the idea of that future state of affairs which we call the 'end' of the conative disposition. Of course, not every such content becomes a fully effective end, in the sense of an end chosen and overtly pursued. Choice is a conative 'activity', while approval is merely a conative 'disposition'. Amongst our many conative dispositions we may be forced by objective conditions to select by the process of 'valuation', assigning degrees of goodness. Some of the conative dispositions will be suppressed by this process of valuation, and only the end placed highest in the valuational scale will become an effectively prosecuted end if the objective conditions enforce selection on this spartan principle. But, in view of all that has been said in Part I, this may be taken as understood. Bearing in mind that, when we are talking of the attribution of goodness, as distinguished from valuation, we are speaking only of ends we have a disposition to adopt, rather than of ends actually chosen, it is still important to stress that, in attributing goodness, what we are doing is expressing the disposition to adopt the state of affairs in question as an end.

It may be felt that this view creates a difficulty over the approval of anything as a 'means'. To say that, in approving, we are adopting something as an end may suggest to some that this is equivalent to saying that we cannot attribute goodness to a 'means'. But this would be a mistaken inference from what has been said. We can perfectly well think of a 'means' as good. If this seems paradoxical, the explanation is quite simple. To call a thing good signifies *that* it is approved; to call it a 'means' is to indicate *why* it is approved.

This point is of importance, not only with regard to the goodness of a 'means', but also with regard to the goodness of what is 'virtuous', 'beautiful', 'wise', and so forth. We can approve of a beautiful picture, a virtuous action, a wise policy or an efficient instrument (a means); but when we use the terms 'beautiful', 'virtuous', 'wise' and 'efficient', we are indicating the characteristics of the thing in question (whether these characteristics be 'intrinsic' or relational does not matter), characteristics which we cognise, and the cognition of which constitutes information about the thing. It is not necessary, for purposes of a theory of the value judgement to say what these characteristics are; but it is necessary to insist that, when we talk of a beautiful picture, virtuous action, wise policy or efficient instrument, these terms signify the content of our cognitive state. They signify why we approve of the things in question, that is to say, why we adopt their creation or maintenance as ends. Thus—concentrating on the question of the goodness of a means—to speak of a thing as an efficient instrument is to speak of it as a means to some end. In so far as a thing is efficacious for the production of a contemplated result, it is a means. If you wish to bring about the result, then you will approve of the means; you will have a conative disposition towards the creation or maintenance of the thing which is the means. You will adopt as an end the creation or maintenance of the thing which is a means. Hence to apprehend and indicate the characteristics of a thing which make it efficacious towards a result (to regard it as a means) does not at all imply that it cannot itself be regarded as good.

The fact that, when we call a thing a 'means' we are referring, not to its goodness, but to those characteristics in virtue of which we attribute goodness to it, is often obscured by our common tendency to distinguish between 'good-as-means' and 'good-as-end' as though we were indicating two different kinds of 'goodness'. But it would be just as correct—and incorrect—to distinguish between 'good-as-beautiful' and 'good-as-end', or between 'good-as-virtuous' and 'good-as-end', or between 'good-as-wise' and 'good-as-end'. 'Beautiful', 'virtuous', 'wise' and 'efficient' indicate cognised characteristics which evoke approval. They do not at all justify us in supposing that there are different kinds of approval corresponding to these objective characteristics.

If this point were more generally recognised it would be very beneficial in disentangling distinct problems which are often jumbled together in moral philosophy, and also in distinguishing between problems of moral philosophy and problems which have little relevance to moral philosophy. Questions in aesthetics, for example, are often treated as though they had something to do with the theory of value; and yet an account of what constitutes beauty has no more to do with the theory of value or goodness than has the engineer's account of the structure of an internal combustion engine. That the beautiful picture can be considered good or be valued, and that the engine can be considered good or be valued, does not imply that the theory of beauty and the theory of heat engines are parts of the theory of value. The same applies with regard to the theory of virtuous action in its relation to the theory of the value judgement. What constitutes virtuous action—if this means action which we ought or have a duty to do—can be understood only by a systematic inquiry into the juridical concepts upon which the notion of obligation is based.

Certainly the moral philosopher is concerned with the theory of virtue (as he is not at all concerned with the theory of beauty or heat engines); and it is part of his business to correlate the theory of virtue (meaning here the theory of obligation) with the theory of the value judgement, because it is his business to elucidate and correlate the fundamental principles operative in the social order, the principles which in their detailed application are investigated by the various social sciences. But this does not justify us in supposing that there is a special kind of value or goodness which is called 'virtue'.

However, to pursue this topic would lead us far from our main point. The main point is this: to say that approval is the adoption of something as an 'end' does not imply that we cannot approve what we regard as a means. It is an end inasmuch as we approve it. It is a means in so far as it is efficacious for the realisation of some other end.

PROPOSITION XV

While a conative attitude is neither true nor false, the expression of approval, as the expression of a total mental state, is to some extent necessarily subject to the criterion of truth and falsity.

This proposition is mainly concerned with the expression of approval, but it is well to remind ourselves at the outset that the language of cognition is not the same as that of approval, and that we cannot expect value judgements to be subject, without remainder, to the criterion of truth in exactly the same way as theoretical judgements. The fact that the statement 'I approve A' is substantially equivalent to 'A is good', and the fact that 'I do not approve A' has an objective reference which the mere denial of cognitive content would not have, are sufficient warning against treating the value judgement as equivalent to a purely theoretical one. To express a mental state which is 'informative about' the objective order and to express a mental state potentially 'formative of' the objective order must have different meanings. Individuals can be opposed with respect to their approvals, just as they can with respect to their beliefs. If they are opposed in belief, they will consider each other as misinformed about the actual nature of the objective order. But if they are opposed in their approvals, the opposition is not essentially in what they believe the objective order to be but in what they want it to be in the future; although this opposition may, in some particular cases, be almost entirely (or even entirely) due to opposed belief on some particular issue. To say that the opposition may be traceable to belief is not to say that the value judgement is purely theoretical; for the removal of the theoretical controversy will result in the same value judgements for both parties only if we suppose that the conative dispositions are in all other respects in harmony. It will not entitle us to say that the value judgement is not expressing a conative disposition.

But while it would be quite improper to identify the value judgement with the theoretical judgement, it would be equally a mistake to say that a value judgement is ever merely the expression of a conative attitude. It is easy to slip into the error of speaking of approval as simply conative when we confine our discussion to the 'nature' of approval. It is when we come to consider the 'expression' of approval that we are forced to recognise that approval is not the conative aspect of a total mental state but the total mental state with the emphasis on the conative aspect.

Even when we recognise that, in speaking of approval, this is a matter of emphasising, rather than of attending exclusively to, the conative element in a mental state, it is by no means easy to avoid becoming confused in discussing the expression of approval in general or the value judgement in particular. The attribution of goodness or badness is the expression of approval or disapproval. To make a value judgement is to attribute goodness or badness. Apparently, then, we are saying that a conative disposition (or the attitude of approval) can be 'expressed' in the form of a statement which is to some extent, or in some sense, true or false. When we talk of 'approval', granting that we are talking of the total mental state which has a cognitive aspect, the emphasis is on the conative side. When we talk of a value 'judgement', granting that the mental state expressed must have a conative aspect, the emphasis is apparently on the cognitive element. How can a conative disposition be expressed in a form such as to suggest that it is primarily a conclusion of cognitive activity?

The difficulty is a real one; but before trying to give an answer, we should look more carefully into the nature of the problem here presented.

Let us note different ways in which approval may be expressed.

Firstly: 'The annual general meeting expressed its warm approval of Mrs Blank's leadership during the past session by unanimously re-electing her to the presidency for the ensuing year.'

Secondly: 'At the conclusion of her song, Elizabeth fled from the stage, and Mr Tittup could hardly persuade her to return and make her bow. But the audience would brook no denial. It clapped and stamped and cheered, and insisted on her doing it all over again.'

Thirdly: 'That the productions of Batch & Co. will be of high quality is now taken for granted; but this latest machine exceeds even their normal standards of efficiency and durability.'

Here we have three different ways of expressing approval. In the *first* case, approval is expressed by the transformation of a disposition into full activity. Mrs Blank's presidency has (it is thought) been an important objective condition of the successful activities of the W.R.I.; and the approval of that condition is expressed by taking the active step of maintaining it in existence for the future; without such active step it would cease to exist. This is the most spontaneous and perhaps the most emphatic way in which we express our approvals. The obvious way of expressing approval of a warm room, a supply of hot water, or the conduct of a government, is to add coals at appropriate intervals, keep the boiler stoked, or return the party with a comfortable majority at the next election.

In the *second* case, we shall probably not be far wrong in saying that the emphasis is on showing that the approval is emphatically there. Objectivists are apt to overstate their case in saying that, when we call things good, we do not intend to convey the information that we have a certain state of mind. Sometimes this is just what we do want to convey. If Elizabeth has any doubt as to our pleasure in her singing, we shall make it quite clear how we are disposed. The sustained applause, put into verbal expression, might be rendered as 'That certainly was *good*!' There is no doubt as to what the 'that' refers to. If there is any doubt as to whether it is approved, the emphatic expression will dispel the doubt. There is a clear expression of the disposition to enjoy more.

In the *third* case, we have a definitely verbal expression of approval, what is called a 'value judgement'. One may suggest that, when we express approval in explicit verbal terms in the form of value judgements, the emphasis is always on the 'that'. Thus the approval of the machine might be rendered: 'We usually think highly of Messrs Batch's products; but, however that may be, there is not the slightest doubt about the appeal of *this* machine.' Objectivists are probably right in supposing that, when we make explicitly verbal value judgements, the meaning or the reference is always directed objectively and not subjectively; but they are certainly wrong in supposing that all expressions of approval are of this type.

Now it is probable that, if all expressions of approval took the form of translating the disposition itself into overt action (as in re-electing Mrs Blank to the presidency), the fact that the 'expression' of the approval took the form of an overt action would obviate any sense of strangeness in the idea that the approval itself is a conative attitude. The sense of strangeness seems to be due to the fact that approval can be expressed in a statement which is open to dispute on the ground of its truth or falsity. The most natural method of expressing approval is, as already stated, the translation of the conative disposition into its appropriate full conative activity on the appropriate occasion; but it also seems to be the case that, if we wish to single out for emphasis just 'what' we approve, the only adequate way of doing so, for the normally developed adult at least in a country with whose language he is familiar, is to express his approval in the form of a statement. The problem then begins to worry us: How can a conative disposition be expressed in a form which is, to all appearance, the same as the expression of a cognitive activity, or the result of a cognitive process? If the expression is like the expression of a cognitive state, must not that which is being expressed be a cognitive state?

Some would evade this difficulty by denying that the 'value judgement' is a real 'judgement', and asserting that the statement 'This is good' is not subject to the criterion of truth and falsity. I do not think that this is a proper solution of the problem. It appears to me that both those who say, 'Since the approval may be expressed in the form of a proposition it must be itself essentially a cognitive activity', and also those who say, 'Since approval is not a cognitive activity the "value judgement" cannot be a real judgement', have failed to notice the pit they are digging for themselves in the theory of knowledge. For there is an exactly similar difficulty which arises in connexion with the expression of 'cognitive states'.

Thus, acting on the well-known maxim, 'If you want to know the time, ask a policeman', I may approach the constable, put the question, and receive the answer '3.45 p.m.'. My response to this information is to thank him and proceed at once to a certain house. Had I not acted thus—had I, for instance, gone to browse over the shelves of a bookshop—anyone who knew my engagements for the day would have been surprised into asking me 'Did you hear what he said? Don't you believe him?' My proceeding at once to the house in question, which is fifteen minutes' walk from where I met the constable, is motivated by the fact that I have a tea engagement there for 4 p.m. My action is a natural expression of my belief that what the policeman tells me is true. My acting in a different way would be regarded, by anyone who knew the circumstances, as an expression of disbelief. Now here is a belief—undoubtedly a cognitive activity—being expressed in a conative form; it is being expressed not by a verbal statement but by an act of will. It does not seem to us strange that cognitive states should be expressed in conative activities. Indeed we often say that a man's beliefs are more 'truly expressed' in what he does than in what he says he believes. Nor is this all that can be said on the matter. Can one express cognitive states in any way other than in some conative activity? We express them by operating our vocal organs, or by taking up a pen and making marks on paper, or by some other type of action.

The point of all this is that, if we argue that the value judgement must be essentially the expression of a cognitive and not a conative attitude because the expression is in a form which is somehow subject to the criterion of truth and falsity, then we are bound to argue that, because belief is expressed in conative activity, it must be a conative and not a cognitive state. There is something seriously wrong with this latter conclusion, as all will agree. There must also be something seriously wrong with the former, for they are both apparently on the same level. No doubt there is a problem to be explained here. We shall have to show how it is that the disposition of approval can be expressed in the form of a value judgement. But the thing to be quite clear about is that this is a problem to be solved, a fact to be explained, and not something to be ignored or denied.

We have already noted the fact that the expression of belief or any other cognitive attitude takes the form of a conative activity. Since, then, from conative activities we may infer a man's beliefs, this means that in relation to some conative activities at least (namely those in which a man is obviously expressing beliefs) we can, in some sense or other, apply the criterion of truth and falsity.

The question, therefore, arises: Is this the case only with respect to some conative activities? Can we apply the criterion of truth only in those cases where the intention is primarily to express belief; or can we apply it to every conative activity in which the expression of approval, and not belief, is primarily intended?

It seems to me that the answer to this question must be in the affirmative; for, even when our primary intention is to express approval, we necessarily express at the same time belief; and in this sense the expression of the mental attitude will be, to some extent or in some sense, subject to the criterion of truth. This is due to the fact (see Proposition XIII) that approval is a response to a prior and continuing cognition of the objective order. The content of the total mental attitude will be partly belief; and the approval, which is the total mental state (with the emphasis on its conative aspect), cannot be expressed without this belief being also expressed. The expression need not be in a verbal form, and the principle applies irrespective of the form which the expression takes. That it does apply when the expression takes a verbal form is clear, for we have in this case what is called a value judgement. Thus, the commendation of Messrs Batch's machine is an expression of approval, and, at the same time, of the belief to which that approval is a response, namely the belief that the reaper will do its job just as well when confronted by a heavy crop on uneven ground as when faced by a normal crop on the alluvial plain.

That it applies also when the expression of approval does not take a definite propositional form seems equally clear. When Mrs Blank is re-elected to the presidency of the local W.R.I., this expression of approval is also an expression of the belief that it is in fact she who has been responsible for the past year's success, that she has the ability and consistency of purpose to ensure good business procedure, safe financial policy, the securing of satisfactory premises, the presence of celebrities, and so on. These beliefs may be true or false, but they are the prior and continuing conditions of the approval, and are expressed in its expression. Similarly, the vociferous applause for Elizabeth assumes, and expresses the assumption, that the sweet sounds really came from her throat and not from that of plain Jane standing in the wing. Again, the ritual belch with which old Ali Abdel Hamid concludes his gargantuan feast of greasy mutton stew expresses, amongst other things, the general anticipation that, for the next five hours at least, his physical state will be pleasantly soporific; and it may provoke the mental comment of his favourite but unfaithful young wife: 'Yes, that's what you think; but Allah, in his inscrutable mercy, calls you even now along a swift and thorny road to Paradise.'

We may commit ourselves without qualification to the assertion that no expression of approval can avoid being at the same time an expression of belief; although it is true that, the more this expression takes a verbal, propositional form, the more will attention be directed to the speaker's belief rather than to the conative element in his mental state. Every expression of approval is thus to some extent also a theoretical judgement. There is every

s

reason for retaining the term 'value judgement' within the vocabulary of moral philosophy.

PROPOSITION XVI

*A value judgement is true or false to the extent that it expresses a
cognitive attitude; and the extent to which a cognitive attitude is
expressed depends upon the extent to which the expression is intended
to create a conative disposition.*

We have seen, in discussing the last proposition, that expressions
of approval, while they all express belief to some extent, can vary
greatly in the extent to which belief rather than conative attitude
is expressed. Indeed the proportions in which conative and cognitive attitudes are expressed can cover such a wide range that it
is not always easy to say whether a judgement should be classified
as a 'value' or as a 'theoretical' judgement. At the one end of the
scale we have such an expression of approval as 'Scrumptious!',
and, at the other, such an expression of disapproval as 'That
picture you are proposing to put in the van with the kitchen
equipment is a famous old master.' The latter statement looks
like a simple piece of information; but what is clearly meant is 'I
strongly disapprove of the picture going in there; put it in a
different van and give it proper protection.' The element of
conative attitude expressed is neither true nor false, but the cognitive attitude expressed is either true or false. It is true or false
that the packer was proposing to put the picture in the kitchen
van, and it is true or false that it is an old master. Thus, taken at
its face value, the whole of the statement is subject to the criterion
of truth, though we know quite well that the speaker is not at all
concerned with the packer's cultural education but with the preservation of the treasure.

What is the reason for this variation in the proportions of
conative and cognitive attitude expressed in expressions of approval and disapproval? Why is it that, while the emphasis in the
state of approval itself is on the conative disposition, the expression
of this state should so often appear to lay the emphasis on a cognitive attitude? The explanation would seem to be that, when

we are merely expressing spontaneously a state of approval, or when we assume the actual existence of a certain conative disposition in others, and are concerned merely to strengthen it or bring it to full conative activity, we tend to let the conative element predominate in our expressions of approval or disapproval; while, if we assume a contrary conative disposition to be operative in the minds of other persons, and wish to create one in keeping with our own, the expression of our approval will give more emphasis to the cognitive element. That is to say, we will tend to include more expression of belief on matters of fact, and thus reap the advantage—and run the risk—of the appeal to reason.

To elaborate this general thesis, let us consider, first, spontaneous expressions of approval and disapproval—'Scrumptious!', 'rotten!', 'how exquisite!', 'confound that noise!': in all these expressions there is some cognitive content, but not very much, although there is a fair amount in the last two. The less the *cognitive* element is expressed, the more does the *affective* tone of the state reveal itself. Perhaps it is roughly true to say that the strength of the affective tone varies inversely with the extent to which cognitive content appears in the expression of approval.

In the second place, if we reflect on those situations in which strong emotional appeals are addressed to people, we find, I think, that the appropriate disposition is assumed to be present without needing to be created, and that the aim of the appeal is to strengthen and confirm it. The elaborate pageantry of state occasions in our own country, of religious services, or of the Italian and German régimes under Mussolini and Hitler, and the assumption of a united nation in Churchill's famous radio talks during the war, are cases in point.

In the third place, when we are aware of a contrary set of approvals and disapprovals in the people to whom we are talking, if we wish to persuade them into the acceptance of our own set, when we have not merely to strengthen some existing disposition but actually to create it, it is the cognitive attitude which finds a suitably increased emphasis in our expression of approval. The expression takes on the character of what is properly called the value judgement, and may even assume the appearance of a bald statement of fact. But it is important to notice that this statement of fact is addressed to some other existing conative disposition in the hearer. The purpose is to lead evidence and suggest inferences with regard to the nature of the objective order such that, when he sees their implications for his own existing conative dispositions, he will respond with the new disposition which we want him to acquire.

Possibly one of the best known illustrations in literature of what has been said under our second and third headings here is the speech of Mark Antony in *Julius Caesar*. He begins, confronted by a hostile audience, by apparently accepting their assessment of Brutus and the other conspirators; then he gradually undermines their beliefs (*First Cit.*: 'Methinks there is much reason in his sayings.' *Sec. Cit.*: 'If thou consider rightly of the matter, Caesar has had great wrong.'); and only when he has created the germ of the necessary disposition to mutiny does he place it in the emotional hot-bed. On a memorable occasion in the Oxford Union a famous, and usually astute, political orator over-estimated the effect of his reasoned argument on the audience, with humiliating consequences when he tried to 'turn on the water-works'.

Of course, what has been said above must be qualified to the extent that people vary greatly in their capacity to distinguish between what is and what is not evidence, what are and what are not valid inferences from the evidence supplied. Sometimes the indication that some statement is widely believed is regarded as conclusive evidence for its truth; and if a statement is made with sufficient 'conviction' or constantly repeated, this may be more convincing to the hearer than a cool matter of fact pronouncement. A clever advocate will not carry, necessarily, the same conviction with the judge on the bench and the members of the public in the court-room. Still, this is a question as to difference of capacity for sifting evidence and testing inferences before reaching theoretical conclusions. It does not affect the point that the creation of conative dispositions must proceed by the creation of belief as to matters of fact in the objective order.

The reason for this difference in the expression of our approvals and disapprovals (when, on the one hand, we can assume the desired disposition in others and wish only to strengthen and confirm it, and when, on the other, we have to assume an opposed disposition which we have to replace by a different one) is that, granted the existence of a conative disposition, it can be strengthened or brought to full conative activity by non-rational sympathetic influence; while the creation of a new conative disposition is a response to one's cognition of the objective order (however efficiently or inefficiently we may use our cognitive powers). This point has already been stressed in an earlier section of the argument. The cognitive content of a total mental state— that which is 'the idea of the end approved'—is not only the cognitive aspect of that state but is also part of our whole cognitive life as unitary self-conscious beings. Since a conative disposition is a response to a prior and continuing awareness of the objective order, it is through changing belief of what in fact this order is, and of what it may become, that our conative dispositions change their character in detail.

Perhaps what has been said may help to explain why objectivists and subjectivists—defenders of the cognitive and defenders of the emotive theories of approval—can both find very suitable examples of 'value judgement' to illustrate their arguments. The defenders of the emotive theory tend to find their main support in expressions of approval which are spontaneous or hortatory— those referred to under our first and second headings. The objectivists, and those who regard approval as essentially cognitive, are apt to insist on the fact that 'people can dispute about what is good and bad', having specially in mind the value judgements coming under our third heading. I do not suggest that the rival schools pay exclusive attention to these different types of expression of approval. I merely suggest that each one builds its main case on one or other of these types before trying to interpret other varieties of expression of approval in terms of the theory so fashioned. In other words, the theories in question take, as the essential element in *approval*, what is in fact the variable element in the *expression* of approval—the affective tone which is prominent when the appeal to belief is slight, or the appeal to belief which is prominent when the intention is not merely to express one's own approval but to induce a corresponding approval in others.

There is one last point which may conveniently be mentioned under this present proposition. In speaking of the significance of the expression of belief in the expression of approval, we have discussed this only in terms of 'inducing a conative disposition towards something', or inducing a person to think of that thing as 'good', for we are concerned in this part of the book with the theory of the attribution of goodness, rather than with the theory of valuation in the narrower sense. But it may be asked whether this is not misleading. Can we ever induce a person to attribute goodness to anything without at the same time making him attribute to it a certain degree of goodness, i.e. some value? I think that, theoretically, it is possible to do so. We attribute values or degrees of goodness to things only when we are faced by the necessity of choosing between them. If a person has conative dispositions to A, B and C, and can satisfy all three, and if we can convince him that the best way to satisfy A is through x, and if the pursuit of x can be undertaken without any sacrifice elsewhere, then he will acquire the disposition to x without ever valuing x, valuation never having been called for. We shall have induced him to consider x good without his attributing to it any particular degree of goodness.

But this is merely to show the theoretical possibility. In actual fact, for most of us, the question of goodness will generally include also the question of degree of goodness. We shall have to 'economise'. We shall be concerned not merely with the 'administrative' and 'technical' question as to what is required to satisfy A, but also with the question whether, and if so how far, we can satisfy A without detriment to the prospects of B and C. Whenever this is the case, the appeal to reason, and therefore the extent to which the cognitive attitude is expressed in our expression of approval, will have to be more complex; for here we have to take account of the whole intricate process of the person's valuational activity. It should be little cause for wonder, therefore, that, in any reasonably live community, it is difficult to say where value judgements end and we have entered the realm of the purely theoretical judgement.

Chapter Nine

THE ULTIMATE GROUND OF THE ATTRIBUTION OF GOODNESS

Up to now, the argument has been that when we attribute goodness we are expressing approval; that the dominant attitude in approval is conative; that it is a conative disposition (as distinguished from a full conative activity) to intervene in the objective order for the purpose of altering or maintaining a certain state of affairs; and that the expression of this attitude contains a varying amount of expression of belief, according as the expression of approval is or is not intended to be persuasive with respect to the approvals and disapprovals of other persons.

In this chapter we shall attempt to push the analysis of our attribution of goodness still farther back, in order, if possible, to discover its ultimate grounds. Since approval is primarily conative, it seems likely that—making due allowance for the presence of cognition and feeling in every mental state—the ultimate ground of the attribution of goodness will be some conative attitude; and the argument of the chapter will be that this is indeed the case. Our notions of goodness spring, in the last resort, from certain behaviour or activity patterns inherent in our nature. These are —and must be—so fundamental that they are not dependent on our conscious wills but manifest our intrinsic psycho-physical nature. This does not mean that the conscious selection and pursuit of ends is a mere illusion, or that it is irrelevant to our conceptions of what is good; but it does mean that, in the last resort, it is our non-teleological and inherited behaviour patterns which set the main directions of our approvals, choices and behaviour. The argument by which it is sought to establish this position may be difficult, for it deals with difficult questions; and I am not completely convinced that, on occasion, the difficulties are not of my own making. However, I shall put the case, as I see it, as clearly

263

as possible. The first stage in the argument (covered under Proposition XVII) will deal with the distinction between 'principal' and 'subsidiary' conative attitudes.

PROPOSITION XVII

Approval may be a principal or a subsidiary conative attitude.

I shall try to show that, while a conative disposition constituting approval may be a subsidiary disposition implying a prior or principal conative attitude, and possibly always is in fact such a subsidiary disposition, it is theoretically possible at least that approval may be an ultimate principal disposition. This whole question is closely bound up with the well-known problem in ethics as to whether 'ultimate ends' are capable of 'proof'; and if we bring out the bearing of the two questions on each other we shall be able to draw some conclusions about the relation of 'ultimate ends' or 'ultimate goods' to 'ultimate conative attitudes', a relation highly significant with respect to the general problem of 'ultimate grounds of approval'.

With regard to the distinction between principal and subsidiary conative attitudes, let us consider once more our previous example of the boys engaged in the rat-hunt. The boy poised ready to strike has a conative disposition, the tendency of which is towards the full activity of killing the rat. Let us consider this disposition as the 'principal' one for purposes of our example. Now, suppose that he notices that the barn door is wide open. This at once strikes him as a state of affairs unfavourable to the complete actualisation of his disposition. The open door is an avenue of escape for the rat if the boy misses with his first blow. His immediate response to the open door is therefore to disapprove; in other words, he strongly approves of a shut door as one of the objective conditions necessary to the actualisation of his principal disposition. The approval will take the form of a subsidiary disposition to create the necessary condition—to have the door shut—and this disposition will, no doubt, express itself in a sharp direction to his assistant to 'Close that door!' Again, if someone enters the barn, comes over to where he is, and obstructs his view, or takes up a position which will interfere with the effective operation of his stick, he will respond with disapproval—he will have the disposition to maintain the previous state of affairs necessary for the actualisation of his principal conative disposition. Thus, assuming that approval is a conative disposition, we can readily see how it can be described as a 'subsidiary conative disposition' implying a principal one. The approval of the shut door, or the approval of a clear field of vision and scope for operations, is the conative disposition towards the shutting of the door or the removal of the person who looks like being an obstruction. This disposition constituting approval is subsidiary, in the sense that it is directed to the creation or maintenance of a specific state of affairs, this state of affairs being a condition for the effective transformation into full activity of the conative disposition to kill the rat. The approval of the shut-door, or of the clear field for operations, is a disposition subsidiary to the principal disposition to kill the rat.

To illustrate the relation between the subsidiary disposition constituting approval and a principal conative attitude which is a full conative activity, and not merely a conative disposition, let us suppose that I am actually engaged in writing, and that someone comes in to talk to me. My first spontaneous reaction, before I know who it is, and before I even interpret the noise of the opening door as connected with the entry of a person, will be one of disapproval. This may at once be succeeded by approval if the intruder is one such as to stimulate dispositions to which I am more generally prone than to the activity on which I am engaged. But if he does not succeed in thus altering the main direction of my mental attitude, if the sense of an interrupted activity is dominant in my mind, if my conative disposition towards the continuance of my writing persists, the initial disapproval of the interruption will continue in force. It may at first be concealed under a show of politeness; but the longer he chatters, the more will the disposition to annihilate the obstruction (not the man but his presence) increase in intensity. The principal conative activity (the business of writing) requires certain objective conditions for its maintenance; and there arises a subsidiary disposition to recreate or maintain these conditions, this subsidiary disposition being the approval of his absence and disapproval of his presence, a disposition which will accept any appropriate occasion or signal to be transformed into the appropriate activity of getting rid of him.

These examples suggest a provisional general conclusion, namely that, if I am engaged in any kind of activity in reasonably satisfactory conditions, I take these conditions for granted and never single any one of them out for conscious approval. I consciously approve only if, for some reason, I am led to contemplate any one of them as possibly absent. My approval will be the disposition towards the maintenance of that condition; and if at any time its existence is threatened, the approval will tend to become transformed into activity directed to its maintenance. Thus, if the room is just at the right temperature, I do not particularly notice it; but if the temperature goes down beyond a certain point, I will get up and mend the fire. The principal activity—or disposition to activity—can be prosecuted only under certain objective conditions, and it is the awareness of any of these conditions as actually or potentially absent which stimulates the subsidiary disposition towards its creation or maintenance.

But this provisional conclusion is merely tentative in the sense that, while it does show quite clearly that the disposition of approval may be a subsidiary one, it only suggests and does not really prove that an attitude of approval cannot be a principal one.

To see whether, theoretically at least, approval could be an ultimate principal disposition, we have to raise the question whether 'the goodness of ultimate ends is capable of proof'. The connexion of the two questions may not be immediately clear to the reader, but I think that this will emerge as we proceed.

We have already seen that, to 'prove' the goodness of anything to a person who does not already regard it as good, I must do so by a process of strictly theoretical demonstration of matter of fact. I have to convince him (by evidence and argument which may or may not be sound, but must carry conviction to him at least) that the objective 'natural' order is such that, if he is to realise the end of some disposition which he already has, he will have to take a line of action which he does not at the moment want to take. When I do convince him of this, then provided that he wills the end supposed, he will react to this new set of beliefs about the objective order with the new conative disposition or approval which I have wished to arouse in him. It follows from this that we can never prove the goodness of the end of a given disposition unless we can relate it, in the person's mind, to some end of an already existing disposition. That is to say, what we can 'prove' to be good must always be the end of a subsidiary disposition implying the existence of a prior or principal disposition; we can never prove the 'end' of a 'finally principal disposition' to be good.

But there is a further important condition of such proof. The person must not only be cognisant of the ends of the principal and of the subsidiary dispositions, but must be *reflectively* cognisant of both. By 'cognisant' here I mean merely that, if there is a conative disposition to any activity, that conative disposition must have its cognitive (and affective) aspects also. But we have accepted[1] the assumption that the term 'approval' cannot be employed with propriety unless the cognitive element in the total mental state is of the 'reflective' level of cognition. That is to say, the person must be aware of his awareness; he must be self-consciously aware of that which is the 'end' of his conative disposition. For convenience, when discussing the cognitive aspect of an attitude of approval, let us refer to the content of cognition which has not reached the reflective level as a 'quasi-end'. If we may be permitted to distinguish in this way between an 'end' (as the content of the reflectively cognitive aspect of a disposition) and a 'quasi-end' (as the content of the sub-reflective cognitive aspect of a disposition), then it will be obvious that, to prove the goodness of anything to a person, the cognitive contents of both his subsidiary disposition (what is to be 'proved good') and his principal disposition (what is presupposed to exist in order that such a proof may be possible) must be genuine 'ends' and not merely 'quasi-ends'. To prove the goodness of keeping the barn door shut during the rat-hunt, it is necessary, not only that the boy should have reflective consciousness of the barn door being shut as a state

[1] See pp. 227-8.

of affairs, but also that he should have reflective consciousness of the killing of the rat as a state of affairs. Otherwise it would be meaningless to say to him 'If you want to get the rat, you should have that door shut'; for he would not know what was meant. There would be no effect upon his beliefs about the objective order sufficient to supply the conditions under which the subsidiary disposition (to get the door shut) could be created. I think that it will be clear, then, that, to prove the goodness of anything, the proof must refer to the end of a subsidiary disposition, and the person to whom the 'proof' is offered must be reflectively aware of the ends of both the subsidiary and the principal disposition.

But all this refers to the conditions required for 'proof' of the goodness of anything, to the conditions when one individual tries to make another individual appreciate the 'reasons' why one disposition should generate another disposition in him. This has all to do with what we may call the 'external' inducement. The conditions of 'internal' inducement are not the same; for while 'external' inducement, in the sense of one person offering proofs or reasons to another, requires reflective awareness of the cognitive content of both principal and subsidiary dispositions, there is a kind of 'internal' inducement to the creation of conative dispositions which does not depend on proofs and 'reasons' but upon 'causes'. It will be easiest to illustrate this if we go well down the biological scale. In fish there is a fundamental conative disposition to develop from the embryonic stage to maturity and to maintain life. There is no doubt, I imagine, that the disposition to eat the fisherman's bait (and the disposition not to eat it in certain circumstances) is a subsidiary disposition which somehow follows from the fundamental disposition to the maintenance of life. There will be cognitive aspects in both these dispositions, but to the best of our knowledge this cognition is unreflective. The contents of the cognitive aspects of the total state will therefore be not 'ends' but 'quasi-ends'. So far as the fundamental disposition to live induces the subsidiary disposition to eat the bait—and I think that this account of the relation of the two dispositions, though not quite accurate, is sufficiently accurate for the present context—this is an instance of a 'cause', not a 'reason', inducing the subsidiary disposition. The unreflective cognitive life of the fish will have something like the continuity of human cognitive life, each disposition will have its cognitive aspect, and the general cognitive field will play an essential part in the process by which a principal conative disposition gives rise to subsidiary dispositions; but the process will go on without any conception of the '(quasi-)ends' so related. The subsidiary disposition arises (with its 'quasi-end') *because* of the existence of the principal disposition (with its 'quasi-end') plus the unreflective cognition of the general objective order, but not through grasp of 'reasons'. The existence of the principal attitude is a cause of, but not a reason for, the growth of the subsidiary. What we suppose to be the characteristic level of the fish's cognitive life is shared by us in part. There are levels of human experience at which subsidiary dispositions, and even full overt activities, are induced when the cognitive contents are not 'ends' but merely 'quasi-ends'. There are the adjustments which we make during deep sleep, for instance, when we grow cold or are irritated in other ways.

Now at this wholly unreflective level of consciousness, neither the principal nor the subsidiary disposition can be called an attitude of approval, for the cognitive condition is lacking. The 'quasi-end' (unreflecting cognised) cannot have goodness attributed to it. There are, therefore, the two extremes: at the upper, we attribute goodness to the 'ends' of both the principal and the subsidiary disposition; at the lower, we attribute goodness to neither of the 'quasi-ends'. The dispositional attitudes are patently there, both at the upper and at the lower extremes; but only in the former case can these dispositional attitudes be identified with states of approval, and their expressions with attributions of goodness.

Between the extremes, however, there is a middle state possible. It is possible to be reflectively aware of the end of a subsidiary conative disposition, but not reflectively aware of the '(quasi-)end' of its principal or inducing disposition. The latter will, in this case, be a cause of the former, and the former will be an attitude of approval—we shall call the end constituting its cognitive content 'good'—but we shall be ignorant of any 'reason' why it is or should be regarded as good. This is quite a common situation in which we find ourselves. We are unable to give any cogent reasons for the goodness of the thing, and we are equally impervious to reasons offered by others professing to show that it is not good. This is where the philosopher's 'intuition' is brought in to cut the knot of the theoretical problem. These things, he will tell us, just *are* good-in-themselves. And so we have the (mistaken) distinction between things which are 'good-as-means' and things which are 'good-as-ends' or 'intrinsically good', the goodness of the former being provable by reason, the goodness of the latter being unprovable by reason and apprehensible only through 'intuition'.

From the foregoing analysis of the two ways in which principal dispositions may participate in creating subsidiary dispositions —either as 'causes' or as 'reasons'—it should be clear that our incapacity to 'prove' the goodness of anything may be due to one or other of two different sets of circumstances. It is admitted (indeed contended) here that we cannot prove the goodness of the end of any disposition which is not subsidiary to some other disposition; but it is also clear that we are able to prove the goodness of a subsidiary end only if we are reflectively conscious of the end of the principal disposition to which it is subsidiary; and we may in fact be reflectively aware of the end of the subsidiary, but not of that of the principal disposition. The end of the subsidiary would, in such a case, be for us 'ultimately good' (for the time-being at least), in the sense that it would be the ultimate end or object of *approval* (implying reflective awareness); but it would not be 'unconditionally good'; it would not be the ultimate ground of our attribution of goodness; it would not be an ultimate, but would be merely a subsidiary, disposition. If we were ever able to extend out reflective awareness to cover the principal disposition which is, for the time being, merely a 'cause' of this subsidiary one, then the latter would cease even to be 'ultimately good' and its goodness would become susceptible to 'reasons'. Reasons might show that, in certain circumstances, it is not good but bad; there could be objective situations, that is, which would imply that the principal disposition would be frustrated rather than assisted by the pursuit of the subsidiary end in question. Our incapacity to 'prove the goodness' of an end may, then, be due to the fact that our reflective awareness extends to it but not to the 'quasi-end' of the disposition which is a cause of it.

But it is at least theoretically possible that the incapacity to 'prove goodness' may have another basis. Supposing we could extend our reflective awareness over the most fundamental of our conative attitudes—over those which are not merely relatively principal attitudes but are ultimately basic conative patterns—then, since we should be aware of the 'ends', and not merely cognise the 'quasi-ends', of those ultimate attitudes, we should be approving those ends. The dispositions or conative attitudes would be 'ultimate as attitudes', and their cognitive contents would also be the objects of 'ultimate approval'. They would be regarded as 'ultimately good' not provisionally but finally— finally, that is, unless the basic patterns of our conative life were to change.

That there must be such ultimate conative attitudes seems clear. When conative dispositions constituting approvals are attitudes induced by prior cognition of the objective order, this prior cognition must itself have a conative correlate in the total mental state. It follows therefore that there is some form of conative attitude which is not derived but is inherent in our psycho-physical life. The argument is not that life as a whole does not have a beginning (that is a metaphysical problem with which I have nothing to do here). The argument is that our psycho-physical life is conative, as well as cognitive and affective, from the outset. That is merely to reaffirm the general psychological theory which has been taken for granted throughout the whole argument. If that theory is sound, then there must be conative attitudes which are intrinsic to our nature. Now, since it is theoretically possible that we should be or become reflectively aware of what those attitudes are, it is therefore theoretically possible that we should be able to conceive of the ends of these attitudes as good; and they will be ultimately good for us so long as our nature remains as it is, and those ends (so long as they remain thus ultimate) will be incapable of proof, because of their status, and not from any imperfection in our cognition.

Now, while much of the argument here has been concerned with the question as to the provability of the goodness of things, that is not the main interest. The proposition is that approval may be a subsidiary or a principal conative disposition; and the discussion of provability was undertaken merely to show that a 'principal' disposition constituting a state of approval need not be interpreted in a relative sense so far as our conative life is concerned. It may be understood in an absolute sense as referring to those basic behaviour patterns which will persist as dispositions so long as our nature remains what it is. I should add that it would be incautious to lay too much stress on this last point. I have emphasised that I am talking of the theoretical possibility that the 'ends' of our most fundamental conative attitudes may emerge into reflective consciousness, and thus be the objects of approval. My personal guess is that this is unlikely to any important extent. Accepting the theoretical possibility that 'ultimate ends' and 'the cognitive content of ultimate conative dispositions' may be one and the same, I think that in fact we remain on a somewhat lower level of cognitive life. It is probable that the 'common demands' which are presupposed in our most general orders of valuation represent the nearest we get to the understanding of our ultimate conative attitudes; and that these 'common demands' are probably all expressive of principal demands in a merely relative, and not in an absolute, sense. But while this will be of great importance for the understanding of practical life, the theoretical possibility of reaching ultimate conative attitudes in reflective consciousness will have to be borne in mind for purposes of the later argument of this chapter.[1]

PROPOSITION XVIII

A principal conative attitude implied in a subsidiary approval disposition need not be teleological, but must be at least organic.

So far, in discussing conative attitudes, we have distinguished

---

[1] See esp. Proposition XXI, pp. 287-8.

between those the content of whose cognitive correlate is an 'end' (reflectively cognised) and those the content of whose cognitive correlate is a 'quasi-end' (unreflectively cognised). This distinction is sometimes equated with that between teleological and non-teleological. That seems to me to be an error. It appears to me that teleological activity is a branch of but not co-extensive with activity towards a reflectively cognised end. This is a point of some importance in the full analysis of the ultimate grounds of the attribution of goodness.

It is necessary to make clear, first of all, the distinction between the terms 'teleological' and 'organic' as here employed. The contrast at once suggested is that between psychical and physiological activity; but that is not the distinction I have in mind; and to avoid misunderstanding I should have preferred to employ some term other than 'organic' had one been available. 'Organic' is legitimate, because in ordinary usage it has a wide application and is used with reference to the mind as well as to the body. It is in this wide sense that I employ the term; and when I speak of an organic activity, as distinguished from a teleological activity, I am referring to a broad range of activities both physiological and psychical whose principal characteristic is that they are 'systematic', and of which teleological activities are a sub-division. That is to say, all teleological activities are organic in this sense, but not all organic activities are teleological.

An activity is organic when it follows a definite pattern and its various manifestations can be seen to be expressions of a whole. As an example we may take the process of development followed by the human organism from the initial union of two cells up to the stage of adult maturity. This is a pattern which had repeated itself through countless ages. As an example of an activity which is not organic, I instance the rolling and bouncing of a stone down a scree slope.

Teleological activity is a sub-division of organic. Perhaps I am using 'teleological' in too narrow a sense; but at any rate the reader will have to bear in mind the sense in which I am using the term. When we speak of an activity as teleological, we imply, I think, (a) that there is a conscious idea or conception of the state of affairs

T

to which the activity is leading, and (*b*) that the conception of that end or state of affairs is a necessary factor in initiating that activity and determining the direction which it takes. Thus the activity of going out to post a letter is teleological, for it satisfies the two conditions. The development of the human organism (subject to an important qualification which will be noted in connexion with a later proposition) is not. When two cells meet, they do not say or think: 'Go to, let us be a second Napoleon.' They have no inkling, one understands, of the pattern of development which they are initiating by their union. Organic development—physiological or psychical—is often spoken of as a manifestation of 'unconscious teleology'; for, to the external observer, it looks like the most marvellously thought out purposive action, though, from the point of view of the developing being, it is known to be nothing of the sort. But it is a pity to confuse issues by speaking of this as teleological in any sense, when the term 'organic' is perfectly suitable to the situation.

Not only do I exclude from the category of 'teleological' activity such activity as implies a mere 'quasi-end' such as the activity of fish in search of food; but I also exclude some activity which is associated with a reflectively cognised 'end' in the proper sense. This is very important in my subsequent argument, and it therefore requires special emphasis at the outset. I lay down two conditions for an activity's admission to the category 'teleological'. Not only must the end of the activity be reflectively cognised, but the conception of an end must be a factor in determining the nature of the activity. To explain briefly—in anticipation of later argument—what this signifies, it is necessary to point out that, on this view, no principal conative activity in the ultimate or absolute sense can be teleological. Only subsidiary activities can be teleological, for only subsidiary activities can fulfil both of the aforesaid conditions. Our basic or 'ultimate' behaviour patterns, even if we are reflectively conscious of, and thus able to approve their ends, are not made what they are by this reflective awareness. The reflective awareness is merely the cognitive aspect of the total psychical state constituting the activity; and therefore cannot be prior to the activity. It is only an activity which arises subsidiary to and by 'reason' of the basic activity pattern which can be teleological. These remarks are not here offered as argument, but are merely offered as an indication of the trend of the subsequent argument for the purpose of clarifying at the outset the sense I attach to 'teleological'.

With this explanation of the meanings of our terms, we now pass to the statement in the proposition, 'the principal activity implied in a subsidiary approval disposition must be at least organic'. The activity may be 'blind' in the sense that there is no conception, in the mind of the being whose activity it is, of the direction in which it is tending, and of the results which will follow. But however 'blind' the principal activity may be in this sense, it must at the very least be a definitely patterned activity. If it were not following a regular pattern, then anything frustrating it would not be resisted, but would be merely acquiesced in; and the flow of the activity would change direction accordingly, as a stone bounces its way down a slope. There would therefore be no disapproval of unfavourable or obstructive conditions. That is to say, unfavourable conditions would not be judged bad; and favourable conditions would not be asserted to be good. There would be no disposition to maintain them. The developing organism, for instance, would not put forth effort, as it clearly does, to manage and adjust the environment to further the pattern of its development. But a developing organism, no matter how non-teleological its activities may be, does not passively conform to environment in this way. It strives to adjust the objective order in suitable ways. At the level of conscious life this moulding of the environment is to a considerable extent teleological; but the moulding has been going on long before the conscious stage.

PROPOSITION XIX

The more distinctly we conceive the trend of any organic activity, the more will its particular expressions take the form of teleological activities.

One of the great problems in Christian theology has been that of reconciling 'God's foreknowledge' with 'man's responsibility', since the former notion seems to require a determinist, and the latter a libertarian, view of human conduct. The same problem arises for the philosophy of dialectical materialism, inasmuch as the world is assumed to be moving from stage to stage in a process determined by certain laws, and at the same time we are supposed to be able to 'assist', or in some sense 'direct', the process by conscious effort, once we apprehend the direction it is taking.

I do not propose to deal with these metaphysical issues. They have their significance in moral philosophy, but they arise in connexion with the problem of freedom rather than in connexion with the theory of the value judgement. Still, they are not wholly unrelated to the question with which our present proposition is concerned; and the solution offered in connexion with our problem may be of some interest to those who deal with the problem of freedom.

In Proposition XVIII we drew a distinction between teleological and organic activity; and it may be suggested that the distinction is so clear-cut that it is hardly proper to speak of teleological activity as a sub-division of organic. Not only are the two conceptions distinct, but (it may be said) activities themselves must fall exclusively under one or other of these headings. An activity cannot be both teleological and organic. Organic activities are not 'motivated', in the proper sense of the term, while teleological activities are, the motive being 'the conception of the end to be realised through the activity'.

Now this view might be the proper one to take if we could feel happy about the assumption that the motive is the 'conception of an end'; but there are some difficulties in the way of adopting such a theory. If we begin by thinking of the motive as the conception of the end, the more we examine the relation of ideas to behaviour, the more do we seem driven to a quite different theory, namely, that consciousness is a mere spectator of processes which go on uninfluenced by it.

I shall try to state this difficulty in the way in which it often appears to those who first begin to reflect on the problem. If the idea or conception of a future state of affairs is the motive or moving force in action, why does this idea sometimes 'motivate' or move us, and sometimes remain a 'mere idea' without practical effect? I can have the clear and distinct idea of putting on my hat and going to the pillar-box with a letter; and I can be quite convinced that this activity is within my power, and yet refrain from carrying out the action. The idea may remain a mere idea without motivating. At other times the idea does become translated into action. What makes the difference? Surely the motive must be something other than the idea—something necessary to link the idea to action? Again, I can have a clear idea of the direction in which my activity is tending, be actually engaged in that activity, and yet be quite convinced that my conception of it has nothing to do with the direction the activity is taking. Thus, when I am a child, I know that I am growing up to be a man. There is the conception of the end, and there is the activity directed towards this end; but the idea seems to be a mere accompaniment, and not in any sense a determinant, of the activity. May it not be the case that our ideas of ends are never really motives, never do in fact influence the course of our activities, but are, in the last analysis, merely the spectators of what is proceeding independently of them?

Thus, when we consider teleological action, that is to say action in which the conception of the end is a necessary factor in determining the direction which the activity takes, and try to explain it in terms of 'motives' consisting of 'ideas' or 'conceptions' of 'ends', the result of our reflections may lead to the conclusion that there is no such thing as teleological action in this sense.

The trouble about this 'spectatorial' theory of the role of consciousness, however, is that, while it does seem to be the inevitable result of analysing the implications of certain facts of experience, it also appears to be flatly contradictory of equally cogent inferences from other facts of experience. While it seems to be the case that our growth from childhood to manhood is an activity independent of consciousness, it seems to be equally true that, when I want to post a letter, the idea of the pillar-box as being at the north, and not at the south end of my street will be a real determinant of the activity in which I engage in going out to post the letter; for this will direct my steps to the right and not to the left when I leave the door of my house.

This antimony seems to arise largely—though not perhaps wholly—from the attempt to regard the 'motive' of action as 'the conception of the end'. A solution may be found through a more careful consideration of what a motive is.

It seems reasonable to assume that a motive, being that which moves to action, must be conative and not cognitive. Hence it will not be the 'idea of the end' considered as a cognitive state. If it be replied that every psychical state is at the same time cognitive, affective and conative, I have no objection to modifying my statement accordingly; we may say that it is reasonable to assume that the motive must be the conative and not the cognitive aspect of the total psychical state. Further, when we speak of a motive, we are thinking of that which initiates an activity in the full sense; what is 'motivated' is not a mere conative 'disposition' or 'activity set' but an overt action. If, then, that for which we are seeking the motive is conative, and if we may assume (as seems reasonable) that the motive must itself be conative, the probability is that the 'motive' will be a conative disposition. That which is motivated is an action, a full conative activity. That which motivates is the conative disposition which, on a given occasion or signal, is transformed from a disposition to a full activity. The disposition to act, or the potential activity, is, on the appropriate occasion, transformed into actual activity.

On this hypothesis that the conative disposition is the motive in the proper sense, how do we relate this disposition to the 'idea of the end' which is so often regarded as the motive? We have already tried to show[1] that the cognitive aspect of a state of approval is the idea of the end approved (in unreflective consciousness the cognitive content correlative to a given disposition is a quasi-end). Considered merely as the cognitive aspect of a total psychical state, the idea or conception of the end does not in any sense motivate or originate action. But the total psychical state of which this conception is the cognitive aspect does originate

[1] See pp. 240-4; 266-72.

or motivate action; for, corresponding to the conception of the end, there is, in the total psychical state, a conative aspect which is the disposition to the activity which will result in the actualisation of that end.

On this theory of the nature of the motive, and of the relation of the idea of the end to the motive, let us see how the theory bears on our proposition that 'the more distinctly we perceive the trend of any organic activity, the more will the particular expressions of that activity take the form of teleological activities'. The argument may be conveniently developed in four phases. We shall try to show: (1) That before it can be a motive, a conative disposition must develop from being a vague general disposition into one of a precise and specific nature by the aid of cognitive clarifications; (2) That this precise focussing of the disposition turns it into a set of particular complementary dispositions; (3) That the activity in which each of these particular dispositions issues must be a teleological activity if the end of the general disposition is reflectively cognised; and (4) That these particular activities will tend to be teleological, even though the general activity of which they are manifestations is, in origin and general character, merely organic and not teleological.

(1) A conative disposition probably begins normally as a vague general disposition towards some form of organic activity, the trend of which is not clearly conceived. Even if the end is more or less well defined, the stages by which it is to be brought about in action will not be clear. Thus, if I arrive at a strange hotel in a strange city and, having written a letter, wish to post it, the end, 'the posting of the letter', may be clear in my mind, and the disposition so far clearly focussed. But, in a sense, the disposition to post the letter will be general and imprecise, because I have not sufficient information about the objective order constituting my environment to know how to go about it. I don't know whether there is a box in the hotel, I don't know if a pillar-box is near and, if so, in what direction it lies. But as I acquire the relevant information, the conative disposition (which, as we have seen, is a response to awareness of an objective order) becomes progressively more specifically directed. If I find out that, by turning left from

the hotel door, turning right, crossing the street and proceeding for 100 yards, I shall come to a post office, then the clarification of my ideas about the objective order will carry with it a correspondingly precise focussing of the disposition. Until it has become so specifically focussed it cannot be a motive to any action. It cannot respond to an 'occasion' by transforming itself into a full conative activity. The 'clarification of the conception of the end' is therefore the necessary antecedent, within the total psychical state, of the 'precise focussing of the conative disposition' which cannot be a motive until it has become so focussed.

(2) If we consider what takes place as the disposition alters from its vaguely general to its concretely focussed form, it is apparent that it is becoming differentiated into a complex of subordinate complementary conative dispositions, corresponding to the various stages in the total activity which will be necessary to get from the hotel to the post office and drop the letter into the box. Each of these stages in the whole has to be focussed— picking up the letter, going down stairs, turning left, turning right, crossing the street, proceeding 100 yards, and finally dropping the letter into the box. The completion of the one stage is the occasion for transforming the disposition relative to the next stage into full activity. There is a total general 'continuing set' or disposition towards the general end, but this is analysable into a complex of particular complementary dispositions constituting a pattern, the completion of the activity appropriate to the one being the occasion for the active expression of the next.

(3) The activity in which each of these dispositions issues must be regarded as teleological, for by a teleological activity we mean one which has, as a necessary condition of its direction and form, the conception of an end. In each of these subordinate activities —the leaving the hotel, the turning left along the street, etc. etc. —the character of the activity has, as a necessary condition, the idea of the general end towards which they are all tending, namely the letter being deposited in the post-box. That which gives direction to each of the subordinate activities within the

whole complex is the idea of the end envisaged in the whole
series, not the particular end which is the cognitive aspect of any
given particular subordinate activity within the general activity
as a whole. The conceptions of the particular ends are simply
the cognitive aspects of the particular subordinate dispositions
(the disposition to go downstairs, e.g. having as its cognitive aspect
the idea of proceeding downstairs, the disposition to turn left
having as its cognitive aspect the idea of turning left, and so forth).
It is important to bear this point in mind since, in discussing the
question whether an activity is teleological or not, what we have
to discover is whether there is any conception of an end which
gives direction to that activity. It is the conception of the general
trend of the activity as a whole, namely its final result in the posting
of the letter, which (on being clarified through increasing knowledge of the objective order within which that state of affairs is to
be embodied) gives rise to each of the particular dispositions constituting a special expression of the general disposition to post the
letter. The ideas of the specific ends, comprising the successive
stages in the carrying out of this total activity, are but the cognitive aspects of the respective particular dispositions; and therefore these ideas of particular ends could not give rise to the dispositions (and hence to the appropriate activities) of which they
are themselves the cognitive aspects.

(4) We come now to the most important, and at the same time
the most difficult, part of the argument. So far we have confined
our attention wholly to activities which are acknowledged to be
teleological. We have explained the teleological nature of subordinate activities within a whole activity by showing that these
subordinate activities would not be what they are in the absence
of an idea of the 'general end' towards which they are all tending.
But the end which we have selected for purposes of illustration is
itself an end of a teleological activity. It is not only the particular
stages in the activity of posting a letter which are purposively
directed; the activity as a whole is purposively directed; for there
is (one may assume) some end for which we are anxious to post
the letter. But what our proposition asserts is that, when we
conceive clearly the trend of even a merely 'organic' (that is,

non-teleological) activity, the subordinate activities which constitute its particular expressions will take the form of teleological activities.

This part of our problem can best be discussed by considering a kind of activity which seems to be quite patently not teleological, and examining the way in which this activity is likely to be influenced by a clear conception of the end towards which it is tending. It has already been suggested that the development of the human being from conception to adult maturity is an organic activity of this type, and not a teleological one, because here we have an instance of an activity pattern being followed out which is not dependent on any conscious purpose on the part of the individual concerned.

Now it is quite true that, if a person lives long enough, this general organic pattern will be followed out in some form or other, irrespective of any purposes which the individual may entertain—provided, of course, that he does not deliberately set his face against continuing to live at all. But the degree to which the development is merely organic varies in the different stages. From conception to birth we are safe in assuming that it is merely organic. The available evidence of when the higher centres of the brain begin to function to any considerable extent suggests that, for at least some months after birth, the process continues to be merely organic. But there comes a stage in comparatively early childhood when teleological activities begin to influence the way in which the general organic development expresses itself. The child becomes aware of the direction in which his growth is tending. He perceives that some day, if he lives, he will be a man. His interest in what this will be like makes him very attentive to what men do and are. His conception of the state towards which he is himself tending becomes filled out and clarified. All men have beards or else shave in the mornings; they are able to scold and grumble with impunity when things don't please them; they are able to read the newspaper at breakfast; they go out to 'work' or 'business' with bags of tools or brief cases; they drive engines; they prescribe nasty medicines which you have to swallow or something dreadful will happen to you; and so on.

As this idea of what manhood means gradually takes shape, the child at the same time begins voluntarily to participate in its realisation, and thus to determine to some extent what will be the final form in which he himself will develop to maturity. He assiduously shaves in the morning (when he remembers) with a clothespin; he has a longing to be a doctor, or a parson, or an engineer, or a soldier. This presumably is why it is possible to keep the majority of children at school for a period of years, and get them voluntarily to co-operate in the fairly arduous business of disciplining their minds and bodies.[1] It explains many of the games they play. Quite obviously it is the explanation of the amusing (and shockingly revealing) actions in which they imitate what they imagine to be grown-up behaviour.

What is happening here is that the conception of the end towards which the child sees the whole process of bodily and mental development to be tending, stimulates in him the growth of conative dispositions towards this end in some specific form; and the more clearly he envisages the concrete character of the end, the more will these dispositions themselves be focussed in specific ways, directed to subordinate ends, and thus influence the form in which the whole process of the development will ultimately embody itself. The process, taken in its general character, is unquestionably a merely organic process. It would go on in some form irrespective of the purposes of the individual. But the concrete form which it takes is largely influenced by the clarity with which he conceives its trend. The conception of the trend arouses dispositions which give that trend specific directions. These dispositions and their corresponding activities are all teleo-

---

[1] It has been suggested to me that I am here crediting young children with a long-sighted, serious purposiveness which bears little relation to the attitudes of children. Possibly. But the reader is invited to cast his mind back to childhood and to ask himself: what sort of consideration did then induce me to apply myself to tasks and to submit to a discipline (admittedly devised for me and imposed on me by others) which did in fact constitute a training for a future status? Supposing I believed firmly that I should cease to exist after my fourteenth birthday, would this have made any difference? Did a long-term view of adult status play any part in determining my behaviour? If such a long-term view did play a part to *any* extent, then to *that* extent the behaviour which constituted my 'growing up' was teleological and not merely organic, although it was a 'teleological particular expression of a process which, in basic, general character, was merely organic'.

logical; for they would not be what they are if the developing individual did not have a conception of the end towards which the general development is tending.

PROPOSITION XX

Teleological activity presupposes the existence of some prior organic activity.

If the argument developed under our last two propositions is valid, this present proposition must also be true.

The argument was that a teleological activity not only presupposes the conception of an end, but also presupposes that this conception of an end arouses the conative disposition of which the teleological activity in question is the overt expression. Now the 'conception of the end' which is a condition of teleological activity, and therefore of the disposition from which that activity issues, cannot possibly be the 'conception of the end' which is the cognitive aspect of the total psychical state of which that disposition is the conative aspect. It must be a conception of an end which exists prior to the existence of the disposition; for otherwise it could not be that which arouses the disposition. To illustrate:

The disposition to proceed down the hotel stairs (as the first stage of activity in posting my letter) is aroused by the conception of an end. But the conception of the end which arouses this disposition to walk downstairs cannot be the conception of walking downstairs; for this is the cognitive aspect of the whole psychical state the conative aspect of which is the disposition to walk downstairs. The conception of an end which makes the activity of walking downstairs teleological is the general conception of 'getting the letter to the post'.

If, then, we attend to a psychical state which has as its cognitive aspect the clear idea of an end (say the walking downstairs) and a conative aspect in the form of a disposition (the disposition to walk downstairs), we must say that, in relation to the conception of an end which is its own cognitive counterpart, any conative disposition must be regarded, not as teleological, but as merely organic; for the cognitive aspect of a psychical state is merely the cognitive aspect of *that* psychical state, and cannot exist before the total state (including its conative aspect) exists. *This* cognitive aspect does not give rise to the conative. The two are aspects of the one state. It follows that, since the conative disposition cannot be aroused by the cognitive aspect of that state of which it is itself a part, any cognitive activity (conception of an end) which can arouse a conative disposition must be the cognitive aspect of a prior mental state.

But if we attend, in turn, to this prior psychical state, the argument forbids us to say that its cognitive aspect can arouse the conative disposition or activity which is its conative complement; for the cognitive aspect cannot exist before the existence of the total state of which it is an aspect. The conative aspect of this prior state will thus be merely organic, unless there is some still earlier conception of an end which has aroused this disposition or activity; and this third conception of an end must, in its turn, be the cognitive aspect of a third psychical state with a conative aspect which will be merely organic, and not teleological, unless there is a still further conception of an end which has aroused it; and so the argument will proceed *ad infinitum*. What the argument signifies is that teleological activity postulates some prior conative activity which is not teleological but merely organic.

It should be noted that this implication is not reciprocal as between teleological and organic activities. The teleological implies the prior existence of the organic; but the organic does not imply, of necessity, the teleological. Organic activity does not presuppose any prior teleological activity, for organic activity does not imply the 'conception of the end' towards which the activity is tending. Nor is teleological activity implied as a necessary consequence of organic; for it seems to be the case that plants and some animals at least can go through the most intricate forms of organic activity without—so far as we can make out— any clear or reflective consciousness of any stage in the process. Hence, although the converse does not hold, it follows from the general line of our argument that teleological activity postulates the existence of prior organic activity.

PROPOSITION XXI

The ultimate ground of the attribution of goodness to anything is the existence, in the individual concerned, of some organic activity characteristic of his nature.

With this proposition we come, substantially, to the end of our analysis of the nature of the attribution of goodness. We began by asking the question: What is the nature of the process in which we attribute goodness to things? And we seemed to find that representatives of all schools of thought could agree on the proposition that, when we attribute goodness or badness, at least one of the things we are doing is expressing approval or disapproval. We saw, next, that approval is best regarded as a total psychical state in which, however, the emphasis is laid on the conative aspect; and that, when we speak of approval, we are thinking of this conative attitude, not as full or overt conative activity, but as a conative disposition to an activity in a certain direction. There are, however, conative dispositions the content of whose cognitive complement is not a reflectively conceived end but merely an unreflectively cognised quasi-end. To dispositions of this latter sort we take it that no one would regard the term approval as appropriate; for approval (at any rate as used in the theory of value judgement) must be associated with the 'judgemental' or reflective level of consciousness. Approval is therefore bound up with the reflective cognition of the end approved.

But we have seen, also, that the reflective cognition of any given end is the cognitive correlate (in the total cognitive-conative-affective mental state) of the conative disposition to *that* particular end. For instance if we are reflectively aware of an end A as approved by us, the conative disposition to A (which we emphasise when we speak of 'approval' of A) is the conative aspect of that total mental state which has the reflective cognition of A as its cognitive aspect.

Let us therefore consider the consequences of this with regard to the question of the ultimate ground of the attribution of goodness. Consider what may be called a 'final' or 'ultimate' approval.[1] By this we do not mean the same as a state in which there is a 'final conative disposition'; for the 'final conative disposition' might be an ingredient in a mental state whose cognitive element had not risen to the reflectively conscious level, and hence the conative disposition could not be called approval (or the total state could not be called one of approval). A final or ultimate approval must be a mental state where the cognitive element is a fully reflective awareness. When we consider an ultimate approval in this sense of a mental state in which there is reflective awareness of the end approved, there are two possibilities:

The *first* possibility is that we are in fact reflectively aware of the end or ends of our ultimate conative dispositions, of the fundamental or ultimate behaviour patterns inherent in our nature. Assuming this to be the case, then it is perfectly clear that the conative attitude or disposition here is not teleological but organic. Teleological activity implies, not only the reflective conception of an end, but also that this conception of the end does itself determine the character and direction of the activity in question. But the reflective conception of the end of an ultimate conative attitude can be nothing other than the cognitive aspect of that total psychical state of which the ultimate conative attitude is the conative aspect. The activity, that is to say, is not determined by the conception of the end but is itself an element in the total psychical state of which the conception of the end is also but an element. The conception of the end would not be present unless the conative disposition were also present. In a total psychical state the awareness of its 'own' end does not make that state teleological in its conative or activity aspect; for this conception of the end is not determining the nature and direction of the activity, but is merely an element in the state of which that activity is also an element.

It is therefore absolutely impossible that an ultimate conative attitude should be teleological, however clearly and reflectively its 'end' may be conceived. It must be merely organic, in the sense defined; and so the ultimate ground of the attribution of

[1] See for fuller elucidation pp. 270-1.

goodness here will be the existence of an organic activity characteristic of our nature.

The *second* possibility is that we cannot in fact become reflectively aware of the fundamental behaviour patterns intrinsic to
our nature (cannot be aware of our ultimate conative dispositions
or attitudes), but only of conative attitudes subsidiary to these
fundamental ones. But in this case, such subsidiary conative
attitudes must necessarily be merely organic and not teleological;
for even though we are reflectively aware of the 'ends' of the
subsidiary attitudes, we are not, *ex hypothesi*, aware of the quasi-
ends of the fundamental behaviour patterns to which those attitudes are subsidiary. Hence the subsidiary attitudes cannot be
what they are, or take the direction they take, because of (i.e.
cannot have been elicited in response to) the conception of an end.
The subsidiary attitudes are 'caused by', but do not arise 'by reason
of', the fundamental behaviour-patterns. There is no awareness
of any end other than the end which is the cognitive correlate of
the activity itself.

Therefore, whether we can or cannot be reflectively aware of
the ends of our ultimate conative attitudes, the ultimate ground of
approval of (of the attribution of goodness to) anything must be
the existence of some organic activity characteristic of our nature,
some fundamental behaviour pattern which is non-teleological.
Approval is the conative disposition towards a reflectively conceived end. If that end is the cognitive content of a subsidiary
attitude, it implies the existence of the ultimate conative attitude;
and if it is the cognitive content of the ultimate itself, that ultimate
behaviour-pattern must itself be merely organic and cannot, as
we have seen, be teleological.

As to what is meant by saying of a person that this organic
activity is 'characteristic' of his nature, our conclusions do not
warrant any inference as to the nature of such activities. We only
know from the foregoing reasoning that there must be such. I do
not propose to embark on metaphysical speculations about the
nature of man as such. Even if profitable, such speculations do
not fall within the province of the theory of the value judgement.

We can, of course, in practical life venture on some broad

generalisations as to what will be the characteristic activities of the human species; and we can say—again in broad outline—how individuals of certain groups will behave; but it is not the business of a general theory of the value judgement to deal with such empirical questions. So far as they are capable of fruitful discussion they will be considered by the mental and social sciences.

Nor is it the function of a general theory of the value judgement to consider the detailed ways in which, under the influence of the concepts of goodness and value, men build up the institutions and 'values' of social and personal life. We cannot deduce, from the mere principles elucidated in the foregoing theory, how these will express themselves in complex concrete circumstances, any more than we can deduce from the principles elucidated in the science of optics how a sunset over the Western Isles will actually appear. But just as the empirical experience of a sunset may be made more intelligible by a knowledge of optics, correlated with a knowledge of geology, meteorology, etc., so the theory of the value judgement, when correlated with other studies, will illuminate the field of human action and, to some extent, enable us to anticipate how men's conceptions of what is good and valuable will tend under given conditions.

PROPOSITION XXII

Value is the place occupied by the content of demand within a rationally integrated 'personal conception of good'.

Our final proposition, which brings together the conceptions of value, rationality and personal conception of good, carries a reference back to our initial statement[1] of the problem of valuation or the comparative value judgement. The problem of valuation, we said, is the problem of explaining how demand is directed in pursuit of a personal conception of good when the individual is confronted by conditions enforcing choice between alternatives. We took this as our first field of inquiry largely because this approach to the problem of the value judgement in general would enable us to profit by the work already done by economists.

---

[1] See Introduction, esp. p. 20; and Chapter I, pp. 35-42.

U

Economics, being essentially a social science, is concerned mainly with the order of exchange; and it develops its theory of valuation only so far as this is necessary for its main purposes. The primary interest of the moral philosopher is to trace the principles of valuation, if possible, right to their ultimate source in the individual mind, to discover those principles which operate whether man is or is not living as a member of society. But while this is the primary interest of the philosopher, he is greatly helped by taking as his starting point the main results of the work of the economist in the systematic study of the 'economic relationship'. When we study the basis of that relationship, we find that it presupposes certain specific things about the individuals who enter into it. They are all pursuing a personal conception of what is good; they are confronted by an objective situation in which they have to choose between alternatives, both of which they consider to be good, but both of which they cannot have; and they employ their rational faculties in deciding which of the alternatives better realises their conception of what is good on the whole. This exercise of reason is what is called valuing the alternatives; and it is in order to reflect back upon the original problem the general results of our inquiry that we state our final proposition in the form 'value is the place occupied by the content of demand' (or the place occupied by any given thing to which we attribute goodness) within a rationally integrated personal conception of good.

It may be thought that our concluding reference should have been to the notion of goodness rather than to that of value, since goodness is the more fundamental of the two. It is true that goodness is more fundamental in the sense that it is the conception indicative of possible membership of a valuational order, and not merely indicative of the specific place occupied in that order. It is more fundamental in the sense that a thing can be considered good without being assigned a value, while a thing cannot be assigned a value without being considered good. But it is just because 'goodness' is more basic or more fundamental in the foregoing sense that it is less important in another sense. In so far as we merely attribute goodness to things, and do not evaluate them, to that extent they may be merely an unco-ordinated collection of things which we approve. If they are to be co-ordinated, they must be evaluated as well as thought good; and this valuation is a function of reason and of reason alone. What is of importance for all practical purposes is to know how men evaluate; for it is by influencing their processes of valuation through the appeal to reason that we are able to influence what they will effectively choose as good. The appeal to reason here does not mean the mere showering of syllogisms on their heads. 'Reason' with them by all means; but the appeal to their reason is something much wider than this, for it includes all those methods by which they may be led to inform themselves about the nature of the objective order constituting their physical and social environment. It is their beliefs about the nature of this order to which their conceptions of what is good, and the arrangement of their relative values, are the responses.

SUMMARY

IN presenting a summary of this whole theory of value judgement (including the attribution of goodness and the attribution of value), it will facilitate appreciation of the salient points if I depart to a considerable extent from the strict order of exposition.

(1) The ultimate ground of all attribution of goodness is the existence in our nature of certain activity-patterns which are not teleological but organic.

(2) As we become increasingly aware of these behaviour-patterns and the directions in which they tend, we take a greater share in determining the particular forms in which they will be manifested; and thus activities, which in general character are organic, become in their particular expressions increasingly teleological.

(3) Our activities, whether organic or teleological, can be carried out only in suitable environmental conditions; and therefore there arise within us many subsidiary conative attitudes directed to the creation or maintenance of the necessary environmental conditions.

(4) Of these subsidiary conative attitudes, some are overt activities and some are merely conative dispositions towards activity—dispositions which will be transformed into overt activity if appropriate occasions arise.

(5) It is to the class of conative dispositions that the conative aspects of the psychical states called states of approval belong; and approvals are mostly, if not indeed entirely, subsidiary conative dispositions; for we do not call a conative disposition a state of approval unless the cognitive aspect of the state reaches the level of reflective awareness of its 'end'.

(6) The expression of approval may take different forms. It may consist in the transformation of the disposition into overt activity; or it may not go beyond a verbal statement; and in this latter case we call the expression a value judgement. At the most elementary level, value judgements are of the form 'This is good', 'That is bad'.

(7) A verbal expression of approval is quite properly called a value 'judgement'; for, while it is primarily the conative disposition which is being emphasised when we speak of approval, no psychical state can be merely conative. It necessarily has its cognitive and affective aspects. Hence the expression of approval, when it takes a verbal form (and even to some degree when it takes the simplest method of becoming overt activity), is subject to some extent to the criterion of truth and falsity.

(8) Now the value judgement in its simplest form, as the mere attribution of goodness rather than the attribution of a degree of goodness, is what the economist would call the expression of 'want' or 'desire'. It is 'demand' in the general sense (not 'effective demand' which the economist generally equates with 'demand' when using the term in a strictly technical sense in formulating, e.g. the laws of supply and demand). It is that psychical attitude in virtue of which the economist attributes 'desiredness' or 'utility' to that to which the attitude is directed. It is a psychical state with the emphasis on the conative disposition towards the creation or maintenance of a state of affairs.

(9) But any particular attribution of goodness, or demand in this general sense, may remain devoid of practical effect if it stands

in competition with other demands of the same subject, the objective conditions rendering necessary a choice between the two or more things demanded. Such enforced choice means enforced 'valuation', the placing of the alternatives in an order of degree of goodness.

(10) When we place things in such a valuational order, the placing is determined by 'opportunity costs'.

(11) The order of value assigned is the inverse of the order of opportunity costs; and for this comparison of costs to be possible, two conditions are necessary: *firstly*, the alternatives in any single valuational order must be considered as expressions of a common demand for that order; and, *secondly*, the common demand being complex, the things evaluated against each other must be, in reality, alternative combinations of things, each combination capable of satisfying to a 'greater or less' degree the complex common demand as a whole. It is to valuation in this sense that 'marginal utility', and the 'law of equilibrium' (the so-called 'law of diminishing utility') relate.

(12) While it is possible for different valuational orders to remain uncorrelated in the same individual mind, this separation can persist only so long as the common demands of the different orders can be satisfied without the one involving opportunity costs for the other. They are all potentially related; and they become actually related when such opportunity costs do arise. For with opportunity cost comes the necessity for choice; and with the necessity for choice comes the necessity to view the common demands of the different orders in a more comprehensive valuational order in relation to a more comprehensive common demand.

(13) This whole theory is appropriately called the theory of 'the value judgement' rather than the theory of 'the attribution of goodness' because, while the attribution of goodness is more fundamental than the attribution of a particular value or degree of goodness, inasmuch as the attribution of goodness is the essential condition of a thing's having membership of any valuational order while the attribution of a value merely assigns a place in such an order, still the attribution of a value includes all that can be meant

in the attribution of goodness, and much more. So far as we merely attribute goodness to things, they are merely an unco- ordinated collection of things approved. To be rationally co- ordinated in 'conditions of scarcity of resources' (the normal, if not indeed the invariable, conditions of life), they must be valued. Hence it is our valuations, rather than our mere attributions of goodness, which normally determine what we effectively regard and pursue as good; and therefore it is normally through our valuations that we can be influenced in practical affairs by our own and others' knowledge and opinions.

(14) It was shown that the ultimate ground of the attribution of goodness (the 'simply positive value judgement') is the exis- tence in our nature of certain organic activity-patterns. But to state the ultimate ground of our comparative value judgements— those value judgements which normally determine what we effec- tively regard as good—we have to do so by reference to the principle of Economy. This is the principle whose operation is popularly described as the search for happiness. It is that principle in our nature, as unitary self-conscious agents, which makes us integrate our different conative dispositions in the pursuit of 'what is good on the whole'.

Chapter Ten

VALUE JUDGEMENT, MORAL JUDGEMENT, AND FREEDOM

In expounding the theory of the value judgement I have tried to make it clear that I have been concerned only with one of the three main problems of ethics. The theory is a theory of the judgement that such and such a thing is 'good' or 'better' than something else. It is not at all concerned with the moral judgement, with assertions to the effect that something ought or ought not to be done. And, of course, it makes no attempt to deal with the third main problem of ethics, the problem of freedom.

But despite this insistence on the limited scope of the work, it is likely that readers will constantly offer objections to the arguments, or to the conclusions, on grounds which are in my view quite irrelevant to the arguments and conclusions themselves. I anticipate that there will be many such criticisms, because I think that most of those who write on moral philosophy are particularly liable to confuse questions concerning the value judgement with questions concerning the moral judgement. It seems to me that it is confusions of this sort which permit them to retain the term 'moral goodness' in whatever technical vocabulary philosophy may be said to possess, to talk of 'ethical sentences' as covering indiscriminately judgements of value and judgements of 'ought-ness', and to be fascinated by the notion that 'goodness' must somehow be an 'intrinsic' property of things so as to provide an 'imperative' ground of behaviour independently of likes and desires.

While, however, I deprecate the introduction of what I consider false issues into the discussion of the value judgement, I have no faith that such issues will be excluded from the minds of readers of this work merely because I say that they are false. If my views on the matter are somewhat out of the main run of contemporary philosophical thought, it is reasonable to suggest that I should place the theory of the value judgement as here developed in a wider context, and thus afford the reader an opportunity of understanding (however much he may reject) my criterion of relevance. To meet this requirement it is necessary to explain how the theory of the value judgement stands in relation to the other main problems of ethics, and give some general hint as to how an ethical theory as a whole would appear with this particular theory of the value judgement as one of the ingredients.

Some general idea of the place occupied by the theory of the value judgement in an ethical system as a whole may be gathered if I say that this book is substantially a greatly enlarged and revised treatment of the ground covered in 'The Meaning of Good'— the first part of Chapter IV of my *Principles of Moral Judgement*. But probably the best method of putting the theory in its context will be to state briefly here the answers which I am inclined to give to the other main problems of ethics. It should not be necessary to add that, in dealing with the moral judgement and the problem of freedom for the limited purposes here in view, the exposition I give will be nothing more than a very brief and quite dogmatic account of the position I hold.

I.   THE THEORY OF MORAL JUDGEMENT

1. THE PROBLEM OF OBLIGATION

As the problem of the value judgement is common to morals and economics, so the problem of obligation is common to morals, law and politics. That this is so is clear from the fact that all three make use of the same fundamental concepts—duty, right, wrong, justice, and so forth. The moral philosopher wants to know the principles upon which, in the last resort, we judge that our duty is to do x rather than y. The legal theorist wants to know the principles upon which a legal order is founded. The political theorist wants to know the principles upon which obedience to authority in the social order is founded. These are different aspects of the one general problem.

But how the problem is to be approached (there have been widely different opinions). Some—e.g. Plato and the mediaeval thinkers—place in the forefront the conception of the connexion between morals, law and politics. Others—e.g. Hobbes, Austin and Kelsen—appear to hold that no legal and political theory can be properly developed unless we begin by emphasising the distinction between morals, law and politics. Both of these extreme views seem to have unfortunate consequences. On the one hand, the initial emphasis on the connexion of law and morals tempts one to deny the distinction between 'law' and 'justice'; and, on the other, initial insistence on the distinction tends to result in a 'positivist' theory of law which makes it hard to understand how moral ideas could have the influence which they have in fact exercised on the development of the legal order.

Now there is a third approach which avoids both extremes. We can begin by asking, not how law 'originates', but how it actually operates as a going concern. It will be agreed that, however legal rules may come into existence, they are of no practical significance except as applied to concrete situations in human life. Surely, then, if we wish to build up a balanced theory of law we should begin by asking: How does law in fact operate? What is 'law in action'? Or, if we want to develop a theory of moral obligation, our first care should be the study of morals in action.

For a study of the principles of obligation, it seems most profitable to approach our problem in the first instance through law, because it is the lawyers who have made the most resolute attempts to analyse the working concepts which are relevant to the problem. That is to say, the theory of moral judgement will be most fruitfully pursued if we begin with the study of 'legal judgement', just as the theory of the value judgement is best approached through study of the analysis made by the economist.

(1) *Law in Action*

Law becomes operative—we have law in action—when legal rules, however they originate, are interpreted and applied to determine the legal rights and duties of the persons concerned in a given issue. For instance, I see a house advertised for sale, make inquiries, and the owner replies that he will sell to me for £2000. I inspect the property, and then write to the owner accepting his offer. I then think that I was foolish to agree; and I write to him again cancelling my acceptance. He brings an action to compel me to carry out the deal. Here is a specific situation in which the law will go into action.

It is of course true that, in probably 999 cases out of 1000, the law becomes active, not through the decisions of courts or professional lawyers, but through commonsense interpretation and application by the persons concerned, or (increasingly in our day) through the interpretation of administrative officials of the State. But, although the Courts function only in a small minority of cases, these cases are usually important, and it is in the activity of Courts that we see by far the most systematic and conscious application of law. It is their procedure, therefore, which shows most clearly the nature of law in action.

Now, if the layman were asked how the Courts go about their business, he would be apt to reply that, knowing all the rules (or at least knowing where to find them if wanted) the Courts first 'clarify the facts of the case' and then proceed to 'subsume the facts under the relevant rule'. But this is too naive an account of what happens. There will be many 'rules of law' applicable to a given 'set of facts'. Thus, in the case of the offer and acceptance of the house for £2000 mentioned above, there is a very relevant rule—'Acceptance of an offer completes a contract'. I have in fact accepted the offer, and it therefore *looks* as though nothing is required but to apply this rule to the case and enforce the obligation against me. But there is also the rule—'A pupil cannot enter into a binding contract', or 'The contractual undertakings of a lunatic are void'. And one or other of these rules *may* be relevant; for I may be under age or lunatic. We cannot, then, take *any* rule in sheer isolation and attempt to apply it; for the facts of the case are always complex, and any given rule applies only to a particular aspect of the case. These rules all qualify each other in the sense that no legal judgement can be given without considering all the important aspects of the case and all the rules relevant to these aspects.

Quite obviously, then, we are concerned with more than simple syllogistic reasoning in the application of law. For one thing, we must have some criterion to determine the relative 'importance' of the aspects of the situation; and this criterion cannot itself be some particular 'rule of law'. For, however we try to make a system of rules absolutely complete so as to provide a rule for every conceivable situation (an ideal of completeness which is in fact impossible of attainment), we shall always be confronted by the question as to the relative importance of different rules if they point towards different solutions for the total situation; and the criterion for determining the relative importance of rules cannot itself be any one or number of the rules whose relative importance is in question.

That is to say, law in action demands something more than a system of rules to be applied in making a judicial decision. There must be a system of rules *plus* some principle or principles in the light of which the rules are 'appropriately' applied. What these principles are will be evident if we reflect on the notion of the judicial process as *ars aequi et boni*.

(2) *Rules and Principles in the Judicial Process*

Judges of great practical experience who have tried to make clear to us what they understand to be their function and procedure often say that Courts are primarily courts of justice rather than courts of law. They do not mean that they are at liberty (much less have a duty) to ignore rules of law and pass judgement according to their own personal convictions of what would be ideally just. They mean that, in interpreting the existing body of law, they can do so only by postulating that the system of rules is intended to express in its various ways two principles in the light of which any given rule is to be applied. The principles are *aequum* (the equitable) and *bonum* (the good). The ultimate analysis of these principles is the business of ethics rather than jurisprudence; and so for the moment we shall confine ourselves to considering the way they actually operate in the judicial process.

(a) *Aequum*

The equitable means, essentially, the proportionately equal. Hence, although the basic notion is that of equality of treatment, to apply this principle will require a fine sense of discrimination when circumstances are complex. But the basic notion itself must always guide the application of rules as such. To 'administer a policy' is not necessarily to apply law. It is, fundamentally, to organise people's activities towards an end; and so the administrator often chafes at the restrictions of law because law does not permit him a sufficiently free hand in treating people *ad hoc*. But to administer or apply a system of law necessarily implies the use of the basic principle of equity, because one cannot apply a rule *as* a rule except by treating in accordance with its terms all cases and persons coming within the definition of its terms. Hence, however immoral or inequitable in general the system of rules may be, to apply any of its rules *as* rules means applying them equitably. For instance, assuming that we should agree in considering the Nazi anti-Semitic legislation immoral and inequitable generally, none of its detailed rules could be applied as rules except equitably, in the sense that, if there were a rule, 'No Jew is capable of owning heritable property', to apply this rule as such, or judicially, involves meting out the same treatment to every person and thing falling within the definitions of its terms.

(b) *Bonum*

The principle of 'the good' is involved in the application of law, as law, in the sense that every Court necessarily assumes that the law-maker has had some end in view in making the rules which are to be applied. The conception of 'good' here has no moral connotation in itself. The Court (provided that the rules come from a recognised legislative authority for that community) does not inquire whether the ends of the law-maker are wise, prudent or moral; but it necessarily assumes there has been some 'end in view'. Sometimes that assumption is wholly implicit because the practical implications of the rule are perfectly clear; but the assumption will become explicit when the meaning is not clear and the rule requires interpretation. The Court has then to look to the 'end' to interpret the rule; and the nature of the end itself may often require interpretation on the *further* assumption that the legislator intends the effect of the rule to be in harmony with the general ends promoted by the body of law in general. The more interpretation required, the more will it be necessary for the Court to approach the point at which it finds its guidance, not in ends explicitly declared by any legislator, but in inference as to what these ends may 'reasonably be assumed to have been'—what would have been a 'reasonable end for a legislator in the situation'.

For instance, take the rule, 'No Jew is capable of holding heritable property'. Who is a 'Jew'? Suppose the German Courts of the time found the broad practice to be that a person was regarded as a Jew if he had an admittedly Jewish grandparent. They would then define 'Jew' in that sense for the case (and all subsequent ones) before them. The assumption would be that the legislator had as the 'end' the prohibition of ownership of heritable property for anyone with that degree of Jewish ancestry. But supposing a further case arose in which it was contended that a person was a Jew because he had a great-great-grandparent admittedly a Jew; the argument being that, since the grandparent (having a grandparent a Jew) was a Jew, then the grandson, having a Jew for a grandparent, must be a Jew. This no doubt would be a perfectly reasonable argument in many respects. But the Court would not be interested primarily in problems of scientific biological classification. It would be concerned with the interpretation of 'ends of legislators'. It would ask itself whether the real intention was to demand from every person claiming to be an Aryan a properly authenticated pedigree back to Adam, and consequently turn the whole country's system of property right into utter chaos. There must have been a 'practicable' objective, and therefore a 'reasonable' objective, one such as a responsible or reasonable legislator would have had in mind. It is this conception of an 'end' underlying anti-Semitism—some end which can be pursued consistently with the operation of a reasonably systematic legal order for Germany—which the Courts would try to envisage, and in accordance with which they would then interpret the scope and

limits of anti-Semitic legislation. Within this context the terms
of the particular rule would be defined and its relevance determined for any given case.

It will be appreciated that I have chosen this illustration of the
way in which the principle of 'the good' operates in the judicial
process in order to exclude any suggestion that 'the good' is
necessarily something which is morally approved or regarded as
'just'. The end envisaged in anti-Semitic legislation is indeed one
which most civilised people disapprove. But for this very reason
it will help to bring more clearly into view the point to be made
in the next stage of the argument. What has been argued up to
now is that any system of rules to be applied as law must be
applied in the light of two principles: firstly, the principle of
equity (the rule must be applied to all persons and things coming
within the definitions of its terms); and secondly, its scope and
relevance must be understood by reference either to the ends
explicitly professed by the legislative authority or to such ends
as the authority may reasonably be understood to have entertained.

(c) Ars Aequi et Boni

While the principle of 'the good' has in itself no specifically
moral connation—it is morally neutral, as the foregoing chapters
setting out a theory of the value judgement have made plain—
nevertheless the interplay of the principles of 'the equitable' and
'the good' in the application of a system of rules is always tending
to adjust the system to the moral standards current in the community. This comes out most clearly when the system of law is
largely a system of 'Common Law' the development of which is
guided by the Courts; and if a government is prepared to give
to Courts the autonomy necessary for their judicial function,
however unlovely the system they are initially called on to
administer, the tendency is for it to be slowly transformed into
something more consonant with current ideas of justice; for if
the system is very bad, the Courts will constantly be faced by
cases in which they cannot really avoid looking to the 'ends' of
the legislator, and at critical stages formulating the 'ends' which

a 'reasonable legislator must have had in mind in making such and such a rule'. This process very often leads to curious interpretations of old rules; but the guiding motive, even in the creation of some of those legal fictions which are later found clumsy and irritating, is the attempt to interpret 'reasonably' and apply equitably ends and rules which, in origin, may have been anything but justly conceived.

The judicial process, then, is a skilled art—*ars aequi et boni*—and it is the interplay of the two principles in the application of rules which gives moral content to the legal order (apart from the moral notions which are influential in the making of the rules themselves). This may appear paradoxical since, at first sight, neither of the principles operating seems to be specifically moral in character. That the idea of 'the good' does not in itself contain the moralising force will be evident from our analysis of the value judgement. The directing influence probably comes therefore from the principle of equity.

But before we can pursue this suggestion, it will be necessary to deal, very briefly, with the sources and concepts of positive law. While, up to now, all the emphasis has been on the point that the application of a system of rules is impossible without the use of the aforementioned principles, it is equally true that principles cannot be applied except through rules. Principles are not 'rules for guiding practice'. They are general regulative concepts which have to be 'schematised' in specific formulae before they can have practical significance. No such formulation can ever state fully the nature and scope of a principle; for every formulation, to be significant at all, must have reference to a context, and contexts are variable. The attempt to apply principles therefore inevitably gives rise to the creation of rules. Rules and principles, then, are necessary complements in any 'order of obligations', any order (whether legal or moral) within which the notions of 'right' and 'duty' are included. What precisely is the distinction between a question of 'legal' and a question of 'moral' duty we are not yet in a position to discuss; but it will, I trust, be obvious that, if principles and rules are essential to both, and if—as has been argued above—'moral' notions are integral to the 'legal' order itself inasmuch as the principle of equity is necessarily applied in the administration of law, then the familiar concepts of a 'legal' order will be operative also in the 'moral'.

Our immediate task, therefore, will be to consider what assistance we can derive, for moral theory, from the analytical work which has been done on the nature of 'positive law'.

While 'law in action' involves the use of both rules and principles, the two things are more conveniently studied separately. The body of rules (particularly the body of rules in force in a political community) is termed 'positive law', and the study of its sources and concepts is the province of jurisprudence; while the analysis of the principles is, broadly speaking, the province of the moral philosopher. We shall consider those questions in general jurisprudence which will be useful in giving us an acquaintance with the sources and concepts of 'positive law' sufficient to grasp their bearing on the problem of moral judgement.

2. POSITIVE LAW: SOURCES AND CONCEPTS

For our present purposes, there are two questions in the general theory of positive law which are important. These questions concern (a) the Sources from which the rules derive, and (b) the nature of the Concepts employed. The treatment of these topics will of necessity be brief, allowing no space for the development of an argument; and it is hoped that the quite dogmatic presentation of the views I hold will be excused in the circumstances.

(a) The most important sources ('source' here meaning what is called a 'legal' as distinguished from a merely 'historical' source) are the Community (giving customary law), Courts or other permanent judicial tribunals (giving precedent or case-law), the Legislature (giving statutory law), and Private Agreement between members of the community (giving what is called conventional law).

Without discussing these different sources in detail, it will be sufficient to say that, on examining the range and degree of authority which each 'source' possesses, we reach a very important conclusion, namely that the range and degree of authority is directly related to the range of persons who have either directly or indirectly participated in the creation of the rules in question. Such a broad generalisation requires much explanation; but it will be remembered that I am not here developing a fully-fashioned theory; I am merely stating dogmatically the views I hold, for the purpose of putting the theory of the value judgement into perspective.

(*b*) The investigation of 'Sources' is of great assistance in defining the 'Concepts'. Law itself (in the sense of positive law) may be defined as 'A system of juridical rules, constituting norms of behaviour for the persons who have directly or indirectly participated in their creation, and directing action or forbearance for the promotion and protection of private and public conceptions of the good'.

This definition of law contains, directly or by implication, references to most of the fundamental concepts of the legal order. 'Personality' has a legal significance which may not be exactly the same as its meaning in psychology or metaphysics. A 'person', in legal terminology, is a being capable of exercising rights and performing duties; and personality may be either 'natural' or 'corporate'. Both natural and corporate persons are real persons in the legal sense of the term; and it is the distinction between natural and corporate persons which probably provides the basis of any systematic, not merely arbitrary, distinction between 'public' and 'private' law. A corporate person is composed of natural persons; and while private law is concerned with the mutual rights and duties of persons (whether natural or corporate) considered as quite separate from and independent of each other, public law is concerned with the mutual rights and duties of a corporate person, on the one hand, and, on the other, any of the persons who together constitute it. As a general rule, however, we speak of public law only when the corporate person called the State is involved.

The definition of personality includes the conceptions of 'right' and 'duty'. Rights and duties are necessarily correlative in the sense that the right (or duty) of *A* always implies the duty (or right) of *B*. But there is a 'logical priority' in the conception of

x

'right'. Just as, in the theory of the value judgement, we found that the conception of 'the marginal unit of utility' is correlative to or complementary to that of 'the marginal unit of equilibrium', though the latter has a logical priority in the sense that the former can be defined only by reference to it; so, while the conceptions of 'right' and 'duty' are correlative or complementary, the latter can be defined only by reference to the former. A 'right' is a sphere of liberty assigned by law to a person, within which he may act or forbear in accordance with his conception of the good; and a 'duty' is the legal demand or demands on another person or persons correlative to the right constituted for a given person.

So much for the main concepts of law so far as it is necessary to deal with these for our present purposes. These are the concepts of 'law' itself, 'person', 'right' and 'duty'.

3. MORAL JUDGEMENT

1. *Legal and Moral Judgement*

But, as we have already seen, 'positive law', or a system of juridical rules, cannot be practically effective—cannot be 'law in action'—without the operation of certain principles. The art of legal judgement is *ars aequi et boni*. The elucidation of these principles is the task of moral philosophy, or ethics, rather than of legal theory in the narrower sense. To attempt the elucidation of these principles is, in effect, to raise the question as to the ultimate grounds of 'obligation'. Why, in the last resort, ought I to do this rather than that? Why, in the last resort, is this a right, or that a duty? This is to ask a question which is at once 'legal' and 'moral'. In saying so, we are not denying the normal and perfectly legitimate distinction which men draw between their 'legal' and their 'moral' rights and duties; we are merely indicating that the principles and the juridical concepts employed are the same in both cases. The distinction between legal and moral rights and duties lies in the fact that the system of rules relevant to the issue is more strictly limited in the case of legal right and duty. A person's moral rights and duties are decided by his own responsible exercise of the art of judgement. He is not limited, in deciding what is ultimately right or wrong for him to do, to the adjustment of a fairly well defined set of rules in the light of the principles of 'the equitable and the good'. In moral judgement the rules of positive law are balanced against other rules which, considered on their merits, are regarded by the person judging as equally relevant to the situation. A person's legal rights and duties, on the other hand, are the rights and duties of the situation as the art of judgement, operating with a fairly well defined set of rules, called the 'body of positive law', adjusts these to each other in the light of the equitable and the good.

That there should be such a distinction between 'legal' and 'moral' is perfectly intelligible. If the members of a community are unable to administer a legal order entirely in their private capacity, if they have recourse to public legislatures and judicial tribunals, either because they cannot themselves see their way through the implications of any given decision, or because they are not sufficiently impartial to make the effort to do so, then they must accept the disadvantages as well as the advantages of a public judiciary. An authoritative public declaration of right must inevitably work with rules which are more limited in their ability to take account of fine detail, because they must be less limited in the range of situations to be covered.

To take a somewhat far-fetched analogy: If the works of art produced in a community were liable to arouse the same passions as questions of personal liberty and reputation, uses of heritable property and commercial contract, and if disagreements over what is and what is not art were likely to produce social unrest in the absence of some public control over what could be publicly exhibited, then there would grow up a distinction between 'personal' and 'public' aesthetic standards analogous to the distinction between 'moral' and 'legal' right and wrong. Privately and informally, people could paint and model and decorate their homes with a wide discretion appropriate to their own and their friends' tastes; but there would have to be certain rules generally acceptable as to art forms, the range of colours permissible, and so forth, governing all work for public display. There would be no essential difference between the 'personal' and 'public' conceptions of 'beauty'; the fundamental criteria would be the same; but, even though the practitioners of 'public art' might be the most distinguished artists in the community, their creations, as public artists, would of necessity be noticeably affected by the limitations within which they were bound to work.

In the same way, the 'positive law' of a community, upon which decisions must be based if people insist upon decisions which will be enforceable by the organs of the State, must consist of rules less able to take account of all the finer details of a situation than the adjustable and more flexible rules which small groups of persons can devise for their special circumstances. The public rules, for instance, must issue from certain well-defined 'sources'; and they will be regarded as valid rules, not because of what the Courts think of their merits, but because they do in fact issue from certain sources. Nevertheless, the fundamental character of moral and legal decisions is the same; they both consist in the art of adjusting rules in the light of the principles of the equitable and the good, and the basic concepts employed are the same.

To repeat, then; it is the business of moral philosophy, in dealing with the 'moral judgement', to grasp the nature of the juridical concepts employed in the operation of a legal order, and to proceed to the elucidation of the principles in the light of which law is applied in juridical judgement. This is another way of saying that moral philosophy is, in this respect, concerned with the ultimate ground of obligation.

(2) *Principles of Legal and Moral Judgement*

The principle of 'equity' is bound up with the notion of respect for personality; it is the principle which was partially formulated by Bentham in the words, 'Each to count as one, and none as more than one', and rather more adequately in the generally Kantian terms, 'Treat persons always as subjects-of-ends, and never merely as potential means to your own ends'.

The conception of 'the good' has been the subject-matter of this book. A person is a being capable not merely of recognising duties, of respecting others as subjects-of-ends; he is himself a subject-of-ends, a 'demander' exercising choice between alternative ends under the influence of the principle of 'economy'. To respect his nature, as such, is to accord him 'rights' and to abide by the duties implied in those rights.

The practice of the *ars aequi et boni*, therefore, assumes that all rules constituting norms for the behaviour of persons in their relations with each other are devised for the promotion of private and public conceptions of 'the good', in the sense of devising a framework within which the mutual respect of persons will permit of those conceptions of the good being pursued. The art of legal and moral judgement is not itself a technique for *securing* the good—not an application of 'technical rules' or 'hypothetical imperatives'. It is the application of a system of 'juridical rules' or 'categorical imperatives' within the framework of which techniques for securing the good can be autonomously employed.

(3) *Moral Judgement and its Ultimate Ground*

That we adopt such systems of rules, and such principles governing their application, implies that we can conceive of, and have a disposition to, conformity to law as such; that is to say, we are able to have, as the motives of action and forbearance, the conformity to a system of rules *because* they are juridical rules defining spheres of autonomy for persons as subjects-of-ends.

Further, since the definition of law is that it is a system of juridical rules 'constituting norms for the persons who have directly or indirectly participated in their creation', there is an important sense in which rules are not ultimately binding on us unless they commend themselves to us as 'fitting'.

This, in turn, implies that there is in each person a faculty of impartial legislation, a power of making rules, not primarily because they secure some self-regarding end of his, nor because they secure the most satisfactory adjustment of his various ends under the guidance of the principle of 'economy', but because they provide for the autonomy of all the persons with whom he is associated. The ultimate ground of the conception of obligation is the capacity in every rational being to legislate impartially for a community of persons.

This power of impartial legislation is something quite distinct from the power to evaluate ends under the influence of the principle of economy. It is not concerned with the co-ordination of ends as having different degrees of goodness; it is concerned with the apprehension of the principles governing an inter-personal order, and of that nice balance of various rules in a given situation which most exactly exemplifies those principles. Hence the emphasis in moral judgement is primarily cognitive, rather than conative (as in the value judgement). Of course it presupposes the conative disposition to social living. If a person were completely indifferent to the social order he would not bother himself about making moral judgements, any more than he would bother making technical calculations as to the means to some result if he were completely indifferent as to whether that result ever came to pass. But while our making moral judgements presupposes an interest in the social order, moral judgements themselves are primarily cognitive in the sense that they are the apprehension of the kind of adjustment of rules which, in given circumstances, exemplify the principles of the inter-personal order. They are therefore the apprehension of something about the objective order rather than the weighing of ends which are alternatives presented by the objective order. They are the apprehension of those actions and forbearances which are categorically imperative under the principles of an inter-personal order. As apprehensions of the objective order of imperatives, they therefore contribute to the setting of the alternatives between which we have to choose in the given situation; our moral judgements are thus, like our ordinary theoretical judgements of fact, constituents in the total apprehension of a situation calling for value judgement or choice as between the possibilities open to us in the pursuit of our total conception of the good.

4. Moral Judgement and Value Judgement

We have now to consider this theory of the moral judgement in relation to the theory of the value judgement expounded in the body of the work.

From time to time we have rejected as 'irrelevant' any criticism of the theory of the value judgement which proceeds upon the assumption that a theory of valuation must provide some 'imperative' ground of valuation or choice which is quite independent of our personal likes and dislikes, our demands and repudiations. But to regard such criticisms as irrelevant to a theory of the value judgement is not to say that they would be irrelevant with regard to a total ethical theory; and it will be clear, from the brief, dogmatic account of the theory of the moral judgement just given, that, in our view, it is the moral judgement, not the value judgement, which presupposes norms independent of our desires and demands. The question now to be considered, therefore, is whether a total ethical theory, which includes a theory of the moral judgement as briefly described above, does give proper weight to two convictions which most moralists regard as fundamental to the moral consciousness, namely (1) the conviction that there is some sense in which moral assessments are incommensurable with 'other valuations', and (2) the conviction that there is an imperative principle operative in experience which has an influence on our valuations and is yet independent of our likes and dislikes.

(1) Moral Judgement and Commensurability of Values

With regard to the first point—the 'incommensurability of moral assessments with other valuations'—the view here taken is that there is an element of truth in the assertion of incommensurability, but that the usual attempts to bring out this truth are vitiated by the confusion of the value with the moral judgement. The point is that moral *judgements* and value *judgements* are incommensurable, for the two kinds of judgement operate with quite different sets of concepts; but any genuine value judgement on that action which a moral judgement indicates as the action which ought to be done is a judgement in accordance with valuational concepts, and it therefore makes the action commensurable in value with alternative actions which may be evaluated against it. It is probably worth while elaborating this point.

A moral judgement—a judgement that such and such an action is the 'right' action, or the action which 'ought' to be done—is a judgement that, in the given situation, this action would be the

nearest approximation to the expression of the principles governing an inter-personal order. It operates within the realm of
juridical concepts—law, personality, right, duty, and so forth; it
is not given in answer to the question, 'What do I think the best
of all the possible alternatives in this situation, in accordance with
my conception of the total good?'; it is an answer to the question,
'What do I think most consistent with respect for the autonomy
of all the persons concerned in this given situation?'. The answer
to this latter question is the answer to the question, 'What,
morally, *ought* to be done?'. It tells us what, in the view of the
person making the judgement, would be the 'virtuous action'.

Quite clearly, then, it would be meaningless to assert that the
designation of an action as 'virtuous' makes it comparable or
commensurable with other actions designated as 'pleasure producing' or 'conducive to knowledge'. It is comparable, so far as
its 'virtue' is being assessed, only with other actions which might
claim to be the virtuous action in the given situation. To call it
virtuous, further (and this is the main point being stressed at
present), is something utterly different from attaching a 'value'
to it in the sense of affirming that 'it would be good to perform
this action' or that 'it would be better to perform this action than
any alternative action open to us in the given situation'. To
ascribe virtue is to make a judgement within the terms of juridical
concepts; to ascribe goodness or value is to make a judgement
within the terms of valuational concepts.

Now this, it seems to me, is the truth underlying the assertion
that 'moral and other values are incommensurable'. But to
attempt to state the truth in this form—'moral and other values
are incommensurable'—is to confuse the issues and encourage the
false inference that 'therefore virtue and other things are incommensurable in value'. It is to ignore the fact that, having decided
that x would be the virtuous action in the given situation, we
may then go on to make a value judgement, asking ourselves, 'Is
it better to do x rather than y?'. It is when we ask this latter
question, assessing the comparative values of x and y in the light
of our total conception of good, that our judgement operates
under valuational concepts, that marginal utility and the law

of equilibrium come into play, the ultimate ground of the judgement being the principle of economy. In all that has just been said, we are simply insisting on the distinction between the two questions, 'What is the morally right act in a given situation?' and 'Do we always choose what we see to be the right act in a given situation?'; and trying to make it clear that the concepts governing our assessment of rightness are juridical, and that those governing our actual choices are valuational or 'economic' in the sense of being grounded on the principle of economy. The 'oughtness' of an action is incommensurable with its 'goodness'; but the same action may be, and often is, assessed both with regard to its oughtness and with regard to its goodness.

That the 'virtue' and the 'goodness' of an action are very different things would be clearer if moral philosophers had been more discriminating in incorporating into the language of philosophy ambiguous terms of popular usage. In this connexion, the term 'moral goodness' is one of the chief sources of confusion. When philosophers talk of 'moral goodness' they are working with a conception which belongs to the sphere of moral judgement but are trying to express it as though it belonged to the field of the value judgement. If this thoroughly misleading term were relegated to its proper place in popular usage and omitted from whatever technical vocabulary ethics may be said to possess, this would be of great advantage in ridding ourselves of unfruitful controversy.

(2) *Imperatives and Value Judgement*

We turn now to the second conviction mentioned—that there is some imperative principle operative in experience which *influences* our valuations but is independent of our likes and dislikes. The theory of the value judgement developed in this work rejected the view that there is any such principle *operative in* the value judgement, either in its simply positive or in its comparative form. The ultimate ground of the simply positive judgement of 'goodness', we said, is the organic behaviour pattern inherent in our nature, expressing itself in conative dispositions; and the ultimate ground of the comparative value judgement is the principle of economy which stimulates us to choose, by reference to opportunity costs, in the light of our total conception of good. The value judgement therefore has an essential reference to our demands, likes and dislikes.

But the theory of the value judgement is not the whole of ethical theory; and it is admitted that there is operative in experience some imperative principle which, while influencing value judgement, is independent of our likes and dislikes. This principle, we hold, comes to light in the analysis of the moral judgement. The question now to be considered is whether, on our theory of the moral judgement, this principle is made more intelligible than it is by those who seek to interpret it by reference to the conception of 'intrinsic goodness' in things such as virtue, knowledge and pleasure.

Let us try, first of all, to locate those experiences which support the conviction that there is some imperative principle independent of our likes and dislikes which nevertheless affects our valuations, and which some philosophers try to explain in terms of a theory of 'intrinsic goodness'.

In trying to identify such facts of experience we can, I think, leave out of account Moore's rarified atmosphere in which beautiful or ugly universes exist without anyone experiencing them. If we are asked to imagine such worlds and to say whether we think that they are or would be good, we are in effect being asked to imagine or think of a world or worlds which no one imagines or thinks about; and it is somewhat difficult to say anything intelligible on this curious condition. We are much safer in giving our attention to real experiences.

Most of us would, I suppose, subscribe to the broad generalisations: 'Knowledge is good', 'Ignorance is bad', 'Pleasure is good', 'Pain is evil'. But it would be unsafe to infer from such general agreement that 'goodness' is something intrinsic to knowledge and pleasure independently of the demands or likings or conative dispositions of those who ascribe goodness to knowledge and pleasure. If knowledge is good, and if goodness is intrinsic to knowledge, then the statement 'Knowledge is good' would be much more than a broad generalisation to which we all assent.

It would be a universal proposition, true with respect to every item of knowledge. 'Malenkov's knowledge of all discoveries made by American atomic scientists is good' would be just as true as 'Malenkov's being kept in ignorance of all discoveries made by American atomic scientists is good' would be false. Presumably Russian government officials would accept the first and reject the second proposition; while it may be suspected that all American government officials—or at least those in possession of a F.B.I. certificate of character—would reject the first and accept the second. This variation in value judgements is much more intelligibly explained on our theory of the value judgement than upon a theory of intrinsic goodness. The essential point is that, as a matter of experience, such conflicting value judgements are made by different people, and made in such situations that we do not suppose that one of them *must* be false. At least one of them must be false if knowledge is intrinsically good; but, on our theory of the value judgement, there is no logical incompatibility between the two statements, the incompatibility being in the conative dispositions which are being expressed. To the extent to which value judgements are subject to a logical criterion (and all value judgements are so subject to some extent, inasmuch as the mental state expressed is not merely 'conative' but also cognitive' and 'affective'), the incompatibility of the conative dispositions is perfectly consistent with logical consistency of the cognitive contents expressed.

One may therefore venture the suggestion that, although the champions of the 'intrinsic' theory devote so much of their attention to the discussion of 'logical' issues, the real basis of their convictions is not that an objectivist theory provides a more 'rationally consistent' theory of the bulk of our value judgements (in point of fact the objectivist theory provides no theory of the value judgement at all, and is content with a metaphysical theory of the nature of the objective order). The basis of their convictions is, almost certainly, *either* an imperfectly understood, but nevertheless strong and enduring dispositional reaction to certain choice situations, *or* the mistaken view that the 'moral imperative' vanishes unless it can be brought within the theory of 'goodness'.

When alternative ends are set before them they may feel a compulsiveness or imperativeness about one of these which is not traceable to any demand or liking of which they are aware in themselves. The 'goodness' of the end thus seems to them to be 'in the thing itself'.

Now so far from denying this compulsive or imperative character which we feel about certain ends, I admit it without reservation. The only question in dispute is the question as to the theoretical interpretation of such a situation. There are two possible explanations which seem to me much more realistic than the one offered by the objectivist.

Firstly, certain situations of this kind can be explained wholly in terms of a theory of valuation without bringing in any specifically 'moral' issue. There are times when we say that we 'just know X to be good, though this cannot be proved'. The 'proof' that something is good takes the form of showing that it is good as subsidiary to something else. But there are cases where the goodness of a thing seems to have an imperative or compulsive claim on our recognition while proof is not only lacking but apparently beyond the range of possibility. The thing seems to be 'just good in itself'.

Now this is the sort of situation which we have dealt with, and of which we have offered an explanation, entirely within the terms of our theory of the value judgement, in Part II, Proposition XVII.[1] Any fundamental conative disposition inherent in our very nature would give rise to this sense of compulsiveness or quasi-imperativeness if we could be reflectively aware of the end to which the fundamental disposition was directed. Or even if we were not dealing with such a fundamental disposition, but merely with a subsidiary disposition, we should have the same sense of compulsiveness if we were reflectively aware of the end of the subsidiary disposition itself but not of the 'principal' disposition to which it was subsidiary. I shall not elaborate the argument here, for to do so would be to repeat what has already been said in the relevant part of the main text.

But, secondly, there are situations when the compulsive quality

[1] Pp. 270-1.

of certain ends cannot be explained within the terms of the value
judgement; and it is situations of this sort which may be illumi-
nated by taking the theory of the value judgement and the theory
of the moral judgement together.

If it be granted (as has been argued in Part II, Proposition XI,
especially pp. 243-4) that the attribution of goodness to something is a conative response to the knowledge or belief that the
thing has certain characteristics, it will readily be admitted that
the knowledge or belief that a certain action would be a virtuous
action, or that a certain action is a 'duty', could be the sort of
knowledge or belief which might induce a conative response, a
disposition to perform that action. In such a situation we should
be attributing 'goodness' to 'the doing of our duty'. It is also
clear that, if the doing of the duty were an alternative in a choice
situation (the doing of the duty entailing the sacrifice of some
other end, and the pursuit of the other end entailing the transgression of the duty), the end consisting of the 'doing of the duty'
would have an imperative or compulsive quality which would be
absent in the other. And this imperativeness would have nothing
whatsoever to do with that sense of compulsiveness which may
be generated by deep-rooted conative tendencies of a non-moral
kind. However strong may be the demand for the attainment of
certain other ends, and however weak the tendency towards the
performance of an unpleasant duty, the sense of imperativeness
which attaches to the latter will not attach to the former.

I think that this account of the situation is substantially correct.
The only question at issue is the question of theoretical explanation. The objectivist wants to say that in such a case we recognise
'intrinsic goodness' or 'intrinsic value' in the doing of the duty.
I say, on the contrary, that the sense of imperativeness attaching
to the doing of the duty has nothing whatsoever to do with the
'goodness' (in the properly valuational sense of the term) of the
action. The imperativeness derives from the fact that a duty *means*
an action prescribed by an imperative or juridical rule. In other
words, the imperativeness we feel with regard to the duty does not
necessarily mean that we attribute to it a greater value, or different
kind of value. It certainly does not mean that we shall choose to

do it as having 'a higher place on a valuational order than the other end'; it means neither more nor less than that we know this to be our *duty* and the other *not* to be our duty. In short, while the end consisting in the doing of the duty has an imperative character independently of our likes and dislikes, this imperativeness is not explicable on a theory of value or value judgement, but only on a theory of the moral judgement.

II. FREEDOM

1. Freedom a Postulate of Value Judgement

The third main problem of moral philosophy—that of freedom—arises through an apparent clash between the postulates of epistemology and those of ethics, or rather between the postulates of scientific and of moral judgement. Scientific judgement presupposes the operation of causality; and moral judgement presupposes the possibility of 'free choice'. To explain anything, we proceed on the assumption that it has a cause or causes. On the other hand, to say that I ought to do something implies that I can do it; and 'I can', in this connexion, implies 'I can also do otherwise'. We do not always do what we ought to do; but if we ought to have done it, then we could have done it even though we did not in fact do so. It is thus, at first sight, difficult to see how the postulates of scientific judgement and those of moral judgement can both be valid.

Now it may seem that this apparent conflict between the postulates of scientific and of moral judgement also arises as between the postulates of value judgement (as explained in this book) and moral judgement. The theory of the value judgement is that choice is always directed to the good as we see it, and, when we are confronted by alternatives, to that alternative which has the higher place in a valuational order in terms of 'opportunity cost'. Now if this be true, if it be the case that we always choose that which has the least opportunity cost, and if it be true that what we know to be our duty may be assessed as having a greater opportunity cost than an alternative line of action, then it follows that we shall always, in such circumstances, choose the non-duty alternative. If this follows from the nature of the 'laws of valuation', how can we continue to hold that the action we did not choose could have been a duty? Can it have been a duty if, according to the laws of valuation or choice, we 'necessarily' chose the non-duty?

Before we can properly appreciate the problem which here confronts us, it is important that we should distinguish it from the familiar Socratic problem with regard to freedom. Socrates held: (1) That all men seek and choose what they regard as good, and what they regard as better rather than what they consider worse; (2) That what is truly good is so independently of our desires and opinions—that 'goodness' is in fact an objective property which we may or may not truly apprehend; and (3) That virtuous action *means* action productive of good. It was because he held all three of these doctrines that he concluded that 'virtue is knowledge', and it is from this paradoxical conclusion that the problem of freedom in its Socratic form arises.

But while our theory accepts Socrates' proposition (1), his proposition (2) seems to us to be plainly inconsistent with any sound analysis of the value judgement; and we reject his proposition (3) as an account of the moral judgement. His theory of the moral judgement is 'utilitarian', while we hold that dutiful action means action in accordance with juridical rules and principles from respect for personality. Plainly, therefore, the problems which arise on a Socratic theory will not be the same as those which will arise on our theory.

How, then, does our theory stand with respect to the problem of freedom? Is it the case, as suggested above, that our theory of the value judgement is 'incompatible' with the postulate of moral judgement in the same way as the postulate of scientific judgement is apparently incompatible with that of moral judgement?

The answer to this question is both 'No' and 'Yes'. The answer is 'No' in the sense that, on our theory of the value judgement, the *value judgement* makes precisely the same assumption of 'freedom' as is made in the moral judgement; and the answer is 'Yes' in the sense that, as a *theory of* the value judgement, our theory makes the same postulate as is made in all scientific judgement. To explain these two points:

The postulate of the moral judgement may be expressed thus: 'There must be a genuine possibility of choice between alternatives —between that which is and that which is not my duty—in a moral situation.' That is to say, when we have set out exhaustively all the relevant conditions in a given situation, that is not and cannot be a 'moral situation' unless, in it, there are alternative modes of action either of which the person concerned can *choose* to do. In the moral situation one action is indicated by a juridical norm, an 'ought', to which a person may, but does not necessarily conform. But this conception of freedom of choice between alternatives is also a fundamental postulate of the value judgement in its comparative form at least; for the theory of the comparative value judgement is a theory to explain our *choices* in those situations where 'alternatives are open to us'. There would be no sense in speaking of the 'valuation' of 'this' alternative as against 'that' one, if it were assumed that one of them was not, in fact, open to us. Thus, if I regard *x* as my duty and *y* as likely to enhance knowledge, and if I must evaluate or choose between *x* and *y* because, in the given conditions, I cannot pursue both, it is clearly postulated, in the process of valuation, that both *x* (doing my duty) and *y* (pursuing this item of knowledge) are alternatives open to me, either of which I may choose. Clearly, then, the postulate of freedom, in this sense of the ability to choose between alternatives, is as fundamental to the value judgement as to the moral judgement.

2. Causality a Postulate of any Theory of Value Judgement

What, then, leads us to suppose that the theory of the value judgement is incompatible with the postulate of freedom? The answer is to be found in a distinction between the postulate of the *value judgement* and the postulate of any *theory of* the value judgement. The value judgement makes the same assumption of 'freedom' as is made in the moral judgement; but if we ever offer a theory of the value judgement to explain how valuation operates, then we are engaged, not in value judgement, but in theoretical analysis of the nature and principles of the value judgement. In attempting to explain how valuations or choices are made, we inevitably employ what are, in principle, causal categories of thought. This employment of the concepts of theoretical explanation is bound to occur, not only in a theory such as the one developed in this book, but also in any attempt whatsoever to theorise about the nature of valuation and choice. It is only those who resolutely decline to offer any theory who are able to avoid the apparent conflict with the postulate of freedom which underlies both the moral and the value judgement. 'Avoid' (not 'overcome') is the operative word here; for we merely evade, and do not overcome difficulties in the interpretation of the value judgement if we decline to put, and refuse to answer, the theoretical issues involved. It is submitted, with all deference, that the usual doctrine of 'libertarianism', which is supposed to set limits to the scope of 'scientific categories of thought', is merely an evasion of one of the great problems of philosophy. For we have either got to abandon any attempt to theorise about valuation and choice, or we have to adopt, in explaining, the postulates of scientific judgement.

3. Freedom and Causality as Complementary Postulates

The point of view adopted in this book is that valuation can be explained as governed by certain principles. The theory advanced therefore proceeds on the postulate of scientific judgement. At the same time, that about which we are theorising, namely the value judgement itself, postulates freedom in precisely the same sense as freedom is postulated in the moral judgement. The question confronting us, therefore, is that of reconciling the postulate implied in the value judgement with the postulate implied in any theory of the value judgement.

My own view on this question is somewhat Kantian in character. Broadly speaking, it denies that there is any real incompatibility between the postulate of scientific judgement and that

Y

of value judgement, because they belong to quite different universes of discourse.

The postulate of scientific judgement may be formulated with reasonable accuracy, perhaps, in the following way: 'Any given event can be "explained" only by showing its relation to some other event antecedent in time.' Thus, if I experience a number of events which I call 'light flashes', I may explain these as 'effects', the causes of which are the opening and shutting of my eyes when my head is turned towards a street-lamp; or I may explain them as the 'effects' of looking towards a lighthouse when the lantern machinery is operating. In either case, the 'explanation' consists in correlating the events with other events antecedent in time. I get what I call the 'real explanation' when I am able to correlate the 'effect-events' with some antecedent events in the absence of which the 'effect-events' do not occur. This I call the establishment of a causal relation between the former and the latter.

Now it is of the first importance to note that the 'establishment of a causal connexion' between A and B is *not* the 'establishment of a necessary, inevitable connexion' between A and B. 'Necessity' belongs entirely to the *a priori concept of causality*. We 'necessarily' assume, if we attempt to explain anything, that, if an event B occurs, there must be some prior event A which is its cause; but this is not to assume a 'necessary' connexion between B and A. No empirical experience can reveal a necessary connexion; but the *a priori* concept of causality drives us to interrogate experience to discover what events are, hypothetically, universally connected in the sense that *if* all other circumstances remain the same, the absence or presence of an event B will be correlated with the absence or presence of A. But all other conditions may not in fact remain the same. The mechanism in the lighthouse may be in fact operating, and I may have my eyes open; but I may have a bag over my head or have my back turned to the lighthouse. The causes—the A's—will thus be present, but the 'effect-events' (seeing light flashes)—the B's—will not. Hence to establish a causal relation between A and B is not to establish a necessary connexion between them. It is merely to establish a hypothetically universal connexion, in the sense that, *if* all other conditions remain the same, the presence or absence of A will be correlated with the presence or absence of B.

Further—and this is a point of the first importance in understanding the relation of the postulate of causality to that of freedom—causal connexions are not between 'things' but between 'events occurring in things'. People often speak of the 'causal connexion' as though it were a 'creative' or 'productive' relationship between 'objects' or 'substances'; and then they become entangled in the insoluble problem of the 'First Cause'. They say: Since everything must have had a cause, there must have been a 'first cause'; and yet this first cause, to exist, must itself have had a cause; and so, *ad infinitum*. The self-contradiction is due to the fact that they misconceive the meaning of 'causality'. Causality is not the creation or production of one 'thing' by another. The lighthouse, for instance, does not cause me. It is certain events in the lighthouse which cause certain events in me. Causality is a relation, not between things, but between events occurring in things; and 'events' are the modifications which things or 'substances' assume, the 'appearances' or 'expressions' in which they reveal themselves, in their reciprocal interaction.

On this conception of causality, it can be argued with real force that the postulates of causality and freedom are not incompatible; that, on the contrary, the concepts of causality and freedom necessarily imply each other. Causality implies what is, in principle, the concept of freedom for the following reasons: Laws of nature, or 'causal laws', are not laws governing the production of one substance or thing by another. They are formulae expressing how one thing or substance will modify itself in response to a modification in some other thing or substance. If then we assume, as we do assume in the *a priori* concept of causality, that the occurrence of a new modification or expression in one substance *necessarily* implies a prior modification in some other substance, and if particular causal laws are formulae stating how substances do in fact 'respond' to each other in this way, this is exactly the same as assuming that substances act in a quasi-teleological manner. It is to assert that, inherent in their nature, there is the capacity to modify their appearance, expression, or characteristic movement, as a response to significant or relevant modifications in the other substances which constitute their 'environment'. The whole universe is thus being conceived as a quasi-teleological order. We very properly confine the term 'teleological order' to an order of self-conscious beings; but, when we think out the implications of the postulate of causality, we see that what it implies is the notion of a quasi-teleological order in the sense that all substances whose modifications can be causally related to the modifications of other substances have a 'creative capacity', the capacity to 'produce' changes in their own appearance or behaviour as responses to other things.

There are, therefore, two quite distinct points of view from which we can and must regard the modifications of substances. From one point of view, modifications of substances are 'events' in space and time to be correlated causally with other events. From another point of view, they are the expressions of the 'creative powers' of the substances of which they are the modifications; and the conception of a creative power in a substance is something quite different from that of a 'cause'. It is not a 'mechanical' but a 'teleological' or 'quasi-teleological' conception.

It is the influence of this quasi-teleological background of our thought—this notion of a creative or productive power which is not simply a link in a causal sequence—that, in our first crude attempts to say what we mean by 'freedom', makes us speak of a 'free act' as an 'uncaused cause'. This is, of course, a contradiction in terms. Every 'cause' is also an 'effect', and there can be no uncaused cause. But there can and must be operative a creative factor which is not capable of being described in causal terms, but which is in some sense the 'creative agency' in substance, expressing itself in the events in space and time which are related to each other in causal terms. What we call this creative agency depends upon the level of being with which we are concerned. When we are dealing with self-conscious rational beings, we call it the conative aspect of our psychical life, 'will', 'desire', and so forth.

On the assumption that the foregoing exposition is acceptable, it will be evident that, when we speak of 'freedom' and 'causality', we are not speaking of two opposed principles which limit each other's fields of operation. We are not, in the first case, speaking of a principle which operates in man's rational nature, and, in the second, of a principle which operates in his physical nature and in the inanimate order. Rather, we are thinking of the total reality —the whole universe inclusive of man—in two different contexts. We can think of the universe as a totality of active agents; and we can think of the behaviour of this totality of active agents as a field for scientific investigation. The postulate of freedom (or quasi-teleology in the non-rational order) is a postulate of active agency or creative action. The postulate of causal necessity is a postulate of the search for knowledge. Both postulates are relevant to the whole universe, in the sense that any event—whether the rolling of a billiard ball or the rational act of conforming to duty—may be regarded *either* as a manifestation of agency *or* as an event to be understood and fitted into a theory. We may wish to understand the processes of moral and value judgement; and in this case we work on the postulate of causality. We may, on the other hand, be faced by a situation calling for a moral or a value judgement; and in this case we work on the postulate of freedom. This awareness of ourselves as agents does not in any way increase our knowledge of ourselves; it is simply the awareness of ourselves as agents, the acceptance of ourselves as 'responsible' for what we do, the 'choosers' between alternative courses of action, one of which may be what we know or believe to be our moral duty.

Hence a theory of choice which professes to explain the nature of valuation in terms of assessment of opportunity costs—a theory to the effect that, while virtuous or dutiful action means action from respect for personality, we shall do what we believe to be our duty only if the assessment of relative opportunity costs indicates the doing of the duty as the line of action with the least opportunity cost in the given choice situation—any such attempt to explain the nature of the value judgement is not in the least inconsistent with the postulate of freedom properly understood. It would be inconsistent with the denial of this postulate, since the theory, after all, is intended as an explanation of the way in which an agent reacts to a situation in which alternative lines of action are open to him.

BIBLIOGRAPHICAL NOTE

(The following works in economics and ethics may be found useful for reference in connexion with the theory of the value judgement.)

ECONOMICS

Cairncross, A. K., *Introduction to Economics* (Butterworth, London).

Fraser, L. M., *Economic Thought and Language* (A. & C. Black, London).

Henderson, Sir H., *Supply and Demand* (Cambridge Economic Handbooks, Cambridge University Press).

Little, I. M. D., *Critique of Welfare Economics* (Oxford University Press).

Macfie, A. L., *Essay on Economy and Value* (Macmillan, London).

Marshall, A., *Principles of Economics* (Macmillan, London).

Robbins, L., *Essay on the Significance of Economic Science* (Macmillan, London).

Wicksteed, P. H., *The Common Sense of Political Economy* (Edited with Introduction by Lionel Robbins, Routledge, London).

ETHICS

Carritt, E. F., *Ethical and Political Thinking* (Oxford University Press).

Ewing, A. C., *The Definition of Good* (Macmillan, New York).

Joseph, H. W. B., *Some Problems in Ethics* (Oxford University Press).

Laird, J., *The Idea of Value* (Cambridge University Press).

Macbeath, A., *Experiments in Living* (Macmillan, London).

Moore, G. E., *Principia Ethica* (Cambridge University Press).

Paton, H. J., *The Good Will* (Library of Philosophy, Allen and Unwin, London).

Perry, R. B., *General Theory of Value* (Longmans, New York).

Ross, Sir W. D., *The Right and the Good* (Oxford University Press).

—— *Foundations of Ethics* (Oxford University Press).

Stevenson, C. L., *Ethics and Language* (Yale University Press).

Urban, W. M., *Valuation* (Library of Philosophy, Allen and Unwin, London).

INDEX OF NAMES

INDEX OF SUBJECTS